Mrs. (Margaret) Oliphant

Who Was Lost And Is Found

A Novel

Mrs. (Margaret) Oliphant

Who Was Lost And Is Found
A Novel

ISBN/EAN: 9783337029562

Printed in Europe, USA, Canada, Australia, Japan

Cover: Foto ©Thomas Meinert / pixelio.de

More available books at **www.hansebooks.com**

WHO WAS LOST AND IS FOUND

A NOVEL

BY

MRS OLIPHANT

WILLIAM BLACKWOOD AND SONS
EDINBURGH AND LONDON
MDCCCXCIV

ORIGINALLY PUBLISHED IN 'BLACKWOOD'S MAGAZINE'

WHO WAS LOST AND IS FOUND.

CHAPTER I.

ONE of the most respected inhabitants of the village, rather of the parish, of Eskholm in Mid-Lothian was Mrs Ogilvy, still often called Mrs James by the elder people who had known her predecessors, who had seen her married, and knew everything about her, her antecedents and belongings. This is a thing very satisfactory in one way, as giving you an assurance that nothing can be suddenly found out about you, no disreputable new member or incident foisted into your family life; while, on the other hand, it has its inconveniences, since it becomes more or less the right of your neighbours to have every new domestic occurrence explained to·them in all its bearings. Great peace, however, had for a long time fallen over the house in which Mrs James Ogilvy was spending the

A

end of her quiet days: no new incident had occurred
there for years: its daily routine to all appearance
went on as cheerfully as could be desired. It was
one of the prettiest houses of the neighbourhood.
Built on the side of a little hill, as so many houses
are in Scotland, it was a tallish two-storeyed house
behind, plunging its foundations deep in the soil, with
an ample garden lying east and south, full of all the
old-fashioned vegetables and most of the old-fashioned
flowers of its period. But in front it was the trimmest
cottage, low but broad, opening upon a little round
platform encircled by a drive, and that, in its turn,
by closely clipped holly-hedges, as thick as a wall
and as smooth. Andrew, the gardener, thought it
more genteel to fill the little flower-border in front
with bedding-out plants in the summer,—red geraniums, blue lobelias, and so forth—never the pansies
and gillyflowers his mistress loved,—and it was only
with great difficulty that he had been prevented from
shutting out the view by a clump of rhododendrons
in the middle of the grass plot. "The view!" Andrew
said in high contempt: but this time his mistress had
her way. The view, perhaps, was nothing very wonderful to eyes accustomed to fine scenery. A bit of
the road that led to Edinburgh and the world was
visible among the trees at the foot of the brae, where
the private path of the Hewan between its close
holly-hedges sloped upward to the house: and be-

hind stretched the full expanse of country,—the towers of the castle making a break among the clouds of trees on one hand, and some of the roofs of the village and the little stumpy church-steeple showing on the other side. Between these two points, and far on either side, the Esk somehow threaded his way, running by village and castle impartially, but indeed exerting himself very much for the Hewan, forming little cascades and bits of broken water at the foot of the steep brae, throwing up glints of sunshine as it were from the depths, and filling the air always with a murmur of friendly companionship of which the inhabitants were unconscious, but of which had it stopped they would have instantly become aware and felt that all the world had gone wrong.

There was a garden-chair placed out here under the window of the drawing-room, where Mrs Ogilvy used to sit during a great part of the summer evenings —those long summer evenings of Scotland, which are so lingering and so sweet. To sit " at the doors " is so natural a thing for the women. They do it everywhere, in all climates and regions. Ladies who were critical said that this was a bad habit, and that there was nothing so becoming for a woman as to sit in her own drawing-room, in her own chair, where she could always be found when she was wanted. But a seat that was just under the drawing-room window, was not that as little different from being inside as could

be ? I agree, however, with the critics that the sentiment was quite different, and that to go indoors at
the right time and have your lamp lighted, and sit
down in your comfortable chair, denotes, perhaps,
a more contented mind and a spirit reconciled to
fate.

It would have been hard, however, to have looked
upon the face of Mrs James Ogilvy as she went about
her little household duties in the morning, or took her
walks about the garden, or knitted her stocking in
the placid afternoon, and to have thought of her as
discontented or struggling with fate. She was about
sixty, a little woman but trim in figure, with a pleasant
colour, and eyes still bright with animation and interest. Perhaps you will think it ridiculous to be
asked to interest yourself in the character and proceedings of an old woman of sixty when there are
so many younger and prettier things in the world:
which I allow is quite true in the general: yet there
may be advantages in it, once in a way. She wore
much the same dress all the year through, which was
a black silk gown of varying degrees of richness (her
best could " stand alone," it was so good), or rather of
newness — for the best gown of one year was the
everyday dress of another, not so fresh perhaps, but
wearing to the last thread, and always looking *good*
to the last, as a good black silk ought to do. Over
this she wore a white shawl, which on superior oc-

casions was of China crape beautifully embroidered,
a thing to be remembered—but often of humbler
material. I recollect one of fine wool with a coloured border printed in what was called an Indian
pine pattern in those days. But whatever the kind
was, she always wore a white shawl. Her cap was
also all white, lace for best, but net for everydays,
trimmed with white ribbons, and tied under the chin
with the same. This dress had been old-fashioned
when she assumed it, and was more than old-fashioned
now; but it suited her very well, as unusual dresses,
it may be remarked, usually do.

And she was kind as kind could be. She could
not refuse either beggar or borrower, unless the one
was a sturdy beggar presuming on the supposed
loneliness of the house and unaware of Andrew in
the background, upon whom she would flash forth
indignant, sending him off "with a flee in his lug,"
as Janet said: or the other a professional spendthrift
of other people's money. Short of these two classes—
and even to them her heart had moments of melting—
she refused nobody within her humble means. But I
will not deceive you by pretending that she was a
woman who went a great deal among the poor. That
fashion of charity had not come into use in her days.
The Scotch poor are *farouche*, they are arrogant, and
stand tremendously on their dignity—which is thought
by many people a fine thing, though, I confess, I don't

think it so; but it was no doubt cultivated more or less by good people like Mrs Ogilvy, who never visited among them, yet was ready to give with a liberality which was more like that of a Roman Catholic lady "making her soul" by such means, than a Scotch Puritan looking upon all she herself said or did as unworthy of regard. They came to her when they were in want; they came for food, for clothes, for coals; for money to pay an urgent debt; for all things that could affect family peace. And they very seldom were sent empty away. It was for this, perhaps, that the other ladies thought a woman should be found in her own chair in a corner of her own drawing-room. But if so, it certainly did not matter much, for Mrs Ogilvy's seat outside answered quite as well.

There was a dining-room and a drawing-room inside, one on each side of the door. The latter was usually called the parlour. It was full of curious things, not exactly of the kind that are considered curious now,— Mrs Ogilvy was not acquainted with *bric-à-brac*,—but there had been two or three sailors in the family, and they had brought unsophisticated wonders, shells, pieces of coral, bowls, sometimes china and precious, sometimes wood and of no value at all: but all esteemed pretty much alike, and given an equal place among the treasures of the house. There was some good china besides of her own, one good portrait, vaguely believed or hoped by the minister and some other connoisseurs of the village to be a Rubens (which meant, I suppose, even in their sanguine imaginations, a copy); and a row of black silhouettes, representing various members of the family, over the mantelpiece. Therefore it will be seen there was great impartiality in respect to artistic value. The carpet was partially covered with a grey linen cloth to preserve it, which gave the room a somewhat chilly look. It was in the dining-room that Mrs Ogilvy chiefly sat. She would have found it a great trouble to change from one to another at every meal. The large dining-table had been placed against the wall, which was a concession to comfort for which many friends blamed her during these years when Mrs Ogilvy had been alone. A smaller round table stood near the fire, her chair, her little old-fashioned stand for book and her work and her occasional newspaper, in the corner. It was all very comfortable, especially on the wintry evenings when the fire sparkled and the lamp burned softly, and everything felt warm and looked bright—as bright as Mrs Ogilvy's face with her white hair under her white cap, and her white shawl upon her shoulders. It might have been a symphony in white, had anybody heard of anything so grand and superior in these days.

It seldom happened, however, that one of the long evenings passed without the entrance of Janet, who at a certain hour in the placid night began always to wonder audibly what the mistress was doing, and

to divine that she would be the better of a word with
somebody, "if it was only you or me." Perhaps
this meant that Janet herself by that time had
become bored by the society of Andrew, her husband
and constant companion, who was a taciturn person,
and who, even if he could have been persuaded to
utter more than one word in half an hour, had no
new subject upon which he could discourse, but only
themes which Janet knew by heart. They were a
most peaceable couple, never quarrelling, working into each other's hands as the neighbours said, keeping
the Hewan outside and inside as bright as a new pin;
and I have no doubt that the sincerest affection, as
well as every tie of habit and long companionship,
bound them together: but still there were moments
very probably when Janet, without using the word
or probably understanding it, was bored. The "fore-
night" was long, and the ticking of the clock, so
offensively distinct when nothing is being said, got on
Janet's nerves; and then she bethought herself of
the mistress sitting all alone in the silence. "I'll just
go ben and see if she wants onything," she said.
"Aweel: I'll take a look at Sandy and see if he's
comfortable," replied Andrew. Sandy was a sleek old
pony with which Mrs Ogilvy drove in to Eskholm
when she had occasion, and sometimes even to Edinburgh, and he held a high place in Andrew's affections.
The one visit was as invariable as the other; and

Sandy, to whom perhaps also the fore-night was long, probably expected it too.

"Well, Janet," Mrs Ogilvy would say, putting aside the newspaper. She did not put aside her stocking, which went on by itself mechanically, but she turned her countenance towards her old servant always with the shining on it of a friendly smile.

"Well, mem—I just came in to see if ye maybe were wanting onything. Andrew he's away taking a look at Sandy. You would think he is a Christian to see the troke there is between that beast and my man."

"Andrew's a good creature, mindful of everybody's comfort," said Mrs Ogilvy.

"I'm saying nothing against that; but it micht be more cheery for me if he were a wee less preceese about what he hears and sees. A man is mair about, he canna miss what might be ca'ed the events of the day. But you and me, mem, we miss them a' up here."

"That's true, Janet; a man that brings in the news is more entertainment in a house than the newspaper itself."

"Whiles," said Janet, moderating the expression. "It's no the clashes and clavers of the toun that I'm wanting, but when onything important is stirring— there's another muckle paper-mill to be set up on our water. It brings wark for the lads—and the lasses too—and ye daurna say, just for the sake of Esk, that is no living thing——"

"I have more courage than you, Janet, for I daur to say it. What! my bonnie Esk no a living thing! What was ever more living than the bonnie running water? Eh, woman, running water is not like anything else in the world! It's just life itself! It sees everything happen and flows on—no stopping for the like of us creatures of a day. It heartens me to think that there's aye some bairns sitting playing by it, or some young thing dreaming her dream, or some woman with her little weans—not you and me, for our time is past, but just other folk."

"I'm no like you, mem. I get little comfort out of that. It's a bonnie stream, and I like the sough of it coming up through the trees; but none of the paper-mills would stop that. And when you think that it will bring siller into the place and wark, and more comfort for the poor folk——"

"Will it do that? God forbid that I should go against what brings work and comfort. It will bring new families, Janet, and strange men to sit and drink, and roar their dreadful songs at the public-house door; and more publics, and more dirty wives and miserable weans. I'm just for doing the best we can with what we have,—and that is not an easy thing."

" And I'm for ganging forward," cried Janet. " The more ye produce the better off ye are—that's what the books ca' an axiom. I carena for the new folk; but it is a grand thing to be making something, and putting work into men's hands to do. Thae poor Millers themselves get but little out of it. They say there's another of them, the little one with the curly head, that is just going like the rest."

" Oh, Janet, the Lord forbid! the little blue-eyed one, that was just the comfort of the house?"

" That's what folk say. I'm no answering for it. In an unfortunate family like that, ye canna have a sair finger but they'll say it's the auld trouble breaking out."

" Poor man, poor man!" cried Mrs Ogilvy. " My heart is wae for him, Janet. He is like the man in the Bible that built Jericho. He has laid his foundations in his first-born, and established his gates on his youngest son. You must tell Andrew that I will want him and Sandy to-morrow to go and inquire. No the bonnie little one that was his comfort!—oh, not her, not her, Janet!"

" Mem, it is aye the Lord that kens best."

" I am not misdoubting that; but I've had many a thought—I would not aye be blaming the Lord. When the seed is put into the ground, we should be prepared for what it will bring forth, and no look for leaves of silver and apples of gold; but why should I speak? for there is little meaning in words, and we are a strange race—oh, just a strange race—following our wild ways."

Mrs Ogilvy had dropped her stocking by this time into her lap, and she wrung her slender hands as she spoke, with a look that was not like the calm of the place. Whether Janet noted this or merely followed the instinct of her wandering record of events, it was impossible to tell from her steady countenance, which did not change.

"And there's to be a wedding up the water at Greenha'. You will mind, mem, Thomoseen, that was once in our ain house here as the girrl, and an awfu' time I had with her, for she would learn nothing. She's grown the biggest woman on a' Eskside, and they call her Muckle Tammy, and mony an adventure she's had since she left my kitchen—having broken, ye will maybe mind, mem, every dish we had. And for her ain sake, thinking it would maybe be a lesson to her, I wanted you to take it off her wages——"

"Yes, yes, I mind. The things would not stay in her hands; they were too big. We have had our experiences with our girrls, Janet," Mrs Ogilvy said, with a smile. She had taken up her knitting again, and recovered her tranquil looks.

"That we have, mem! if I was to make out a chronicle—but some of them have turned out no so ill after a'. Weel, Muckle Tammy, she has gotten a man."

"He will likely be some small bit creature," the mistress said.

"They say no—a clever chield, and grand wi' a garden, and meaning to grow vegetables for the market at Edinburgh; for she is a lass with a tocher, her mother's kailyard and her bit cottage, and nothing for him to do but draw in a chair and sit down."

"I doubt there'll be but little comfort inside," said Mrs Ogilvy. "If it had been her to look after the kail and the cabbages, and him to keep everything clean and trig; but there's no telling. A change like that works many ferlies. You must just see, Janet, if there is anything she is wanting for her plenishing—some linen, or a few silver teaspoons, or a set of china, or a new gown."

"They a' ken there will be something for them in the coffers at the Hewan," said Janet; "but, mem, if ye will be guided by me, you will let it be no too much. If only one of these dishes had been stoppit off her wages it would have been a grand lesson: but ye will never hear a word! A set of chiney! they would a' be broken afore ever she got them hame."

"Let it be the silver spoons then, Janet; they are the things that last the best. And now, if you were to cry in Andrew, we might read our chapter, and get ready for our beds."

This was the invariable conclusion of these evening colloquies. And Janet went "ben" to her kitchen and then to the garden door, and "cried upon" Andrew, still conversing with the pony in the stable. And then there was a great turning of keys and drawing of bolts, and the house was closed up for the night. And finally the pair went into the parlour, where Mrs Ogilvy, with her clear little educated voice read "the chapter," usually from one of the Gospels, and read in sequence night by night. Janet was of opinion that she never understood so well as when her mistress read, and indeed Mrs Ogilvy had a little pride in her reading, which was very clear and distinct with its broad vowels. The little prayer which was read out of a book did not please Andrew so much, who was of opinion that prayers ought never to be previously invented and written, but come, as he said, "straught from the hairt." He had himself indeed thought on occasion that he could have poured forth the sentiments that moved the family with more unction and expression than was in the sometimes faltering voice and pause for breath which affected his mistress when she read these "cauld words out of a book"; but Andrew knew his own place: or if he did not know, Janet did.

What was there to catch the breath, and make the voice falter, in the printed words and amid all that deep calm of waning life? It was at the prayer for the absent that Mrs Ogilvy for fifteen years past had always broken down. Nay, not broken down: she was too deeply sensible that to make an exhibition of private feeling while leading the family devotions would have been irreverent and unseemly; but she was not capable of going on quite smoothly without a pause over that petition, "Those who are absent of this family, be Thou with them to bless them, and bring them home in Thy good time if it be Thy blessed will." Every night there came to Janet's eyes as she knelt a secret tear; and every night it seemed to Andrew that if he might speak "straught from the hairt" instead of that cauld prayer that was printed, the Lord would hear. I need not say that even in a Scotch book of domestic worship the words were varied from day to day, but the meaning was always the same. They left the mistress of the house in a certain commotion of mind when her old servants had bidden her good night and withdrawn. She had a way then of walking about the room, sometimes pausing as if to listen. There was deep silence about the Hewan, uplifted on its little brae, and with few houses near,—nothing to be heard except the distant murmur of the Esk, and the rustling of the trees. But the night has strange mysteries of sound for which no one can account. Sometimes something came that seemed like a step on the gravel outside, sometimes, fainter in the distance, what might have been the swing of the gate, sometimes a muffled knock as at the door. She knew them all well, and had been deceived by them a thousand times; nor was she undeceived yet, but would stop and raise her head and hold her breath, waiting for perhaps some second sound to follow to give meaning to it. But there never came any second sound, or at least there never was, never had been, any meaning in them. She listened, holding up her head, and then drooped it again, going on upon her little measured walk. "At ainy moment!" she would say sometimes to herself.

Over the front door of the cottage, which was not without a little pretension, there was what we used to call a fanlight: and in this summer and winter every night a light burned till morning. People shook their heads at it as a piece of foolish sentiment and very extravagant; and Andrew grudged a little the trouble it caused him. But there it burned all the year round, every night through.

CHAPTER II.

IN the summer evenings Mrs Ogilvy sat on the bench outside the parlour window. I have never forgotten the sort of rapture with which the long summer evenings in Scotland impressed my own mind when I rediscovered them, so to speak, after a long interval of absence. The people who know Scotland only in the autumn know them not. By that time all things have grown common, the surprises of the year are over; but in June those long, soft, pearly, rosy hours which are neither night nor day, which melt by indescribable degrees out of the glory of the sunset into everything that is soft and fair, through every tint and shining colour and mingling of lights, until they reach that which is inconceivable — surround us with a heavenly atmosphere all their own, the fusion of every radiance, the subdual of every shade. There are no shadows in that wonderful light any more than there is any sun. The midnight sun must be a very spectacular sort of performance in comparison. To people who live in it always, however, it will probably appear no such great thing.

Mrs Ogilvy was not aware that there was anything that was not most ordinary in these June nights. She loved them, but knew no reason why. She sat in the sweet air, in the silence, sometimes feeling herself as if suspended between air and sky, floating softly in space with the movement of the world: and in her thoughts she was able even sometimes to detach herself from Then and Now, those two dreadful limits of our consciousness, and to catch a glimpse of life as it is rounded out, and some consciousness of the beginning and the end, and the sequence and connection of all things. Sometimes: but perhaps not very often, for these gleams of discovery are but gleams, and fly like the flashes of lightning which suddenly reveal to us a broad country, a noble city lost in the darkness. On such occasions the great sphere overhead, the great landscape stretching into distance, the glimpses of houses, great and small, amid the warm surrounding of the trees, the murmur of the Esk low in the glen, filling all the air with sound, affected her with an extraordinary calm. She used to think sometimes that this was the Peace that passeth understanding which descended upon her, hushing all her thoughts, stilling every sigh. It came but seldom in that height of blessing, but often in a less perfect way, as she sat and pondered upon the great still world revolving round, and she an atom in the boundless breadth of being, which by-and-by would drop, while the world went on.

But at other times it appeared to her more strange still that in all these miles and miles of distance, of solid earth and growing trees, and the hopeful harvests that were coming, there was one little thing, so little in fact, so insignificant in the midst of all, that was throbbing and throbbing and disturbing the quiet, unmoved by the peace of the sky and the earth and all the beautiful things between them — thinking its own small thoughts, and troubling, and living — till all the quiet throbbed and thrilled with it, the one thing that was out of harmony. The centre of her thoughts, or rather the cause of them all, night and day, was a thing that had happened fifteen years ago, a thing that most people had forgotten—a small matter to the world — just the going away of a heedless young man. It was not that she was always thinking of him, for her thoughts rambled and wandered through all the heavens and earth; but that he was the centre of all, the pivot on which they turned, the beginning and the end of everything. He had gone away — he had left his home, having already

erred and strayed—and he had been heard of no
more. She was not complaining or finding fault
with God for it: she would sometimes wonder with
a little wistfulness why God never listened to her, did
not somewhere seize that wandering boy and bring
him back—to satisfy her before she died. But then
there were many things to be considered, Mrs Ogilvy
knew and acknowledged to herself in the philosophy
that had grown out of her much thinking. Robert
was not a bairn, nor was God a mere benevolent
patron, to seize the lad without rhyme or reason, and
set him back there, because she wearied Him with
crying. She had wanted God to be that, many
times in her long period of trouble; but by dint
of time and thought a different sense of things had
come to her. God was not a good fairy: He was
the great God of heaven and earth. He had
Robert to think of as well as his mother, and
thousands and millions of other things. Often in
the weariness of her heart she asked nothing for
Robert, said nothing, but sat there before the Lord
with the boy's name on her heart put before Him.
And that was all she was doing now.

Of all that landscape there was one point to which
her eyes turned the oftenest, and which drew her
away out of herself, as if by some charm of movement and going. And that was the piece of road
which lay at the foot of the brae, with her own

garden-gate opening into it, and the two lines of
the holly-hedges on either side. Often she would
be drawn back from her thinking by the sight of
a figure on the road, which turned out to be a very
common figure,—sometimes a beggar, or a man with
a pack, a travelling merchant, or, more familiar still
than that, a postman on his way home, or a lad that
had been working later than usual. But whatever
the man was, the sight of him always gave Mrs Ogilvy
a sharp sensation. "At any moment!" she had said
to herself so long that it had entered into her very
soul. "At any moment!"—she was conscious of this
night and day. Through all that she was doing she
had always one ear listening for any new step or
sound. And you may think how much more strong
that habitual watchfulness was when she looked out
in the evening, the time when everybody comes home,
upon the road by which he must come, if he ever
came. A hundred times and a hundred more she
had watched that road, with her eyes

> "Busy in the distance shaping things
> That made her heart beat thick."

Often and often she had seen a man detach himself
from the white strip of the road, and heard her own
gate click and swing, and watched a head moving
upward over the line of the hedge. But it never
was any one except the most simple, the most natu-

rally to be expected visitor — perhaps the minister,
perhaps Mr Miller from the paper-mill, perhaps some
friend of Andrew's and Janet's. Her heart beat in
her ears, in her throat, for a dreadful moment, and
then stood still. It was not he: how should it?
She rose up with no heart at all, everything stopped
and hushed, and said, "How are you to-night, Mr
Logan? What a bonnie evening for a walk," or
"How are you, Mr Miller; sit down and take a rest
after your climb." She said nothing about her disappointment; and, indeed, who could say she was
disappointed? It just was not Robbie: and she
had no more reason to think that it would be him
than that the night would suddenly turn into day.

On this particular evening it was Mr Logan, the
minister, who gave her this thrill of strong expectation, this disappointment — which was not a disappointment. He found nothing that was out of
the way in her peaceful looks, neither the one sensation nor the other, but sat down beside her, pleased
with this conclusion to his summer evening's walk,
and the delightful air and pleasant view, and the
calm of the Hewan, in which everybody said there
was such an atmosphere of repose and peace. Mr
Logan was a country minister of what is now called
the old school. He was not a man who had ever
thought of making innovations or disturbing the old
order of affairs. His services were just the same as

they had been when he was ordained some thirty
years before. He had baptised a great part of his
parishioners, and married the others, so that there
were only the quite old folk, patriarchs of the parish,
who could remember the time when he was first
"placed" at Eskholm, and opposed by some, though
always "well likit" by others. He was considered
by Mrs Ogilvy and many ladies of the parish to be
a very personable man, comely in his grey hair, with
a good presence and a good voice, and altogether a
wyss-like man. This description, which is so common
in Scotland, has nothing to do with the wisdom of
the person described, who may be very wyss-like
without being at all wise. Mr Logan sat down and
stretched out discreetly his long legs. He had the
shadow, or rather the subdued light, of a smile
hovering about his face. He looked as if he had
something agreeable to tell.

"And how is Susie?" Mrs Ogilvy said.

"Susie," he said, with a change of expression which
did not look quite so genuine as the lurking smile.
"Oh, Susie, poor thing, she is just in her ordinary;
but that is not very well——"

"Not well! Susie? But she has just been wonderful in her health and her cheery ways."

"Ay, ay! she has kept up to the outside of her
strength; but I have never thought she was equal
to it. You will do me the justice to remember that

I always said that. These big boys are too much
for her; and now that they're coming and going to
Edinburgh every day, and all the trouble of getting
them off in the morning, with sandwiches for George
who is in his office, and a piece for Walter and Jamie
who are at the school: and the two little ones all
the day at home, and me on the top of all, that am
perhaps accustomed to have too much attention paid
to me——"

The lurking smile came forth again, much subdued,
so that nobody could ask the minister brutally, "What
are you smiling at?"

"Dear me," said Mrs Ogilvy, "I am very much
astonished. I have always thought there was nobody
like Susie for managing the whole flock."

"She is a good girl, a very good girl; but it's too
much for her, Mrs Ogilvy. I've always said so. She
takes after her mother, and you know my—wife was
far from strong."

The little pause he made before that simple word
wife was as when a man who has married a second
time says "my first wife."

Mrs Ogilvy was startled and stared; but she did
not take any notice of this alarming peculiarity. She
said, "I cannot think Susie delicate, Mr Logan. She
has none of the air of it. And her mother at her
age——"

"Ah, her mother at her age! I must take double

care that nothing interferes with Susie. It is an anxious position for a man to have a family to look after that is deprived of a mother's care."

"It is so, no doubt," said Mrs Ogilvy; "but with Susie——"

"Poor thing! who just strains every faculty she has. There are some women who do these kind of things with no appearance of effort," said Mr Logan, shaking his head a little. "You will have heard there was a marriage in the parish yesterday. They would fain have had it in the church, in their new-fangled way. But I said our auld kirk did not lend itself to that sort of thing, and I would like it better in their own drawing-room, or if they preferred it, mine."

"Yes, yes," said Mrs Ogilvy, "I heard of it. The English family that have taken the little house near the Dean. I did not think it was big enough to have a drawing-room."

"Well, an English family is rather a misnomer: they can scarcely be called English, though they come from the south—and a family you can call it no longer, for this was the last daughter, and there's nothing but Mrs Ainslie herself left."

"She's a well-put-on, well-mannered woman, and well-looking too: but I know nothing more about her," Mrs Ogilvy said.

"She is all that," replied the minister, with a little fervour unnecessary in the circumstances. "We

were at the little entertainment after, Susie and me.
Everything was just perfectly done, and nobody
neglected, and without a bit of fuss or flutter such
as is general in these cases——"

"Do you think it is general?" said Mrs Ogilvy,
with that natural and instantaneous impulse of self-
defence which is naturally awakened by excessive
praise bestowed upon the better methods of a stranger.
"We are maybe not much used to grand entertainments
in a landward parish like this, where there are not
many grand folk."

"Oh, there was nothing particularly grand about
it," said the minister, with the air of lingering pleasantly in recollection over an agreeable subject. "These
simple sort of things are so much better; but it takes
a clever person to see just what is adapted to a country
place. I was saying to Susie this morning it's a grand
thing to bring people together like yon—and no expense
to speak of when you know how to go about it——"

"And what did Susie think?" Mrs Ogilvy asked.

"My dear lady," said the minister, "nobody will
say I am one to take down the ladies or give them
a poor character; but they are maybe slower of the
uptake than men—especially when it's another lady,
and one with gifts past the common, that is held up
for their example."

"I thought you were too wise a man to hold up
anybody for an example."

"You're always sensible, Mrs Ogilvy. That is just what I should have remembered: but perhaps I am too open in my speech at all times. I've come to speak to Susie as if she knew things and the ways of the world just as well as me."

Mr Logan was a little vague about his pronouns, which arose not from want of grammar, but from national prejudice or prepossession.

"And so she does," said Mrs Ogilvy, with a little surprise. "She's young still, the dear lassie; but it's very maturing to the mind to be in a position like hers, and she is just one of the most reasonable persons I know."

"Ah, yes," said the minister, with a sigh, which did not interrupt the lurking smile; "but it's a very different thing to have a companion of your own age."

At this she began to look at him with more attention than she had as yet shown, and perceived that there was a little flush more than ordinary on the minister's face. Had he come to make any revelation? Mrs Ogilvy had all the natural prejudices, and she was resolved that at least she would do nothing to help him out. She sat demurely and looked at him, while he, leaning forward, traced lines upon the gravel with the end of his stick. The faint imbecility of the smile about his lips, made of vanity and pleasure and a little shame, always irritating to women, called forth an ironical watchfulness on her part.

" There is but one way of having that," he continued ; "a man's a sad wreck in many cases when he's left a widower, as you may say, in the middle of his days,—

> ' My strength he weakened in the way,
> My days of life he shorten-ed.'

This is not the usual sense in which the words are used, but it just comes to that. You will know by yourself, Mrs Ogilvy. You were widowed young."

" I have never taken myself to be a rule for other folk," she said.

" Well, you don't do that; but still how are you to judge of other folk's feelings but according to what you feel yourself ? "

The lady made no reply. No, she would not help him! if he had any ridiculous thing to say to her, he should muddle through it the best way he could. She would not hold out a little finger to help him up to dry land.

" Well," he said, after a pause, with a little sigh, " to return to Susie. She's not equal to her present charge, not equal to it at all. Three big boys on her hands, and the two little ones, not to count all the family correspondence with the others in India and Australia, and all that. There is a great deal of care connected with a large family that people never think of." He paused for sympathy, but it was not a point

upon which his present listener could speak : he went
on with a slight and momentary feeling that she was
selfish not to have entered into this trouble, notwithstanding that it was so different from her own. "And
these growing laddies want a firm hand over them—
they want authority—not just a sister that they can
tease and fleech——I maybe ought from the first," he
said, slowly and tentatively, "to have taken the
burden more upon myself."

"It would have left less burden upon Susie ; but I
think for my part she is quite equal to it," Mrs Ogilvy
said.

When a man condescends to blame himself, he
expects as his natural due that he should be reassured.
Mr Logan felt that his old friend and parishioner, to
whom he had come half for sympathy, half for encour-
agement, was not nearly so sympathetic a person as he
thought.

"I see we'll not agree in that; and I am sure I
hope you're the one that is in the right. Well," he
said, getting up slowly, "I'm afraid I must be going.
This is a long walk for me at this hour of the night;
and they'll be waiting for me at home."

"You'll let me know," Mrs Ogilvy said, as she
walked with him along the little platform round the
plot of grass. "You'll let me know—when things
have gone further."

"When things have gone further?" he cried, with

a sudden redness and look of surprise: then added, shaking his head, "What things there are to go further, and how far they can go, is a mystery to me. You must be referring to something in your own mind."

And the good-night was a little formal with which he went away.

It was time to go in. The light was fading at last, growing a little paler, and ten had struck on the big clock. The lamp had been lighted in the drawing-room for Mrs Ogilvy to read the chapter by, though there was no real need for it. Janet, who had come out for her mistress's work and her footstool, lingered, as was her wont, before she "cried upon" Andrew for that concluding ceremonial of the day.

"Did you ever hear that there was any word of the minister—— ? But perhaps I should not speak on the small authority I have," Mrs Ogilvy said.

"Speak freely, mem; I can aye bear it—and better from you than from some other folk."

Andrew had strong Free Church inclinations. He was given to disrespectful speech of the ministers of the Auld Kirk in general, and of Mr Logan in partic- ular, calling him a dumb dog that could not bark— which roused Janet to her inmost soul. She was not satisfied even with her mistress, though she had never forsaken the Kirk of her fathers. Janet bore her burden, as the only perfectly orthodox person in the house, with great solemnity and a sense of suffering for the right. "Say what you will, mem; you may be sure I will have heard worse. I can put up with it," Janet said.

"You are just a very foolish person to speak in that tone to me. Am I one to find fault with the minister without cause? Nor am I finding fault with him. He has a right to do it if he likes. I would not say that it was expedient."

"Eh, mem, if ye would but put me out of my pain! What is it? He is a douce man, that would do harm to nobody. What is he going to do?"

"Indeed, Janet, I cannot tell. It is just some things he said. Was there ever any lady's name named—or that caused a silly laugh, or made folk speak?"

"Named!" said Janet, — "with our minister? 'Deed, and that there have been—every woman born that he has ever said a ceevil word to. You ken little of country clashes, mem, if you're surprised at that. Your ainsel' for one, and we ken the truth there is in that."

"They were far to seek if they named me," said Mrs Ogilvy, drawing herself up with dignity; "but there is a lady he is very full of. I do not ask you to inquire, for I hate gossip; but if it should come your way from any of the neighbours, I would like to hear what they say. Poor Susie! he says she is not able for so much work, that he is feared she

will go like her mother.   Now, she's not like her
mother either in that or any other thing.   There's
trouble brewing for my poor Susie—if you hear anything, let me know."

"And you never heard who the leddy was?" Janet
said.

"I have heard much more—a great deal more,"
Mrs Ogilvy cried, very inconclusively it must be
allowed, "than I had any wish to hear!"

CHAPTER III.

THIS was the ordinary of the life at the Hewan. A great deal of solitude, a great deal of thought, an endless circling of mind and reflection round one subject which shadowed heaven and earth, and affected every channel in which the thoughts of a silent much-reasoning creature can flow: and at the same time much acquaintance with a crowd of small human events making up the life of the neighbourhood, with which, practically speaking, Mrs Ogilvy had nothing to do, yet with which, in the way of sympathy, advice, and even criticism, she had a great deal to do. Such half confidences as that of Mr Logan were brought to her continually—veiled disclosures made for the purpose of finding out how such and such things looked in the eyes of a woman who was very discreet, who never repeated anything that was said, and who had the power of intimating an opinion as veiled as the disclosure by delicate

C

methods without putting it into words. She sat on
her modest height, a little oracle wrapped in mystery
as to her own inner life, impartial and observant as
to that about her. How she had come to be an
authority in the village it would be difficult to tell.
She was not a person of noted family or territorial
importance, which is a thing which tells for so much
in Scotland. Perhaps it was chiefly because, since
the great misfortune of her life, she had retired
greatly from the observation of the parish, paying
no visits, seeing only the people who went to see
her, and as for her own affairs confiding in nobody,
asking no sympathy — too proud in her love and
sorrow even to allow that she was stricken, or that
the dearest object of her life was the occasion of all
her suffering. Neighbours had adjured her not "to
make an idol" of her boy; and after the trouble
came they had shaken their heads and assured her
in the first publicity of the blow that God was a
jealous God, and would not permit idolatry. To
these speeches she had never made any reply: and
scarcely any one to this day knew whether his mother
had ever heard from Robert, or was aware of his
movements and history. This position had been very
impressive to the little community. It is a kind of
pride with which in Scotland there is a great deal of
sympathy.

On the other hand she had never rejected the

appeal, tacit or open, of any one who came to her.
The ladies of the village were almost a little servile
in the court they paid to this old lady. They liked
to know what Mrs Ogilvy thought of most things
that went on, and to have her opinion of any stranger
who settled among them; and if a rumour rose in
the village, where rumours are so apt to rise, nobody
knows how, there was sure to be a concourse in the
afternoon, unpremeditated and accidental, of visitors
eager to hear, but very diffident of being the first to
ask, what the lady of the Hewan thought. Now
the suggestion that the minister of Eskholm was
about to make a second marriage, overturning the
entire structure of life, displacing his daughter, who
had been the mistress of the manse for many years,
and inflicting a new and alien sway upon his big
boys and his little girls, all flourishing under the
cheerful sovereignty of Susie, was such an idea as
naturally convulsed the parish from one end to the
other. And there was little doubt that this was the
question it was intended to discuss, when two or
three of these ladies met without concert or pre-
meditation in the afternoon at the Hewan; and Janet,
half proud of the concourse, half angry at the trouble
involved, had to spend all the warm afternoon serving
the tea. If such was the purpose, however, it was
entirely foiled by the unlooked-for appearance of a
lady not at all like the ladies of Eskholm—a stranger,

with what was considered to be a strongly marked "English accent," the very person who was believed to have led the minister astray. The new-comer was good-looking, well-dressed, and extremely anxious to please; but as the only method of doing so which she could think of was to take the lead of the conversation, and to assume the air of the principal person, the expedient perhaps was not very successful. But for the moment even Mrs Ogilvy was silenced. She allowed her hand to be engulfed in the two hands of the stranger held out to her; and even gave to this frank and smiling personage in her consternation the place of honour, the seat by herself. The English lady, Mrs Ainslie, was not shy; and the little hostile assembly in the drawing-room of the Hewan, which had assembled to discuss the danger to the minister of this alarming siren in their midst, was changed into an audience of civil listeners, hearing the siren discourse.

"Oh, I like it beyond description," she said. "It has become the most important place in the world to me! What a thing providence is! We came here thinking of nothing, meaning to spend six weeks, or at the most two months. And lo! this little country retreat, as we thought it, has become—I really can't speak of it. My daughter, my only remaining one, the last—whom I have sometimes thought the flower of the flock——"

"You will have a number of daughters?"

"I am a grandmother these four or five years," said the stranger, spreading out her hands, and putting herself forth, and her still fresh attractions, with a laugh and a pardonable boast. The ladies of Eskholm, all listening, felt a movement among them, a half-perceptible rustle, half of interest, half of envy. This was what it was to be English, to have a house in London, to move about the world, to introduce your girls and have them properly appreciated. How can you do that in a small country place? Some of these ladies were grandmothers too, and no older than Mrs Ainslie, but not one of them could have succeeded in declaring with that light and airy manner, See how young, how fresh, how unlike a grandmother I am! They looked at her with admiration modified by disapproval. They had meant to discuss her, to organise a defence against her; and here she was in command of everybody's attention, the centre of the group!

"I am sure," the lady continued, "it is the truest thing to say that marriages are made in heaven. We came here, Sophie and I, thinking of nothing—just for a few weeks in the summer: and here she is happily married! and, for all I know, I may spend the rest of my life in the place. She is my youngest, and to be near her is such an attraction. Besides, I have made such excellent friends—friends that I hope to keep all my life."

"It is not everybody that is so fortunate," Mrs Ogilvy said. None of the audience gave her the least assistance. They were fascinated by the confidence of the stranger, her pleasure in her own good fortune, and her freedom from any of that shyness which silenced themselves.

"Fortunate is really too little to say. Fancy, all all my girls have made love-matches, and my sons-in-law adore their wives—and me. Now, I think that is a triumph. They are all fond of me. Don't you think it is a triumph? If ever I feel inclined to boast, it is of that."

"You are perhaps one of those," said Mrs Ogilvy, somewhat grimly, "that, as we say in this country, a'body likes,—which is always a compliment—in one way."

"That ah-body likes," cried Mrs Ainslie with outstretched hands, and an imitation which had a very irritating effect on the listeners. "Thank you a hundred times. It is a very pretty compliment, I think."

"That awbody likes," repeated Mrs Ogilvy, putting the vowel to rights. "We do not always mean it in just such a favourable sense."

"It means a person that makes herself agreeable—with no real meaning in it," said one.

"It means just a whillie-wha," said another.

"It means a person, as they say, with a face like a fiddle, and no sincerity behind."

Mrs Ainslie put up her hands again. "Oh, how am I to understand so much Scotch? I must ask Mr Logan," she said.

And then again there was a pause. She dared to mention him! in the face of all those ladies banded together for his defence.

"What a delightful man he is," she proceeded—"so learned, and so clever, and so good! I don't know that I ever met with such a man. If he were only not so weighed down with these children. Dear Mrs Ogilvy, don't you think it is dreadful to see a poor man so burdened. If he had only some one to keep order a little and take proper care of him. My heart sinks for him whenever I go into his house."

Then there was a universal outcry, no longer capable of being controlled. "I cannot see that at all," cried one. "He has Susie," cried two or three together. "And where could he find a better? I wish, indeed, he was more worthy of such a daughter as that."

It was an afternoon of surprises, and of the most sensational kind, for just as the ladies of Eskholm were warming to this combat, in which so much more was meant than met the eye, and, a little flushed with the heat of the afternoon and the tea and rising temper, were turning fiery looks toward the interloper, the door opened quietly, without any preliminary bell or even knock at the door, and Susie Logan herself— Susie, in behalf of whom they were all so ready to do battle—walked quietly in. Susie herself was quite calm, perfectly fresh, though she had been walking in the hottest hour of the day,—her white straw hat giving a transparent shade to the face, her cotton dress so simple, fresh, and clean. Nobody ever managed to to look so fresh and without soil of any kind as Susie, whatever she might do.

There was a sudden pause again, a pause more dramatic than before, for the speakers had all been in full career, and some of them angry. Susie was very familiar at the Hewan—she was like the daughter of the house. She stopped short at the door and looked round, too much at home even to pretend that she did not see how embarrassing her appearance was. "I must have interrupted something?" she said.

"Oh no, no, Susie." "How could you interrupt anything?" "You are just the one that would know the most of it, whatever we were discussing," the ladies hastened to say, one taking the word from another. Mrs Ogilvy held out her hand without moving. "Come in, come in," she said; "and ye can leave the door a little open, Susie, for we're all flushed a little with the heat and with our tea."

Mrs Ainslie was the one who gave Susan the most marked reception. She alone got up and took the girl in her arms. "How glad I should have been," she said, "had I known I was to meet you here."

"Now, Susie, I will not have this," said Mrs Ogilvy;

"sit down and do not make yourself the principal
person, my dear; for I was thinking it was me this
lady was glad to see. As we are talking of marriages,
I would like to know if anybody can tell me about that
big lassie Thomasine that I've been hearing of—a
creature that has a cottage and a kailyard, and not
much of a head on her shoulders. Will he be a
decent man?"

There were some who shook their heads, and there
were some who answered more cordially—Thomasine's
husband had been as much discussed in the parish as
a more important alliance could have been. And
under the shelter of this new inquiry most of the
guests stole away. Mrs Ainslie herself was one of
the last to go. She put once more an arm round
Susie. "Are you coming, my love? I should like to
walk with you," she said.

"Not yet, Mrs Ainslie," said Susan, with rising
colour. She freed herself from the embrace with a
little haste. "I have not seen Mrs Ogilvie for a long
time."

"You have not seen me either," said the stranger
playfully and tenderly, shaking a finger at her; "but
it is right that new friends, even when they're dear
friends, should yield to old friends," she said, with a
little sigh and smile. She made a very graceful exit
considering all things, and Susie's presence prevented
even the lingerer who went last from murmuring a

private word as she had wished. When they were all
gone, Susie placed herself by her old friend's side.

"They worry you, these folk; they come to you
with all their clashes. What was it this time?   I
saw they were stopped by me. It was not that old
business," said Susie, with a blush, "about Johnny
Maitland? I thought that was all past and gone."

"It was not that—it was rather this lady, this
English person that stopped all their mouths before
you came in. She is a very wyss-like woman, though
her manners are strange to me. As I said to your
father, she's well put-on and well looking. Do you
like her, Susie?"

"Me! I've no occasion not to like her, Mrs Ogilvy."

"I was not asking that. Do you like her, Susie?"

Upon which Susie began to laugh. "What can I
say?—

'I dinna like ye, Doctor Fell,
    The reason why I canna tell.'

I've no occasion not to like her. She is always very
kind, a little too kind, to me—I am not fond of all
that kissing—but it is perhaps just her way. I am
not very fond of her, to tell the truth."

"Nor am I, Susie; but she is maybe well enough if
we were not prejudiced."

"Oh yes, she is well enough,—she is more than
that; and papa thinks there is nobody like her," she
added, with a laugh.

" Ah! your papa has an opinion on the subject ? "

" And why not ? He has a great eye for the ladies. Did you not know that ? I think I like her the less because he makes so much of her. There was that party she had for the marriage, I never hear the end of it. It was all so nice, and so little trouble, and no fuss, and no expense, and so forth. How can he tell it was no expense ?—all the things were sent out from Edinburgh ! " said Susie, offended in her pride of house-keeping; " and as for the sandwiches and things, I have seen the very same in Edinburgh parties, and not so very new either. I could make them perfectly myself ! "

" My dear, that is the way of men," said Mrs Ogilvy; " a bit of bread-and-butter in a strange place they will take for a ferlie: whereas it's only a piece for the bairns at home."

" Oh, papa is not so bad as that," said Susie; " and I'm very silly to mind. Now, just you lean back in your big chair and be quiet a little; and I will go ben to Janet and bring you a little new-made tea."

" I like to see you do it, Susie. I like to take it from your hand. It is not for the tea——"

" No, it is not for the tea," said the girl; and, though she was not fond of kissing, as she said, she touched Mrs Ogilvy's old soft cheek tenderly with her fresh lips, and went away briskly on her errand with a tear in her eye. Perhaps it is something of a misnomer to call Susie Logan a girl. I fear she must have been thirty or a little more; but she had never left her home, and though she was full of experience, she retained all the freshness and openness of youth. Her hazel eyes were limpid and mildly bright; her features good if not remarkable; her colour fresh as a summer morning. Nowhere could she go without carrying a sense of youth and life with her; and here in this still existence at the Hewan among the old people she was doubly young, the representative of all that was wanting to make that house bright. She alone could make the mistress yield to this momentary indulgence, and permit herself to look tired and to rest. And for her Janet joyfully boiled the kettle over again, though she had just been congratulating herself on having finished for the day.

Susan went back and administered the tea, that cordial which is half for the body and half for the mind, but which swallowed amid a crowd of visitors fulfils neither purpose: and then she seated herself by Mrs Ogilvy's side. "How good it is to feel they're all gone away and we are just left to our two selves!"

"Have you anything particular to say to me, Susie?"

"Oh no, nothing particular; everything is just in its ordinary: the little ones are sometimes rather a handful, and if papa would get them a governess I would be thankful. They mean no harm, the little

things; but the weather is warm and the day is long,
and they are not fond of their lessons—neither am I,"
said Susie, with a laugh, "if the truth were told."

"And you are finding them a little too much for
you—that is what your father was saying——"

" I find them too much for me! did papa say that?"
cried Susie, alarmed; "that was never, never in my
head. I may grumble a little, half in fun; but too
much for me, Mrs Ogilvy! me that was born to it,
the eldest daughter! such a thing was never, never
in my mind——"

" I told him so, my dear, but he would not believe
me; he just maintained it to my face that it was too
much for you, and your health was beginning to fail."

" What would he mean by that?" said Susie, sitting
up very upright on her chair. A shadow came over
her brightness. "Oh, I hope he has not got any new
idea in his head," she cried.

" Maybe he will be thinking of a governess for the
little ones, Susie."

" It might be that," she acknowledged in subdued
tones. "And then," she added, with again a sudden
laugh, "I heard *that* woman—no, no, I never meant to
speak of her so—I heard Mrs Ainslie saying to him
it would be a good thing. I would rather not have
the easement than get it through her hands."

" Oh fie! Susie, fie! she would have no ill motive:
you must not take such things into your head."

"It is she that makes me feel as if it were too much," cried Susie, "coming in at all hours following me about the house. I get so tired of her that I am tired of everything. I could just dance at the sight of her: she puts me out of my senses; and always pitying me that want none of her pity! It must be kindness, I suppose," said Susie, grudgingly; "but then I wish she would not be so kind." After this there was a pause. The talk came to an end all at once. Mrs Ainslie and her doings dropped out of it as if she had gone behind a veil; and Susie looked in her old friend's face, with the tenderest of inquiring looks, a question that needed not to be spoken.

"No word still, no word?" she rather looked than said.

"Never a word: not one, not one!" the elder woman replied.

Susie put her head down on Mrs Ogilvy's knee, and her cheek upon her friend's hand, and then gave way to a sudden outburst of silent tears, sobbing a little, like a child. Mrs Ogilvy shed no tear. She patted the bowed head softly with her hand, as if she had been consoling a child. "The time's very long," she said,—"very long, and never a word."

After a while Susie raised her head. "I must, perhaps, not be very well after all," she said, with an attempt at a smile; "or why should I cry like that?

It is just that I could not help thinking and minding. It was about this time of the year——"

"The fifteenth of this month," Mrs Ogilvy said; "to-morrow, and then it'll be fifteen years."

They sat for a little together saying nothing; and then Susie exclaimed, as if she could not contain herself, "But he'll come back—I'm just as sure Robbie will come back! He will give you no warning; he was never one for writing. You will just hear his step on the road, and he will be here."

"That is what I think myself," Mrs Ogilvy said.

And while they were sitting together silent, there suddenly came into the silence the click of the gate and the sound of a step. And they both started, for a moment almost believing that he had come.

CHAPTER IV.

THE continued disappointment, which was no disappointment but only the fall of a fancy, a bubble of fond imagination in which there was no reality at all —happened once more, while these two ladies sat together and listened. And then the shadow of a man crossed the open window—a little man—who, not knowing he was seen, paused to wipe his bald head and recover his breath before he rang the bell at the open door. The house was all open, fearing nothing, the sunshine and atmosphere penetrating everywhere.

"It is Mr Somerville, my man of business. It will only be something about siller," Mrs Ogilvy said in a low tone.

"I will go away, then," said Susie. She paused a little, holding her old friend's hands. "And if it's any comfort," she said, "when you're sitting alone and thinking, to mind that there is one not far away that is thinking too—and believing——"

" It is a comfort, Susie—God bless you for it, my
dear——"

" Well, then, there are two of us," she said, with a
smile beaming out of the tearfulness of her face, "and
it will be easier when this weary month is past."

Susie, in her fresh summer dress, with her sweet
colour and her pleasant smile, met, as she went out,
the old gentleman coming in. She did not know him,
but gave him a little bow as she passed, with rural
politeness and the kindness of nature. Susie was not
accustomed to pass any fellow-creature without a salutation. She knew every soul in the parish, and every
soul in the parish knew her. She could not cross any
one's path without dropping, as it were, a flower of
human kindness by the way, except, of course, when
she was in Edinburgh or any other large and conventional place, where she only thought her goodwill to
all whom she met. The visitor, coming from that
great capital and used to the reticences of town life,
was delighted with this little civility. He seized his
hat, pulling it once more off his bald head, and went
into the Hewan uncovered, as if he had been going
into the presence of the Queen. It gave him a little
courage for his mission, which, to tell the truth, was
not a very cheerful mission, nor one which he had
undertaken with any alacrity. It was not that Mrs
Ogilvy's income had sustained any diminution, or that
he had a tale of failing dividends and bad investments

D

to tell. What she had was invested in the soundest
securities, It did not perhaps bring her in as much as
would now be thought necessary; but it was as safe
as the Bank of England, and the Bank of Scotland,
and the British Linen Company, all rolled into one.
Her income scarcely varied a pound year by year.
There was very little for her man of business to do
but to receive the modest dividends and send her the
money as she required it. She would have nothing to
do with banks and cheque-books. She liked always
to have a little money in the house—but there was
little necessity for frequent meetings between her and
the manager of her affairs. He would sometimes come
in on rare occasions when he had taken a long walk
into the country : but Mr Somerville was not so young
as he once had been, and took long walks no more.
Therefore she looked at him not with anxiety but
with a little curiosity when he sat down beside her.
She was far too polite to put, even into a look, the question, What may you be wanting ? but it caused a little
embarrassment between them for the first moment.
She, however, was more at ease than he was—for she
expected nothing more than some question or advice
about money, and he knew that what he had to say
was something of a much more troublous kind. This
made him prolong a little the questions about health
and the remarks on the weather which form the inevitable preliminaries of conversation with such old-

fashioned folk. When they had complimented each
other on the beautiful season, and the young crops
looking so well, and new vegetables so good and
plentiful, there came a little pause again. Mrs Ogilvy
was leaning back a little in her chair, very peaceful,
fearing no blow, when the old gentleman, after clear-
ing his throat a great many times, began—

"You will remember, Mrs Ogilvy—it is a thing you
would be little likely to forget—a commission that you
charged me with, in confidence—it is now a number
of years ago——"

She raised herself suddenly in her chair, and drew
a long breath. The expression of her countenance
changed in a moment. She said nothing, nor was it
necessary : her look, the changed pose of her person
leaning towards him, her two hands clasped together
on the arm of her chair, were enough.

"You must not expect too much, my dear lady—it
is perhaps nothing at all, perhaps another person altogether; but at least, for the first time, it appears to me
that it is something in the shape of a clue. I have
been very cautious, according to your directions, but
all the same I have made many inquiries : and none
of them have ever come to anything."

" I know, I know."

" This, if there's anything in it, is no credit of
mine, it is pure accident." Mr Somerville paused
here to feel in his pockets for something. He tried

his breast-pocket, and his tail-pockets, and all the other mysterious places in which things can be hidden away. "I must have left it in my overcoat," he said. "One moment, if you permit, and I'll get it before I say more."

Mrs Ogilvy made no movement, while she sat there and waited. She closed her eyes, and there came from the depths of her bosom a low sigh, which was something like the breath of patience concentrated and condensed. She was perfectly still when he went back again, full of apologies: after having made a great rustling and searching of pockets in the outer hall, he came back with a newspaper in his hand.

"We have a good deal of business with America," he said. "I can scarcely tell you how it began. One of our clients had a son that went out, and got on very well in business, and one thing followed another; what with remittances home, and expenses out, and money for the starting of farms, and so forth, — and then being laid open to the temptation of American investments, which, as a rule, pay very well, and all our poor customers just give us no peace till we put their money on them. This makes it very necessary for us to know the state of the American stock market, and how this and that is going. You will not maybe quite understand, but so it is."

"I understand," Mrs Ogilvy said.

"And this one, you see, was sent to us a day or two ago with this object. It's from one of the towns in what's called the wild West, just a ramshackle sort of a place, half built, and not a comfortable house in it. But they've got a newspaper, such as it is. And really valuable to us for the last week or two, showing the working of a great scheme."

Would the man never be done? He laid the newspaper across his knee, and pointed his words with little gestures made over it. A glance would have been enough to show her what it was. But no, let patience have its perfect work. By moments she closed her eyes not to see him, and spoke not a word.

"Well, you see, the business of overlooking these American investments comes upon me; and I get a great many of their papers to glance at—trashy things, full of personal gossip, the most outrageous nonsense. I don't often look beyond the share lists. But this morning, when I first came into the office, this thing was lying on my table. I had glanced at it, and taken what was of use in it yesterday. It's just a wonder how it got there again. I gave another glance at it by pure chance, if you'll believe me, as I slipped on my office-coat. And my eye was caught by a name. Well, it was

only an *alias*, among a lot of others; but I've been
told that away there in these wild places you can
never tell which may be a man's real name—as
like as not the fifth or sixth *alias* in a long line."

He looked up at her by chance, and it seemed
to him as if his client had fainted. Her face was
drawn and perfectly white, the eyes half closed.
"Bless me!" he cried, starting up; "it's been more
than she could bear. What can I do?—some
water, or maybe ring the bell."

He was about to do this when she caught him
with one hand, and with the other pointed to the
paper. Something like "Let me hear it," came
from her half-closed lips.

"That I will! that I will!" he cried. It was a relief that she could speak and see. He took up the
paper, and was—how long—a year? of finding the place.

"It's just this," he said; "it's an account of a
broil in which some of those wild fellows got
killed: and among the lot of them that was present, there was one, an Englishman they say—but
that's nothing, for they call us all Englishmen abroad.
Our fathers would never have stood it; but what can
you do? it's handiest when all's said—an Englishman that had been about a ranch, and had been a
miner, and had been a coach-driver, and I don't know
all what; but this is his name, 'Jim Smith, *alias*
Horse - breaking Jim, *alias* James Jones, *alias* Bob

the Devil, *alias,*'" here he held up his finger to
arrest her attention, "' Robert Ogilvy. It is suspected that the last may be his real name.' "

Mrs Ogilvy was incapable of speech. She signed
for the paper, raising herself a little in her chair.

"That is just all there is: you would not understand the story. I've just carefully read it to you.
Well, madam, if you will have it." The old gentleman was much disturbed. He let her take the
paper because he could not resist it, and then he
went of his own accord and rang the bell. "Will
ye bring a little wine, or even a drop of brandy?"
he said, going to meet Janet at the door, "if your
mistress ever takes it. She has had a bit shock,
and she's not very well."

She had got the paper in her hands. The touch
of that real thing brought her back more or less
to herself. She sat up and held it to the light,
and read it every word. There was more of it than
Mr Somerville had read. It was an account of a
tumult at which murder had been done — no accident, but cold-blooded murder, and the names
given were of men more or less involved. The last
of these, perhaps, therefore, the least guilty, was
this man of many names, Robert Ogilvy — oh, to
see it there in such a record! The bonnie name,
all breathing of youth and cheerful life, with the
face of the fresh boy looking at her through it!—

Robbie, her Robbie, *alias* Jim, *alias* Bob, *alias*——
She clasped her hands together with the paper between them, and "O Lord God!" she said, in tones
wrung out of her very heart.

"Just swallow this, swallow this, my dear lady;
it will give you strength. She has had a bit shock.
She will be better, better directly. Just do everything you can for her, like a good woman. I was
perhaps rash. But she'll soon come to herself."

"I am myself, Mr Somerville, I am not needing
any of your brandy. I cannot bide the smell of
it. Janet, take it way. I have got some news that
I will tell you after. Mr Somerville, I will have
to take time to think of it. I cannot get it into
my mind all at once."

"No, no," he said, soothingly, "it was not to be
expected. I was too rash. I should have broken
it to you more gently: a wee drop of wine, if you
will not have the brandy? — though good spirit
is always the best."

"I want nothing," she said; "just give me a moment to think." And then out of that bitterness
of death there came a low cry—"Oh, his bonnie
name, his bonnie name!"

"Ay," said the old gentleman, full of sympathy,
"that is just what I thought—my old friend's name,
douce honest man! that never did anything to be
ashamed of in all his days."

The blood came back to her face with a rush. "And how can you tell," she said, "whether there's anything to be ashamed of there? You said yourself it was a wild place. They cannot be on their p's and q's as we are, choosing their company. I am a decent woman myself, and have been, as you say, all my days; but who could tell what kind of folk I might have got among had I been there?"

She rose up and began to walk about the room in sudden excitement. "He would interfere to help the weak one," she said. "If there was a weak side, he would be upon that; he would be helping somebody. Him—murder a man! You were his father's friend, I know; but did you ever see Robbie Ogilvy, my son?—and, if not, man! how daur you speak, and speak of shame and my laddie together, to me?"

Mr Somerville was so taken my surprise that he could not find a word to say. "I thought," he began —and then he stopped short. Had not shame already been busy with Robbie Ogilvy's name? But however much he had been in possession of his faculties and recollections, silence was the wiser way.

"There is one thing," Mrs Ogilvy said; "if this be true, and if it be *him*—there will be a trial, and he will need defence. He must have the best defence, the best advocate. You will send somebody

out at once without losing a day. Oh, I'm old, I'm
weak, I'm an old woman that knows nothing! I've
never been from home. But what is all that. What
is all that to my Robbie? I think, Mr Somerville, I
will go myself."

"You must not think of that," he cried. "A wild
unsettled country, and miles and miles, in all proba-
bility, to be done on horseback, and no certainty
where to find him—if it is him—on one side of the
continent or the other. For, you will see, none of
them were taken. Not the chief person, who will
doubtless be a very different sort of person, nor—
any of the others. They will all be away from that
place like the lightning. They will not bide to be
put through an interrogatory or stand their trial.
I will tell you what I will do. I will write to our
correspondents most particularly. I will bid them
employ the sharpest fellow they can find about there
to follow him and run him down."

"Run him down!" she cried, with a mixture of
horror and indignation,—"my boy! You use words
that are ill chosen and drive me out of my senses,"
she added, with a certain dignity. "But you are
well meaning, Mr Somerville, and not an injudicious
person in business so far as I have seen. You will
write to no correspondents. There must be sharp
fellows here, and men that have been about the
world. You will send one of them. If I go my-

self or not, I will take a little time to think; but
without losing a day or a moment you will send one
of them."

"It will be a great expense, Mrs Ogilvy—and the
other way would be better. I might even cable to our
correspondents: that means telegraph. It's another
of their new-fangled words."

"The one need not hinder the other. You can do
both. Cable, as you call it——"

"It is very expensive," he said.

"Man!" cried Mrs Ogilvy, towering over him,
"what am I caring about expense?—expense! when
it's *him* that is in question. It will be the quickest
way. Cable or telegraph, or whatever you call it;
and since there's nothing that can be done to-night,
send the man wherever you may find him — to-
morrow."

"You go very fast," he cried, panting as if for
breath.

"And so would you, if it was your only son, your
only child, that was in question. And I will think.
I will perhaps set out to-morrow myself."

"To-morrow is the Sabbath-day," said Mr Somerville, with an indescribable sensation of relief.

This damped Mrs Ogilvy's spirit for the moment.
"It's not that I would be kept back by the Sabbath-
day," she said; "for Him that was the Lord of the
Sabbath, He just did more on that day than any

other, healing and saving: and would He put it against me? Oh no! I ken Him too well for that. But since it's not a lawful day for travelling, and there's few trains and boats, send your cable to-night, Mr Somerville. Let that be done at least, if it is the only thing we can do."

"There will still be time; but I will have to hurry away," said the old gentleman reluctantly, "to Edinburgh by the next train."

And then there ensued a struggle in the mind of the hostess, to whom hospitality was second nature. "I did not think of that; and you've had a hot journey out here, and nothing to refresh you. Forgive me, that have been just wrapped up in my own concerns. You will stay and take—some dinner before you go back."

"No, no," he said; "it's a terrible thing for you to refuse a dinner to a hungry man. You never did the like of that in your life before. But it's best I should go. There's a train in half an hour. I'll take a glass of the wine you would not take, and I'll be fresh again for my walk to the station. It's not just so warm as it was."

"You will stay to your dinner, Mr Somerville."

"No; I could not swallow it, and you could not endure to see me eating it and losing time."

"Then Andrew shall put in the pony, and drive you down to Eskholm," Mrs Ogilvy said. This was a relief to her, in the unexampled contingency of sending a visitor unrefreshed from her house— a thing which perhaps had never happened in her life before.

She went out to her habitual place outside a little later, at her usual hour. She was not capable of saying anything to Janet, who followed her wistfully, putting herself forward to bring out her mistress's cushion, her footstool, her book, her knitting, one after another, always hoping to be told what Mrs Ogilvy had promised to tell her after. But not a word did her mistress say. She did not even sit down as she usually did, but walked about, quickly at first, then with gradually slackening steps, sometimes pausing to look round, sometimes stooping to throw away a withered leaf, but always resuming that restless walk which was so unlike her usual tranquillity. She had her hand pressed upon her side, as one might press a handkerchief upon a wound. And indeed she had the stroke of a sword in her heart, and the life-blood flowing. Robert Ogilvy, Robbie Ogilvy, the bonnie name! and after the silence of fifteen years to hear it now as in the 'Hue and Cry,' at the end of all that long string of awful nicknames. It was only now that she had full time to realise it all. Yesterday at this time what would she not have given for any indication that he was living and where he was! She

would have said she could bear anything only to
know that he was safe, and to have some clue by
which he could be found. And now she had both, and
a wound gaping in her heart that required both her
hands to cover it, to prevent her life altogether from
welling away. Robert Ogilvy, Robert Ogilvy—oh, his
bonnie name!

After a while, her forces wearing out, she sat down
in her usual place, but not with her usual patience
and calm. Was that what could be called an answer
to her prayers?—the sudden revelation of her son,
for whom she had cried to God for all these years
night and day, in anguish and crime and danger?
Oh, was this an answer? Her eyes wandered by habit
to the landscape below and the road which she had
watched so often, the white road, white with summer
dust, upon which every passing figure showed. There
was a passing figure now, walking slowly along as far
as she could see. On another day she would have
wondered who the man was. She took no interest
in him now, but saw him pass and pass again as if
it were the merest accident. It was not until she
had seen him pass three or four times that her attention was roused. A big figure, not one she could
identify with any of the usual passers-by, strangely
clad, and carrying a cloak folded over one shoulder.
A cloak? what could a man like that want with a
cloak—an old-fashioned cumbrous thing. Whatever

he wanted, he kept his face towards the Hewan. Sometimes he passed very slow, lingering at every step; sometimes very fast, as if he were pursued. Other figures went and came—the farmers' gigs, a few carriages of the gentry going home. It was late, though it was still so light. What was that man doing loitering always there? Her attention was more and more drawn to the road. At last she saw that nobody except this one man was within sight, not a wheel audible, not a creature visible. The figure seemed to hesitate, and then all at once with a dart approached the gate, which swung at his touch. Was he coming here? Who was he? Long, long had she watched and waited. Was he coming home at last this June day,—this night of all nights? And who was he, who was he, the man that was coming? It will only be some person with a message—it will only be some gangrel person, Mrs Ogilvy said to herself.

CHAPTER V.

THE footstep came slowly up the sloping path. The holly-hedges were high, and for some time nothing more was visible than a moving speck over the solid wall of green. There is something in awaiting in this way the slow approach of a stranger which affects the nerves, even when there is little expectation and no alarm in the mind. Mrs Ogilvy sat speechless and unable to move, her throat parched and dry, her heart beating wildly. Was it he? Was it some one pursuing him — some avenger of blood on his track? Was it no one at all—some silly messenger, some sturdy beggar, some one who would require Andrew to turn him away? These questions went through her head in a whirl, without any volition of hers. The last was the most likely. She waited with a growing passion and suspense, yet still in outward semblance as the rose-bush with all its buds showing white, which stood tranquilly in the dimness behind her. It was growing dark; or rather it was growing dim, everything still visible, but vaguely, as if a veil had dropped between the eye and what it saw. When the man came out at the head of the path, detached and separate from all the trees and their shadows, upon the little platform, a thrill came over the looker-on. He seemed to pause there for a moment, then advanced slowly.

A tall big man, loosely dressed so as to make his proportions look bigger : his features, which there would not in any case have been light enough to see, half lost in a long brown beard, and in the shade of the broad soft hat, partly folded back, which covered his head. He did not take that off or say anything, but came slowly, half reluctantly forward, till he stood before her. It seemed to Mrs Ogilvy that she was paralysed. She could not move nor speak. This strange figure came into the peaceful circle of the little house closing up for the night, separated from all the world—in silence, like a ghost, like a secret and mysterious Being whose coming meant something very different from the comings and goings of the common day. He stood all dark like a shadow before the old lady trembling in her chair, with her white cap and white shawl making a strange light in the dim picture. How long this moment of silence lasted neither knew. It became intolerable to both at the same moment. She burst

E

forth, "Who are you, who are you, man?" in a
voice which shook and went out at the end like the
flame of a candle in the air. "Have you forgotten
me—altogether?" he said.

"Altogether?" she echoed, painfully raising herself
from her chair. It brought her a little nearer to him,
to the brown beard, the shadowed features, the eyes
which looked dimly from under the deep shade of
the hat. She stood for a moment tottering, trembling,
recognising nothing, feeling the atmosphere of him
sicken and repel her. And then there came into that
wonderful pause a more wonderful and awful change
of sentiment, a revolution of feeling. "Mother!"
he said.

And with a low cry Mrs Ogilvy fell back into
her chair. At such moments what can be done but
to appeal to heaven? "Oh my Lord God!" she
cried.

She had looked for it so long, for years and years
and years, anticipated every particular of it: how
she would recognise him afar off, and go out to meet
him, like the father of the prodigal, and bring him
home, and fill the house with feasting because her
son who had been lost was found: how he would
come to her all in a moment, and fling himself down
by her side, with his head in her lap, as had been
one of his old ways. Oh, and a hundred ways besides,
like himself, like herself, when the mother and the

son after long years would look each other in the
face, and all the misery and the trouble would be
forgotten! But never like this. He said "Mother,"
and she dropped away from him, sank into the seat
behind her, putting out neither hands nor arms.
She did not lose consciousness—alas! she had not
that resource, pain kept her faculties all awake—
but she lost heart more completely than ever before.
A wave of terrible sickness came over her, a sense
of repulsion, a desire to hide her face, that the
shadows might cover her, or cover him who stood
there, saying no more: the man who was her son,
who said he was her son, who said "Mother" in a
tone which, amid all these horrible contradictions,
yet went to her heart like a knife. Oh, not with
sweetness! sharp, sharp, cutting every doubt away!

"Mother," he said again, "I would have sworn
you would not forget me, though all the world forgot me."

"No," she said, like one in a dream. "Can a
mother forget her——" Her voice broke again, and
went out upon the air. She lifted her trembling
hands to him. "Oh Robbie, Robbie! are you my
Robbie?" she said in a voice of anguish, with the
sickness and the horror in her heart.

"Ay, mother," he said, with a tone of bitterness
in his voice; "but take me in, for I'm tired to
death."

And then a great compunction awoke within her:
her son, for whom she had longed and prayed all
these years — and instead of running out to meet
him, and putting the best robe on him, a ring on
his hand, and shoes on his feet, he had to remind
her that he was tired to death! She took him by
the hand and led him in, and put him in the big
chair. "I am all shaken," she said: "both will and
sense, they are gone from me: and I don't know
what I am doing. Robbie, if ye are Robbie——"

"Do you doubt me still, mother?" He took off
his hat and flung it on the floor. Though he was
almost too much broken down for resentment, there
was indignation in his tone. And then she looked at
him again, and even in the dimness recognised her
son. The big beard hid the lower part of his face,
but these were Robbie's eyes, eyes half turned away,
sullen, angry—as she had seen him look before he
went away, when he was reproved, when he had done
wrong. She had forgotten that ever he had looked
like that, but it flashed back to her mind in a moment
now. She had forgotten that he had ever been anything but kind and affectionate and trusting, easily
led away, oh, so easily led away, but nothing worse
than that. Now it all came back upon her, the
shadows that there had been to that picture even
at its best.

"Robbie," she said, with faltering lips, "Robbie, oh,

my dear! I know you now," and she put those trembling lips to his forehead. They were cold—it could not feel like a kiss of love; and she was trembling from head to foot, chiefly with emotion, but a little with fear. She could not help it: her heart yearned over him, and yet she was afraid of this strange man who was her son.

He did not attempt to return the salutation in any way. He said drearily, " I have not had bite nor sup for twelve hours, nothing but a cup of bad coffee this morning. My money's all run out."

" Oh, my laddie!" she cried, and hurried to the bell but did not ring it, and then to the door. But before she could reach the door, Janet came in with the lamp. She came unconscious that any one was there, with the sudden light illuminating her face, and making all the rest of the room doubly dark to her. She did not see the stranger sitting in the corner, and gave a violent start, almost upsetting the lamp as she placed it on the table, when with a half laugh he suddenly said, "And here's Janet!" out of the shade. Janet turned round like lightning, with a face of ashes. " Who's that," she cried, " that calls me by my name?"

" We shall see," he said, rising up, " if she knows me better than my mother." Mrs Ogilvy stood by with a pang which words could not describe, as Janet flung up her arms with a great cry. It was true:

the woman did recognise him without a moment's hesitation, while his mother had held back—the woman, who was only the servant, not a drop's blood to him. The mother's humiliation could not be put into words.

"Janet," she said severely, mastering her voice, "set out the supper at once, whatever is in the house. It will be cold; but in the meantime put the chicken to the fire that you got for to-morrow's dinner: the cold beef will do to begin with: and lose not a moment. Mr Robert,"—she paused a moment after those words,—"Mr Robert has arrived suddenly, as you see, and he has had a long journey, and wants his supper. You can speak to him after. Now let us get ready his food."

She went out of the room before her maid. She would not seem jealous, or to grudge Janet's ready and joyful greeting. She went into the little dining-room, and began to arrange the table with her own hands. "Go you quick and put the chicken to the fire," she said. Was she glad to escape from his presence, from Robbie, her long absent son, her only child? All the time she went quickly about, putting out the shining silver, freshly burnished, as it was Saturday; the fresh linen, put ready for Sunday; the best plates, part of the dinner-service that was kept in the dining-room. "This will do for the cold things," she said; "and oh, make haste, make haste

with the rest!" Then she took out the two decanters
of wine, the port and the sherry, which nobody drank,
but which she had always been accustomed to keep
ready. The bread was new, just come in from the
baker's, everything fresh, the provisions of the Saturday market, and of that instinct which prepares the
best of everything for Sunday—the Sabbath—the
Lord's day. It was not the fatted calf, but at least
it was the best fare that ever came into the house,
the Sunday fare.

Then she went back to him in the other room: he
had not followed her, but sat just as she had left him,
his head on his breast. He roused up and gave a
startled look round as she came in, as if there might
be some horrible danger in that peaceful place.
"Your supper is ready," she said, her voice still
tremulous. "Come to your supper. It is nothing
but cold meat to begin with, but the chicken will
soon be ready, Robbie: there's nothing here to
fear——"

"I know," he said, rising slowly: "but if you had
been like me, in places where there was everything
to fear, it would be long before you got out of the
way of it. How can I tell that there might not be
somebody watching outside that window, which you
keep without shutter or curtain, in this lonely little
house, where any man might break in?"

He gave another suspicious glance at the window

as he followed her out of the room. "Tell Janet to
put up the shutters," he said.

Then he sat down and occupied himself with his
meal, eating ravenously, like a man who had not seen
food for days. When the chicken came he tore it
asunder (tearing the poor old lady's heart a little, in
addition to all deeper wounds, by the irreverent rend-
ing of the food, on which, she had also remarked, he
asked no blessing), and ate the half of it without stopping. His mother sat by and looked on. Many a
time had she sat by rejoicing, and seen Robbie, as she
had fondly said, "devour" his supper, with happy
laugh and jest, and questions and answers, the boy
fresh from his amusements, or perhaps, though more
rarely, his work—with so much to tell her, so much
to say,—she beaming upon him, proud to see how
heartily he ate, rejoicing in his young vigour and
strength. Now he ate in silence, like a wild animal,
as if it might be his last meal; while she sat by, the
shadow of her head upon the wall behind her showing
the tremor which she hoped she had overcome, trying
to say something now and then, not knowing what to
say. He had looked up after his first onslaught upon
the food, and glanced round the table. "Have you no
beer?" he said. Mrs Ogilvy jumped up nervously.
"There is the table-beer we have for Andrew," she
said. "You will have whisky, at least. I must have
something to drink with my dinner," he answered,

morosely. Mrs Ogilvy knew many uses for whisky, but to drink it, not after, but with dinner, was not one that occurred to her. She brought out the old-fashioned silver case eagerly from the sideboard, and sought among the shelves where the crystal was for the proper sized glass. But he poured it out into the tumbler, to her horror, dashing the fiery liquid about and filling it up with water. "I suppose," he said again, looking round him with a sort of angry contempt, "there's no soda-water here?"

"We can get everything on Monday, whatever you like, my—my dear," she said, in her faltering voice.

Afterwards she was glad to leave him, to go up-stairs and help Janet, whose steps she heard overhead in the room so long unused—his room, where she had always arranged everything herself, and spent many an hour thinking of her boy, among all the old treasures of his childhood and youth. It was a room next to her own—a little larger—"for a lad has need of room, with his big steps and his long legs," she had many a time said. She found Janet hesitating be-tween two sets of sheets brought out from Mrs Ogilvy's abundant store of napery, one fine, and one not so fine. "It's a grand day his coming hame," Janet said. "Ye'll mind, mem, a ring on his finger and shoes on his feet: it's true that shoon are first necessaries, but no the ring on his finger."

"Take these things away," said Mrs Ogilvy, with

an indignation that was more or less a relief to her, pushing away the linen, which slid in its shining whiteness to the floor, as if to display its intrinsic excellence though thus despised. She went to the press and brought out the best she had, her mother's spinning in the days when mothers began to think of their daughter's "plenishing" for her wedding as soon as she was born. She brought it back in her arms and placed it on the bed. "He shall have nothing but the best," she said, spreading forth the snowy linen with her own hands. Oh! how often she had thought of doing that, going over it, spreading the bed for Robbie, with her heart dancing in her bosom! It did not dance now, but lay as if dead, but for the pain of its deadly wounds.

"And, Janet," she said, "how it is to be done I know not, but Andrew must hurry to the town to get provisions for to-morrow. It will be too late to-night, and who will open to him, or who will sell to him on the Sabbath morning, is more than I can tell; but we must just trust——"

"Mem," said Janet, "I have sent him already up Esk to Johnny Small's to get some trout that he catched this afternoon, but couldna dispose o' them so late. And likewise to Mrs Loanhead at the Knowe farm, to get a couple of chickens and as many eggs as he could lay his hands on. You'll not be surprised if ye hear the poor things cackling. We'll just thraw their necks the morn. I maun say again, as I have aye said, that for a house like this to have nae resources of its ain, no a chicken for a sudden occasion without flying to the neebors, is just a very puir kind of thing."

"And what would become of my flowers, with your hens and their families about?"

"Flooers!" said Janet, contemptuously: and her mistress had not spirit to continue the discussion.

"And now," she said, "that all's ready, I must go down and see after my son."

"Eh, mem, but you're a proud woman this night to say thae words again! and him grown sic a grand buirdly man!"

The poor lady smiled—she could do no more—in her old servant's face, and went down-stairs to the dining-room, which she found to her astonishment full of smoke, and those fumes of whisky which so often fill a woman's heart with sickness and dismay, even when there is no need for such emotion. Robert Ogilvy sat with his chair pushed back from the table, a pipe in his mouth, and a tumbler of whisky-and-water at his hand. The whisky and the food had perhaps given him a less hang-dog look, but the former had not in the least affected him otherwise, nor probably had he taken enough to do so. But the anguish of the sight was not less at the first glance to his mother, so long unaccustomed to the habits of

even the soberest men. She said nothing, and tried
even to disguise the trouble in her expression, heart-
wrung with a cumulation of experiences, each adding
something to those that had gone before.

"Your room is ready, Robbie, my dear. You will
be wearied with this long day—and the excitement,"
she said, with a faint sob, "of coming home."

"I do not call that excitement," he said: "a man
that knows what excitement is has other ways of
reckoning——"

"But still," she said, with a little gasp accepting
this repulse, "it would be something out of the
common. And you will have been travelling all
day. How far have you come to-day, my dear?"

"Don't put me through my catechism all at once,"
he said, with a hasty wrinkle of anger in his forehead.
"I'll tell you all that another time. I'm very tired,
at least, whether I've come a short way or a long."

"I have put your bed all ready for you—Robbie."
She seemed to say his name with a little reluctance:
his bonnie name! which had cost her so keen a pang
to think of as stained or soiled. Was it the same
feeling that arrested it on her lips now?

"Am I bothering you, mother, staying here a little
quiet with my pipe? for I'll go, if that is what you
want."

She had coughed a little, much against her will,
unaccustomed to the smoke. "Bothering me!" she

cried: "is it likely that anything should bother me
to-night, and my son come back?"

He looked at her, and for the first time seemed
to remark her countenance strained with a wistful
attempt at satisfaction, on the background of her
despair.

"I am afraid," he said, shaking his head, "there is
not much more pleasure in it to you than to me."

"There would be joy and blessing in it, Robbie,"
she cried, forcing herself to utterance, "if it was a
pleasure to you."

"That's past praying for," he replied, almost roughly,
and then turned to knock out his pipe upon the edge
of the trim summer fireplace, all so daintily arranged
for the warm season when fires were not wanted.
Her eyes followed his movements painfully in spite
of herself, seeing everything which she would have
preferred not to see. And then he rose, putting the
pipe still not extinguished in his pocket. "If it's
to be like this, mother," he said, "the best thing for
me will be to go to bed. I'm tired enough, heaven
knows; but the pipe's my best friend, and it was
soothing me. Now I'll go to bed——"

"Is it me that am driving you, Robbie? I'll go
ben to the parlour. I will leave you here. I will do
anything that pleases you——"

"No," he said, with a sullen expression closing over
his face, "I'll go to bed." He was going without

another word, leaving her standing transfixed in the
middle of the room—but, after a glance at her, came
back. "You'll be going to church in the morning,"
he said. "I'll take what we used to call a long lie,
and you need not trouble yourself about me. I'm a
different man from what you knew, but—it's not my
wish to trouble you, mother, more than I can help."

"Oh, Robbie, trouble me!" she cried: "oh, my
boy! would I not cut myself in little bits to please
you? would I not—— I only desire you to be
comfortable, my dear—my dear!"

"You'll make them shut up all these staring open
windows if you want me to be comfortable," he said.
"I can't bear a window where any d——d fellow
might jump in. Well, then, good-night."

She took his hand in both hers. She reached up
to him on tiptoe, with her face smiling, yet convulsed with trouble and pain. "God bless you,
Robbie! God bless you! and bless your home-
coming, and make it happier for you and me than
it seems," she said, with a sob, almost breaking
down. He stooped down reluctantly his cheek towards her, and permitted her kiss rather than received it. Oh, she remembered now! he had done
that when he was angered, when he was blamed,
in the old days. He had not been, as she persuaded
herself, all love and kindness even then.

But she would not allow herself to stop and think.

Though she had herself slept securely for years, in the quiet of her age and peacefulness, with little heed to doors and windows, she bolted and barred them all now with her own hands. "Mr Robert wishes it," she said, explaining to Janet, who came in in much surprise at the sound. "He has come out of a wild country full of strange chancy folk— and wild beasts too, in the great forests," she added by an after-thought. "He likes to see that all's shut up when we're so near the level of the earth."

"I'm very glad that's his opinion," said Janet, "for it's mine; no for wild beasts, the Lord preserve us! but tramps, that's worse. But Andrew's not back yet, and he will be awfu' surprised to see all the lights out."

"Andrew must just keep his surprise to himself," said the mistress in her decided tones, "for what my son wishes, whatever it may be, that is what I will do."

"'Deed, mem, and I was aye weel aware o' that," Janet said.

CHAPTER VI.

THE next day was such a Sunday as had never been passed in the Hewan before. Mrs Ogilvy did not go to church: consequently Sandy was not taken out of the stable, nor was there any of the usual cheerful bustle of the Sunday morning, the little commotion of the best gown, the best bonnet, the lace veil taken out of their drawers among the lavender. Nobody but Mrs Ogilvy continued to wear a lace veil: but her old, softly tinted countenance in the half mask of a piece of net caught upon the nose, as was once the fashion, or on the chin, as is the fashion now, would have been an impossible thing. Her long veil hung softly from her bonnet behind it or above it. It could cover her face when there was need; but there never was any reason why she should cover her face. Her faithful servants admired her very much in her Sunday attire. Janet, though she was so hot a churchwoman, was not much of a churchgoer. Somebody, she said, had to stay at home to look after the house and the dinner, even when it was a cold dinner: and to see the mistress sit down without even a hot potatie, was more than she could consent to: so except on great occasions she remained at home, and Andrew put a mark in his Bible at the text, and told her as much as he could remember of the discourse. It was a "ploy" for Janet to come out to the door into the still and genial sunshine on Sunday morning, and see the little pony-carriage come round, all its polished surfaces shining, and Sandy tossing his head till every bit of the silver on his harness twinkled in the sun, and Andrew, all in his best, bringing him up with a little dash at the door. And then Mrs Ogilvy would come out, not unconscious and not displeased that the old servants were watching for her, and that the sight of her modest finery was a "ploy" to Janet, who had so few ploys. She would pin a rose on her breast when it was the time of roses, and take a pair of grey gloves out of her drawer, to give them pleasure, with a tender feeling that made the little vanity sweet. The grey gloves were, indeed, her only little adornment, breaking the monotony of the black which she always wore; but Janet loved the lustre of the best black silk, and to stroke it with her hand as she arranged it in the carriage, loath to cover up its sheen with

F

the wrapper which was necessary to protect it from
the dust. Nothing of all this occurred on the dull
morning of this strange Sabbath, which, as if in
sympathy, was grey and cheerless—the sky without
colour, the landscape without sunshine. Mrs Ogilvy
came out to the door to speak to Andrew as he
ploughed across the gravel with discontented looks
—for to walk in to the kirk did not please the
factotum, who generally drove. She called him to
her, standing on the doorstep drawing her white
shawl round her as if she had taken a chill. "Andrew," she said, "I know you are not a gossip; but
it's a great event my son coming home. I would
have you say little about it to-day, for it would
bring a crowd of visitors, and perhaps some even
on the Sabbath: and Mr Robert is tired, and not
caring to see visitors. He must just have a day
or two to rest before everybody knows."

"I'm no a man," said Andrew, a little sullen,
"for clashes and clavers: you had better, mem, say
a word to the wife." Andrew was conscious that
in his prowl for victuals the night before he had
spread the news of Ogilvy's return,—"and nae mair
comfort to his mother nor ever, or I am sair mis-
taen"—far and wide.

"Whatever you do," Mrs Ogilvy said, a little subdued by Andrew's looks, "do not say anything to
the minister's man."

She went back, and sat down in her usual place between the window and the fireplace. The room was full of flowers, gathered fresh for Sunday; and the Bible lay on the little table, the knitting and the newspapers being carefully cleared away. She took the book and opened it, or rather it opened of itself, at those chapters in St John's Gospel which are the dearest to the sorrowful. She opened it, but she did not read it. She had no need. She knew every word by heart, as no one could do by any mere effort of memory: but only by many, many readings, long penetration of the soul by that stream of consolation. It did her a little good to have the book open by her side: but she did not need it— and, indeed, the sacred words were mingled unconsciously by many a broken prayer and musing of her own. She had gone to her son's room, to the door, many times since she parted with him the night before; but had heard no sound, and, hovering there on the threshold, had been afraid to go in, as she so longed to do. What mother would not, after so long an absence, steal in to say again good-night—to see that all was comfortable, plenty of covering on the bed, not too much, just what he wanted; or again, in the morning, to see how he had slept, to recognise his dear face by the morning light, to say God bless him, and God bless him the first morning as the first night of his return? But

Mrs Ogilvy was afraid. She went and stood outside the door, trembling, but she had not the courage to go in. She felt that it might anger him—that it might annoy him—that he would not like it. He had been a long time away. He had grown a man almost middle-aged, with none of the habits or even recollections of a boy. He would not like her to go near him—to touch him. With a profound humility of which she was not conscious, she explained to herself that this was after all "very natural." A man within sight of forty (she counted his age to a day—he was thirty-seven) had forgotten, being long parted from them, the ways of a mother. He had maybe, she said to herself with a shudder, known—other kinds of women. She had no right to be pained by it—to make a grievance of it. Oh no, no grievance: it was "very natural." If she went into the parlour, where she always sat in the morning, she would hear him when he began to move: for that room was over this. Meantime, what could she do better than to read her chapter, and say her prayers, and bless him—and try "to keep her heart"?

Many, many times had she gone over the same thoughts that flitted about her mind now and interrupted the current of her prayers, and of the reading which was only remembering. There was Job, whom she had thought of so often, whose habit was, when his sons and daughters were in all

their grandeur before anything happened to them, to
offer sacrifices for them, if, perhaps, in the carelessness
of their youth, they might have done something amiss.
How she had longed to do that! and then had reminded
herself that there were no more sacrifices, that there
had been One for all, and that all she had to do was
but to put God in mind, to keep Him always in
mind: that there was her son yonder somewhere
out in His world, and maybe forgetting what his
duty was. To put God in mind!—as if He did
not remember best of all, thinking on them most
when they were lost, watching the night when
even a mother slumbers and sleeps, and never,
never losing sight of them that were His sons
before they were mine! What could she say then,
what could she do, a poor small thing of a woman,
of as little account as a fly in the big world of
God? Just sit there with her heart bleeding, and
say between the lines, "In my Father's house are
many mansions"—and, "If a man love me, my
Father will love him, and we will come unto him,
and make our abode with him:" nothing but "my
Robbie, my Robbie!" with anguish and faith con-
tending. This was all mixed up among the verses
now, those verses that were balm, the keen sharpness
of this dear name.

She was not, however, permitted to remain with
these thoughts alone. Janet came softly to the door,

want them least is just the time they are like to
come."

"We'll just steek the doors and let them chap till
they're wearied," said Janet, promptly. "They'll think
ye've gane away like other folk, for change of air."

"I'm loth to do that—when folk have come so far,
and tired with their walk. Do you think, Janet, you
could have the tea ready, and just say I have—stepped
out to see a neighbour, or that I'm away at the manse,
or——? I would be out in the garden out of sight,
so it would be no lee to say I was out of the house."

"If it's the lee you're thinking of, mem—I'm no
caring that," and Janet snapped her fingers, "for
the lee."

Neither mistress nor maid called it a lie, which
was a much more serious business. The Scottish
tongue is full of those *nuances*, which in other
languages we find so admirable.

"Oh, Janet!" cried Mrs Ogilvy again, between
laughing and crying, "I fear I'll have but an ill
character to give you — washing out a shirt on
Sunday and caring nothing for a lee!"

"If we can just get Andrew aff to his kirk in
the afternoon. I'll no have him at my lug for
ever wi' his sermons. Lord, if I hadna kent better
how to fend for him than he did himsel', would
he ever have been a man o' weight, as they say
he is, in that Auld Licht meetin' o' his, and speak-

ing ill o' a' the ither folk? Just you leave it to
me. Bless us a'! sae lang as the dear laddie is
comfortable, what's a' the rest to you and me?"

"Oh, Janet, my woman!" said the mistress, holding out her hand. It was so small and delicate that
Janet was seized with a compunction after she had
squeezed it in her own hard but faithful one, which
felt like an iron framework in comparison. " I
doubt I've hurt her," she said to herself; "but I
was just carried away."

And Mrs Ogilvy was restored to her musing
and her prayers, which presently were interrupted
again by sounds in the room overhead — Janet's
step going in, which shook and thrilled the flooring,
and the sound of voices. The mother sat and listened,
and heard his voice speaking to Janet, the mas-
culine tone instantly discernible in a woman's house,
speaking cheerfully, with after a while a laugh. His
tone to her had been very different. It had been full
of involuntary self-defence, a sort of defiance, as if he
felt that at any moment something might be de-
manded of him, excuse or explanation — or else
blame and reproach poured forth upon him. The
mother's heart swelled a little, and yet she smiled.
Oh, it was very natural! He could even joke and
laugh with the faithful servant-woman, who could
call him to no account, whom he had known all
his life. If there was any passing cloud in Mrs

Ogilvy's mind it passed away on the instant, and the only bitterness was that wistful one, with a smile of wonder accompanying it, "That he could think I would demand an account—me!"

He came down-stairs later, half amused with himself, in the high collar of Andrew's gala shirt, and with a smile on his face. "I'm very ridiculous, I suppose," he said, walking to the glass above the mantelpiece; "but I did not want to vex the woman, and clean things are pleasant."

"Is your luggage — coming, Robbie?" she ventured to say, while he stood before the glass trying to fold over or modify as best he could the spikes of the white linen which stood round his face.

"How much luggage do you think a man would be likely to have," he said impatiently, standing with his back towards her, "who came from New York as a stowaway in a sailing-ship?"

She had not the least idea what a stowaway was, but concluded it to be some poor, very poor post, with which comfort was incompatible. "My dear," she said, "you will have to go into Edinburgh and get a new outfit. There are grand shops in Edinburgh. You can get things—I mean men's things—just as well, they tell me, as in London."

She spoke in a half-apologetic tone, as if he had been in the habit of getting his clothes from London, and might object to a less fashionable place

— for indeed the poor lady was much confused, believing rather that her son had lived extravagantly and lavishly than that he had been put to all the shifts of poverty.

"I've had little luggage this many a day," he said, — "a set of flannels when I could get them for the summer, and for winter anything that was warm enough. I've not been in the way of sending to Poole for my clothes." He laughed, but it was not the simple laugh that had sounded from the room above. "What did I ever know about London, or anything but the commonest life?"

"Just what we could give you, Robbie," she said, in a faltering tone.

"Well!" he cried impatiently. And then he turned round and faced her—Andrew's collars, notwithstanding all his efforts, giving still a semi-ludicrous air, which gave the sting of an additional pang to Mrs Ogilvy, who could not bear that he should be ridiculous. He confronted her, sitting down opposite, fixing his eyes on her face, as if to forestall any criticism on her part. "I've come back as I went away," he said with defiance. "I had very little when I started,—I have nothing now. If you had not kept me so bare, and never a penny in my pocket, I might have done better : but nothing breeds nothing, you know, mother. It's one of the laws of the world."

"Robbie, I gave you what I had," she exclaimed, astonished, yet half relieved, to find that it was she who was put on her defence.

"Ay, that's what everybody says. You must have kept a little more for yourself, however, for you seem very comfortable: and you talk at your ease of a new outfit, while I've been glad of a cast-off jacket or an old pair of breeks that nobody else would wear."

"Oh Robbie, Robbie!" she cried in a voice of anguish, "and me laying up every penny for you, and ready with everything there was — at a moment's notice!"

"Well, perhaps it's better as it is," he said: "I might just have lost it again. You get into a sort of a hack-horse way — just the same round, and never able to get out of it—unless when you've got to cut and run for your life."

"Robbie!"

"I'll tell you about that another time. I don't know what you're going to do with me, now you've got me here. I'm a young fellow enough yet, mother —a sort of a young fellow, but not good for anything. And then if this affair comes up, I may have to cut and run again. Oh, I'll tell you about it in time! It's not likely they'll be after me, with all the loose swearing there is yonder, and extraditions, and that kind of thing; but I'm not one that would stand being had up and examined—even if I was sure I should get off: I'd just cut and run."

"Is there any danger?" she said in a terrified whisper.

He burst out laughing again, but these laughs were not good to hear. "Of what do you think? That they might hang me up to the first tree? But till it blows over I can be sure of nothing—or if any other man turns up. There is a man before whom I would just cut and run too. If he should get wind that I was here"—he gave a suspicious glance round. "And this confounded house on a level with the ground, and the windows open night and day!"

"Who is it? Who is the man?" she said. She followed every change of his face, every movement, every question, with eyes large with panic and terror.

What he said first, he had the grace to say under his breath out of some revived tradition of respect, "Would you be any the wiser if I told you a name—that you never heard before?" he said.

"No, Robbie, no. But tell me one thing, is it a man you have wronged? Oh Robbie, tell me, tell me that, for pity's sake!"

"No!" he shouted with a rage that overcame all other feelings. "Damn him! damn him! it's he that has never done anything but hunt and harm me."

"Oh, God be thanked!" cried his mother, suddenly rising and going to him. "Oh Robbie, my
dear, the Lord be praised! and God forgive that
unfortunate person, for if it's him, it's not you!"

He submitted unwillingly for a moment to the
arm which she put round him, drawing his head
upon her breast, and then put her not ungently
away. "If there's any consolation in that, you can
take it," he said: "There's not much consolation in
me, any way." And then he reached his large hand
over the table to her little bookcase, which stood
against the wall. "I can always read a book," he
said, "a story-book; it's the only thing I can do.
You used to have all the Scotts here."

"They are just where they used to be, Robbie,"
she said, in a subdued tone. She watched him, still
standing while he chose one; and throwing himself
back in his chair, began to read. It added a little
sense of embarrassment, of confusion and disorder,
to all the heavier trouble, that he had thrown himself
into her chair, the place in which she had sat through
all those years when there was no one to interfere
with her. Glad was she to give up the best place
in the house to him, whatever he might please to
choose; but it gave her a feeling of disturbance
which she could not explain, not being even aware
at first what it was that caused it. She did not
know where to sit, nor what to do. She could not

go back to fetch her open Bible, nor sit down to read it, partly because it would be a reproach to him sitting there reading a novel — only a novel, no reading for Sabbath, even though it was Sir Walter's; partly because it would seem like indifference, she thought, to occupy herself with reading at all, when at any moment he might have something to say to her again.

CHAPTER VII.

PERHAPS it would be well for Janet's sake not to
inquire into the history of that Sabbath afternoon.
Friends arrived from Edinburgh, as Mrs Ogilvy had
divined, carefully choosing that day when they were
so little wanted. There were some people who
walked, keeping up an old habit: the walk was
long, but when you were sure of a good cup of
tea and a good rest at a friend's house, was not
too much for a robust walker with perhaps little
time for walking during the week: and some—but
they kept a discreet veil on the means of their con-
veyance — would come occasionally by the wicked
little train which, to the great scandal of the whole
village, had been permitted between Edinburgh and
Eskholm in quite recent days, by the direct influence of the devil or Mr Gladstone some thought,
or perhaps for the convenience of a railway director
who had a grand house overlooking the Esk higher

up the stream. It may well be believed, however, that nobody who visited Mrs Ogilvy on Sunday owned to coming by the train. They could not resist the delights of the walk in this fine weather, they said, and to breathe the country air in June after having been shut up all the week in Edinburgh was a great temptation. They all came from Edinburgh, these good folks: and there was one who was an elder in the Kirk, and who said that the road had been measured, and it was little more, very little more, than a Sabbath-day's journey, such as was always permitted. Sometimes there would be none of these visitors for weeks, but naturally there were two parties of them that day. Mrs Ogilvy, out in the garden behind the house, sat trembling among Andrew's flower-pots in his tool-house, feeling more guilty than words could say, yet giving Janet a certain countenance by remaining out of doors, to justify the statement that the mistress just by an extraordinary accident was out. Robert was in his room up-stairs with half a shelf-ful of the Waverleys round him, lying upon his bed and reading. Oh how the house was turned upside down, how its whole life and character was changed, and falsity and concealment became the rule of the day instead of truth and openness! And all by the event which last Sabbath she had prayed for with all the force of her heart. But

G

she did not repent her prayer. God be thanked, in spite of all, that he had come back, that he that had been dead was alive again, and that he that had been lost was found. Maybe—who could tell?—the prodigal's father, after he had covered his boy's rags with that best robe, might find many a thing, oh many a thing, in him, to mind him of the husks that the swine did eat!

Meantime Janet gave the visitors tea, and stood respectfully and talked, now and then looking out for the mistress, and wondering what could have kept her, and saying many a thing upon which charity ·demands that we should draw a veil. She had got Andrew off to his kirk, which was all she conditioned for. She could not, she felt sure, have carried through if Andrew had been there, glowering, looking on. But she did carry through; and I am not sure that there was not a feeling of elation in Janet's mind when she saw the last of them depart, and felt the full sweetness of success. The sense of guilt, no doubt, came later on.

"And I just would take my oath," said Janet, "that they're all away back by *that* train. Ye needna speak to me of Sabbath-day's journeys, and afternoon walks. The train, nae doubt, is a great easement. I ken a sooth face from a leeing one. They had far ower muckle to say about the pleesure of the walk. They're just a' away back by the train."

"It's not for you and me to speak, Janet, that have done nothing but deceive all this weary day!"

"Toots!" said Janet, "you were out, mem, it was quite true, and just very uncomfortable—and they got their rest and their tea. And I would have gathered them some flowers, but Mrs Bennet said she would rather no go back through the Edinburgh streets with a muckle flower in her hands, as if she had been stravaigin' about the country. So ye see, mem, they were waur than we were, just leein' for show and appearance—whereas with us (though I leed none—I said ye were oot, and ye *were* oot) it was needcessity, and nae mair to be said."

Mrs Ogilvy shook her head as she rose up painfully from among the flower-pots. It was just self-indulgence, she said to herself. She had done harder things than to sit in her place and give her acquaintances tea; but then there was always the risk of questions that old friends feel themselves at liberty to ask. Any way, it was done and over; and there was, as Janet assured her, no more to be said. And the lingering evening passed again, oh so slowly—not, as heretofore, in a gentle musing full of prayer, not in the sweet outside air with the peaceful country lying before her, and the open doors always inviting a wanderer back! Not so: Robert was not satisfied till all the windows were closed, warm though the evening was, the door locked, the shutters bolted, every precaution taken, as if the peaceful Hewan were to be attacked during the night. He caught Andrew in the act of lighting that light over the door which had burned all night for so many years. "What's that for?" he asked abruptly, stopping him as he mounted the steps, without which he could not reach the little lamp.

"What it's for I could not take it upon me to tell you. It's just a whimsey of the mistress. They're full of their whims," Andrew said.

"Mother, what's the meaning of this?" Robert cried.

She came to the parlour door to answer him, with her white shawl and her white cap—a light herself in the dim evening. It was perhaps too dim for him to see the expression in her eyes. She said, with a little drawing of her breath and in a startled voice, "Oh, Robbie!"

"That's no answer," he said, impatiently. "What's the use of it? drawing every tramp's attention to the house. Of course it can be seen from the road."

"Ay, Robbie, that was my meaning."

"A strange meaning," he said, shrugging his shoulders. "You'd better leave it off now, mother. I don't like such landmarks. Don't light it any more."

Andrew stood all this time with one foot on the steps and his candle in his hand. "The mistress,"

he said darkly, in a voice that came from his boots,
."has a good right to her whimsey—whatever it's for."

"Did we ask your opinion?" cried Robert, angrily.
" Put out the light."

" You will do what Mr Robert bids you, Andrew,"
Mrs Ogilvy said.

And for the first time for fifteen years there was
no light over the door of the Hewan. It was right
that it should be so. Still, there was in Mrs Ogilvy's
mind a vague, unreasonable reluctance—a failing as
if of some visionary hope that it might still have
brought back the real Robbie, the bonnie boy she
knew so well, out of the dim world in which, alas!
he was now for ever and for ever lost.

Robert talked much of this before he went up-stairs
to bed. Perhaps he was glad to have something to
talk of that was unimportant, that raised no exciting
questions. " You've been lighting up like a light-
house; you've been showing all over the country, so
far as I can see. But that'll not do for me," he said.
" I'll have to lie low for a long time if I stay here,
and no light thrown on me that can be helped. It's
different from your ways, I know, and you have a
right to your whimseys, mother, as that gardener
fellow says—especially as you are the one that has
to pay for it all."

" Robbie," she cried, " oh, Robbie, do not speak like
that to me!"

"It's true, though. I haven't a red cent; I haven't a brass farthing: nothing but the clothes I'm standing in, and they are not fit to be seen."

"Robbie," she said, "I have to go in to Edinburgh in the morning. Will you come with me and get what you want?"

"Is that how it has to be done?" he said, with a laugh. "I thought you were liberal when you spoke of an outfit; but what you were thinking of was a good little boy to go with his mother, who would see he did not spend too much. No, thank you: I'll rather continue as I am, with Andrew's shirt." He gave another laugh at this, pulling the corners of the collar in his hand.

Mrs Ogilvy had never allowed to herself that she was hurt till now. She rose up suddenly and took a little walk about the room, pretending to look for something. One thing with another seemed to raise a little keen soreness in her, which had nothing to do with any deep wound. It took her some time to bring back the usual tone to her voice, and subdue the quick sting of that superficial wound. "I am going very early," she said; "it will be too early for you. I am going to see Mr Somerville, whom perhaps you will remember, who does all my business. There was something he had taken in hand, which will not be needful now. But you must do—just what you wish. You know it's our old-fashioned way here to

do no business on the Sabbath-day; but the morn,
before I go, I will give you—if you could maybe tell
me what money you would want——?"

"There's justice in everything," he said, in a tone of
good-humour. "I leave that to you."

Then he went to his room again, carrying with him
another armful of Waverleys. Was it perhaps that
he would not give himself the chance of thinking?
It cheered his mother vaguely, however, to see him
with the books. It was not reading for the Sabbath-
day; but yet Sir Walter could never harm any man:
and more still than that—it was not ill men, men
with perverted hearts, that were so fond of Sir Walter.
That was Robbie—the true Robbie—not the man that
had come from the wilds, that had come through crime
and misery, that had run for his life.

She left him a packet of notes next morning before
she went to Edinburgh. This must not be taken as
meaning too much, for it was one-pound notes alone
which Mrs Ogilvy possessed. She was glad to be
alone in the train, having stolen into a compartment
in which a woman with a baby had already placed
herself. She did not know the woman, but here she
felt she was safe. The little thing, which was trouble-
some and cried, was her protection, and she could
carry on her own thoughts little disturbed by that
sound: though indeed after a while it must be
acknowledged that Mrs Ogilvy succumbed to a temp-

tation almost irresistible to a mother, and desired the
woman to "give me the bairn," with a certainty of
putting everything right, which something magnetic
in the experienced touch, in the soft atmosphere of
her, and the *frôlement* of her silk, and the sweetness
of her face, certainly accomplished.   She held the
baby on her knee fast asleep during the rest of the
short journey, and that little unconscious contact with
the helpless whom she could help did her good also.
And the walk to Mr Somerville's office did her good.
On the shady side of the street it is cool, and the little
novelty of being there gave an impulse to her forces.
When she entered the office, where the old gentleman
received her with a little cry of surprise, she was
freshened and strengthened by the brief journey, and
looked almost as she had looked when he found her,
fearing no evil, in the great quiet of the summer
afternoon two days before.   He was surprised yet
half afraid.

"I know what this means," he said, when he had
shaken hands with her and given her a seat.   "You've
made up your mind, Mrs Ogilvy, to make that dreadful journey.   I see it in your face—and I am sorry.
I am very sorry——"

"No," she said; "you are mistaken.   I am not
going.   I came to ask you, on the contrary, after
all we settled the other day, to do nothing
more——"

"To do nothing more!—I cabled as I promised, and I've got the man ready to go out——"

"He must not go," she said.

"Well——I think it is maybe just as wise. But you have changed your mind very quick. I will not speak the common nonsense to you and say that's what ladies will do: for no doubt you will have your reasons—you have your reasons?"

She looked round her, trembling a little, upon the quiet office where nobody could have been hidden, scarcely a fly.

"Mr Somerville," she said, "you were scarcely gone that day—oh, how long it is ago I know not —it might be years!—you were scarcely gone, when my son came home."

"What?" he cried, with a terrifying sharpness of tone.

Her face blanched at the sound. "Was it an ill thing to do? Is there danger?" she cried; and then with deliberate gravity she repeated, "You were scarcely gone when, without any warning, my Robbie came home."

"God bless us all!" said the old gentleman. "No; I do not know that there is any danger. It might be the wisest thing he could do—but it is a very surprising thing for all that."

"It is rather surprising," she said, with a little dignity, "that having always his home open to him,

and no safeguards against the famine that might
arise in that land—and indeed brought down for
his own part, my poor laddie, to the husks that the
swine do eat—he should never have come before."

"That's an old ferlie," said Mr Somerville; "but
things being so that he should have come now—
that's what beats me. There's another paper with
more particulars: maybe he was well advised. It's
a far cry to Lochow. That's a paper I have read
with great interest, Mrs Ogilvy, but it would not
be pleasant reading for you."

"But is there danger?" she said, her face colouring
and fading under her old friend's eye, as she watched
every word that fell from his lips.

"Well," he said, "with a thing like that hanging
over a man's head, it's rash to say that there's no
danger; but these wild offeecials in the wild parts
of America—sheriffs they seem to call them—riding
the country with a wild posse, and a revolver in
every man's hand—bless me, very unlike our sheriffs
here!—have not their eyes fixed on Mid-Lothian nor
any country place hereaway, we may be sure. They
will look far before they will look for him here."

"But is it him—him, my son—that they are looking
for, my Robbie?" she said, with a sharp cry.

"I think I can give you a little comfort in that
too—it's not him in the first place, nor yet in the
second. But he was there—and he was one of them,

or supposed to be one of them. Mistress Ogilvy,"
said the old gentleman, slowly and with emphasis,
"we must be very merciful. A young lad gets mixed
in with a set of these fellows—he has no thought
what it's going to lead to—then by the time he
knows he's so in with them, he has a false notion
that his honour's concerned. He thinks he would
be a kind of a traitor if he deserted them,—and all
the more when there's danger concerned. I have
some experience, as you will perhaps have heard,"
he said, after a pause, with a break in his voice.

"God help us all!" she said, putting out her hand,
her eyes dim with tears. He took it and grasped
it, his hand trembling too.

"You may know by that I will do my very best
for him," he said, "as if he were my own." Then
resuming his business tones, "I would neither hide
him nor put him forward, Mrs Ogilvy, if I were
you. I would keep him at home as much as possible. And if the spirit moves him to come and
tell me all about it—— Has he told you——?"

"Something—about not being one to stand an
examination even if he should get off, and about some
man—some man that might come after him: but
he will not explain. I said, Was it a man he had
wronged? and he cried with a great No! that it
was one that had wronged him."

"Ah! that'll just be one of them: but let us

hope none of these American ruffians will follow
Robert here. No, no, that could not be; but, dear
me, what a risk for you to run in that lonely house.
I always said the Hewan was a bonnie little place,
and I could understand your fancy for it, but very
lonely, very lonely, Mrs Ogilvy. Lord bless us! if
anything of that kind were to happen——! But
no, no; across half the continent and the great Atlantic—and for what purpose? They would never
follow him here."

"I have never been frighted of my house, Mr
Somerville; and now there is my son Robbie in it,
a strong man, bless him!—and Andrew the gardener—and plenty of neighbours less than half a
mile off—oh, much less than half a mile."

"Do you keep money in the house?"

"Money! very little—just enough for my quarter's
payments, nothing to speak of—unless when William
Tod at the croft comes up to pay me my rent."

"Then keep none," said Mr Somerville; "just take
my word and ask no questions—keep none. It's
never safe in a lonely house; and let in no strange
person. A man might claim to be Robert's friend
when he was no friend to Robert. But your heart's
too open and your faith too great. Send away your
money to the bank and lock up your doors before
the darkening, and keep every strange person at a
safe distance."

"But," said Mrs Ogilvy, "where would be my faith then, and my peace of mind? Nobody has harmed me all my days—not a living creature— if it were not them that were of my own house," she added, after a moment's pause. "And who am I that I should distrust my neighbours?—no, no, Mr Somerville. There is Robbie to take care of me, if there was any danger. But I am not feared for any danger—unless it were for him—and you think there will be none for him?"

"That would be too much to say. If he were followed here by any of those ill companions—— Mind now, my dear lady. You say Robert will take care of you. It will be far more you that will have to take care of him."

"I have done that all his days," she said, with a smile and a sigh; "but, oh, he is beyond me now—a big, strong, buirdly man."

They were Janet's words, and it was in the light of Janet's admiration that his mother repeated them. "I am scarcely higher than his elbow," she said, with a more genuine impulse of her own. "And who am I to take care of a muckle strong man."

"Mind!" cried the old gentleman, with a kind of solemnity, "that's just the danger. If there's cronies coming after him, Lord bless us, it may just be life or death. Steek your doors, Mrs Ogilvy, steek your doors. Let no stranger come near you. And

mind that it is you to take care of Robert, not him
of you."

She came away much shaken by this interview.
And yet it was very difficult to frighten her, notwithstanding all her fears.   Already as she came
down the dusty stairs from Mr Somerville's office,
her courage began to return.   Everybody had warned
her of the danger of tramps and vagabonds for the
last twenty years, but not a spoon had ever been
stolen, nor a fright given to the peaceful inhabitants
of the Hewan.   No thief had ever got into the
house, or burglar tried the windows that would
have yielded so easily.   And it could not be any
friend of Robbie's that would come for any small
amount of money she could have, to his mother's
house.   No, no.   Violence had been done, there had
been quarrels, and there had been bloodshed.   But
that was very different from Mr Somerville's advices
about the money in the house.   Robbie's friends
might be dangerous men, they might lead him into
many, many ill ways; but her little money—no, no,
there could be nothing to do with that.   She went
home accordingly almost cheerfully.   To be delivered
from her own thoughts, and brought in face of the
world, and taught to realise all that had happened
as within the course of nature, and a thing to be
faced and to be mended, not to lie down and die
upon, was a great help to her.   She would lock

the doors and fasten the windows as they all said. She would watch that no man should come near that was like to harm her son. To do even so much or so little as that for him, it would be something, something practical and real. She would not suffer her eyelids to slumber, nor her eyes to sleep. She would be her own watchman, and keep the house, that nothing harmful to her Robbie should come near. Oh, but for the pickle money! there was no danger for that. She would like to see what a paltry thief would do in Robbie's hands.

With this in her mind she went back, her heart rising with every step. From the train she could see the back of the Hewan rising among the trees —not a desolate house any longer, for Robbie was there. How ill to please she had been, finding faults in him just because he was a boy no longer, but a man, with his own thoughts and his own ways! But to have been parted from him these few hours cleared up a great deal. She went home eagerly, her face regaining its colour and its brightness. She was going back not to an empty house, but to Robbie. It was as if this, and not the other mingled moment, more full of trouble than joy, was to be the mother's first true meeting with her son after so many years.

CHAPTER VIII.

WHEN Mrs Ogilvy reached, somewhat breathless, the height of the little brae on which her own door, standing wide open in the sunshine, offered her the usual unconscious welcome which that modest house in its natural condition held out to every comer, it was with a pang of disappointment she heard that Robert had gone out. For a moment her heart sank. She had been looking forward to the sight of him. She had felt that to-day, after her short absence, she would see him without prejudice, able to make allowance for everything, not looking any longer for her Robbie of old, but accustomed and reconciled to the new—the mature man into which inevitably in all these years he must have grown. She had hurried home, though the walk from the station was rather too much for her, to realise these expectations, eager, full of love and hope. Her heart fluttered a little: the light went out of her eyes for a moment; she sat down, all the strength gone out of her. But this was only for a moment. "To be sure, Janet," she said, "he has gone in to Edinburgh to—see about his luggage. I mean, to get himself some—things he wanted." Janet had a long face, as long as a winter's night and almost as dark. Her mistress could have taken her by the shoulders and shaken her. What right had she to take it upon her to misdoubt her young master, or to be so anxious as that about him—as if she were one that had a right to be "meeserable" whatever might happen?

"Could he not have gane with you, mem, when you were going in yoursel'?"

"He was not ready," said Mrs Ogilvy, feeling herself put on her defence.

"You might have waited, mem, till the next train——"

"If you will know," cried Mrs Ogilvy, indignant, "my boy liked best to be free, to take his own way— and I hope there is no person in this house that will gainsay that."

"Eh, mem, I'm aware it's no for me to speak—but so soon, afore he has got accustomed to being at hame —and with siller in his pouch." •

"What do you know about his siller in his pouch?" cried the angry mistress.

"I saw the notes in his hand. He's aye very

nice to me," said Janet, not without a little pleasure in showing how much more at his ease Robert was with her than with his mother, "and cracks about everything. He just showed me in his hand—as many notes as would build a kirk. He said: 'See how liberal——'" Janet stopped here, a little confused; for what Robert had said was, "See how liberal the old woman is." She liked to give her mistress the tiniest pin-prick, perhaps, but not the stab of a disrespect like that.

"I wish to be liberal," said Mrs Ogilvy. "I am very glad he was pleased: and I knew he was going, —there was nothing out of the way about it that you should meet me with such a long face. I thought nothing less than that he must be ill after all his fatigues and his travels."

"Oh, no a bit of him," said Janet—"no ill: I never had ony fears about that."

Mrs Ogilvy by this time had quite recovered herself. "He will have a good many things to do," she said. "He will never be able to get back to his dinner. I hope he'll get something comfortable to eat in Edinburgh. You can keep back the roast of beef till the evening, Janet, and just give me some little thing: an egg will do and a cup of tea——"

"You will just get your dinner as usual," said Janet, doggedly, "as you did before, when you were in your natural way."

When she was in her natural way! It was a cruel speech, but Mrs Ogilvy took no notice. She did not fight the question out, as Janet hoped. If she shed a few tears as she took off her things in her bedroom, they were soon wiped away and left no traces. Robbie could not be tied to her apron-strings. She knew that well, if Janet did not know it. And what could be more natural than that he should like to buy his clothes and get what he wanted by himself, not with an old wife for ever at his heels? She strengthened herself for a quiet day, and then the pleasure of seeing him come back.

But it was wonderful how difficult it was to settle for a quiet day. She had never felt so lonely, she thought, or the house so empty. It had been empty for fifteen years, but it was long since she had felt it like this, every room missing the foot and the voice and the big presence, though it was but two days since he came back. But she settled herself with an effort, counting the trains, and making out that before five o'clock it would be vain to look for him. He would have to go to the tailor's, and to buy linen, and perhaps shoes, and a hat — maybe other things which do not in a moment come to a woman's mind. No; it could not be till five o'clock, or perhaps even six. He would have a great many things to do. She would not even wonder, she said to herself, if it were later. He would, no doubt, just walk about

a little and look at things that were new since he
went away. There were some more of these statues
in the Princes Street Gardens. Mrs Ogilvy did not
care for them herself, but Robbie would. A young
man, noticing everything, he would like to see all
that was new.

A step on the gravel roused her early in the afternoon—the swing of the gate, and the sound of the
gradually nearing footstep. Ah, that was him! earlier
than she had hoped for, knowing she would be anxious,
making his mother's heart to sing for joy. She watched
discreetly behind the curtain, that he might not think
she was looking out for him, or had any doubts about
his early return. Poor Mrs Ogilvy! she was well
used to that kind of disappointment, but it seemed
like a blow full in her face now, a stroke she had
not the least expected, when she saw that it was not
Robbie that was coming, but the minister—the minister of all people—who had the right of old friend-
ships to ask questions, and to have things explained
to him, and who was doubtless coming now to ask
if she had been ill yesterday,—for when had it happened before that she had not been in her usual
place in the kirk? She sat down faint and sick,
but after a moment came round again, saying to herself that it would have been impossible for Robbie
to get back so soon, and that she richly deserved a
disappointment that she had brought on herself.

When Mr Logan came in she was seated in her usual chair (she had moved it from its old place since Robert seemed to like that, placing for him a bigger chair out of the dining-room, which suited him better), and having her usual looks, so that he began by saying that he need not ask if she had been unwell, for she was just as blooming as ever. Having said this, the minister fell into a sort of brown study, with a smile on his face, and a look which was a little sheepish, as if he did not know what more to say. He asked no questions, and he did not seem even to have heard anything, for there was no curiosity in his face. Mrs Ogilvy made a few short remarks on the weather, and told him she had been in Edinburgh that morning, which elicited from him nothing more than a " Dear me ! " of the vaguest interest. Not a word about Robbie, not a question did he ask. She had been alarmed at the idea of these questions. She was still more alarmed and wondering when they did not come.

" I had a call from Susie — the other day," she said at last. Was it possible that it was only on Saturday—the day that was now a marked day, above all others, the day that Robbie came home !

" Ay ! " said the minister, for the first time looking up. " Would she have anything to tell you ? I'm thinking, Mrs Ogilvy, Susie has no secrets from you."

" I never heard she had any secrets. She is a real

upright-minded, well-thinking woman. I will not say
bairn, though she will always be a bairn to me——"

"No, she's no bairn," said the minister, shaking
his head. Two-and-thirty well-chappit, as the poor
folk say. She should have been married long ago,
and with bairns of her own."

"And how could she be married, I would like to
ask you," cried Mrs Ogilvy, indignant, "with you
and your family to look after? And never mother
has done better by her bairns than Susie has done
by you and yours."

"I am saying nothing against that. I am saying
she has had the burden on her far too long. I told
you before her health is giving way under it," the
minister said. He spoke with a little heat, as of
a man crossed and contradicted in a statement of
fact of which he was sure.

"I see no signs of that," Mrs Ogilvy said.

"I came up the other night," he went on, "to open
my mind to you if I could, but you gave me no en-
couragement. Things have gone a little further since
then. Mrs Ogilvy, you're a great authority with
Susie, and the parish has much confidence in you.
I would like you to be the first to know—and perhaps you would give me your advice. It is not as
to the wisdom of what I'm going to do. I am just
fairly settled upon that, and my mind made up——"

"You are going—to marry again," she said.

He gave a quick look upward, his middle - aged countenance growing red, the complacent smile stealing to the corners of his mouth. " So you've guessed that ! "

" I have not guessed it—it was very clear to see ——both from her and from you."

" You've guessed the person, too," he said, the colour deepening, and the smile turning to a confused laugh.

" There was no warlock wanted to do that; but what my advice would be for, I cannot guess, Mr Logan, for, if your mind's fixed and all settled——"

" I did not say just as much as that; but——well, very near it. Yes, very near it. I cannot see how in honour I could go back."

" And you've no wish to do so. And what do you want with advice ? " Mrs Ogilvy said.

She was severe, though she was thankful to him for his preoccupation, and that he had no leisure at his command to ask questions or to pry into other people's affairs.

" Me," he said ; " that's but one side of the subject. There's Susie. It's perhaps not quite fair to Susie. I've stood in her way, you may say. She's been tangled with the boys—and me. There's no companion for a man, Mrs Ogilvy, like the wife of his bosom ; but Susie—I would be the last to deny it— has been a good daughter to me."

"It would set you ill, or any man, to deny it!" cried Mrs Ogilvy. "And what are you going to do for Susie, Mr Logan? A sister that keeps your house, you just say Thank you, and put her to the door; but your daughter—you're always responsible for her——"

"Till she's married," he said, giving his severe judge a shamefaced glance.

"Have you a man ready to marry her, then?" she asked, sharply.

"It's perhaps not the man that has ever been wanting," said the minister, with a half laugh.

"And how are you going to do without Susie?" said Mrs Ogilvy, always with great severity. "Who is to see the callants off to Edinburgh every morning, and learn the little ones their lessons? It will be a great handful for a grand lady like yon."

"That's just a mistake that is very painful to me," said Mr Logan. "The lady that is going to be—my wife——"

"Your second wife, Mr Logan," said Mrs Ogilvy, with great severity.

"I am meaning nothing else—my second wife—is not a grand lady, as you all suppose. She is just a sweet, simple woman—that would be pleased to do anything."

"Is she going to learn the little ones their lessons, and be up in the morning to give the boys their breakfasts and see them away?"

Mr Logan waved his hand, as a man forestalled in what he was about to say. "There is no need for all that," he said—" not the least need. The servant that has been with them all their days is just very well cap- able of seeing that they get off in time. And as for the little ones, I have heard of a fine school—in England."

Mrs Ogilvy threw up her arms with a cry. "A school—in England !"

"Which costs very little, and is just an excellent school—for the daughters of clergymen—but, I confess, it's clergymen of the other church : it is not proved yet if a Scotch minister will be allowed——"

"A thing that's half charity," said Mrs Ogilvy, scornfully. "I did not think, Mr Logan, that you, that are come of well-kent folk, would demean your- self to that."

"She says—I mean, I'm told," said the poor man, "that it's sought after by the very best. The English have not our silly pride. When a thing is a good thing and freely offered——"

"You will not get it, anyway," said Mrs Ogilvy, quickly. "You're not a clergyman according to the English way. You're a Scotch minister. But if all this is to be done, I'm thinking it means that there will be no place for Susie at all in her father's house."

"She will marry," the minister said.

"And how can you tell that she will marry ? Is she to do it whether she will or not ? There might be more reasons than one for not marrying. It's not any man she wants, but maybe just one man."

Mrs Ogilvy thought she was well aware what it was that had kept Susie from marrying. Alas, alas! what would she think of him now if she saw him, and how could she bear to see the wonder and the pain reflected in Susie's face?

"I thought," said Mr Logan, rising up, "that I would have found sympathy from you. I thought you would have perceived that it was as much for Susie I was thinking as for myself. She will never break the knot till it's done for her. She thinks she's bound to those bairns; but when she sees they are all provided for without her——"

"The boys by the care of a servant. The little ones in a school that is just disguised charity——"

"You're an old friend, Mrs Ogilvy, but not old enough or dear enough to treat my arrangements like that."

"Oh, go away, minister!" cried the mistress of the Hewan. She was beginning to remember that Robbie's train might come in at any moment, and that she would not for the world have him brought face to face with Mr Logan without any warning or preparation. "Go away! for we will never agree on this point. I've nothing to say against you for marrying. If your heart's set upon it, you'll do it, well I know; but to me Susie and the bairns are the first thing, and not the second. Say no more, say no more! for we'll never agree."

"You'll not help me, then?" he said.

"Help you! how am I to help you? I have nothing to do with it," she cried.

"With Susie," he repeated. "I'll not quarrel with you: you mean well, though you're so severe. There is nobody like you that could help me with Susie. You could make her see my position—you could make her see her duty——"

"If it is her duty," Mrs Ogilvy said.

She could scarcely hear what he said in reply. Was that the gate again? and another step on the gravel? Her heart began to choke and to deafen her, beating so loud in her ears. Oh, if she could but get him away before Robbie, with his rough clothes, his big beard, his air of recklessness and vagabondism, should appear! She felt herself walking before him to the door, involuntarily moving him on, indicating his path. I think he was too deeply occupied with his own affairs to note this; but yet he was aware of something repellent in her aspect and tone. It was just like all women, he said to himself: to hear that a poor man was to get a little comfort to himself with a second wife roused up all their prejudices. He might have known.

It was time for Robbie's train when she got her visitor away. She sat down and listened to his foot-

steps retiring with a great relief. That sound of the
gate had been a mistake. How often, how often had
it been a mistake! She lingered now, sitting still,
resting from the agitation that had seized upon her
till the minister's steps died away upon the road.
And as soon as they were gone, listened, listened over
again, with her whole heart in her ears, for the others
that now should come.

It was six o'clock past! If he had come by this
train he must have been here, and there was not another for more than an hour. He must have been
detained. He must have been looking about the new
things in the town, the new buildings, the things that
had been changed in fifteen years, things that at his
age were just the things a young man would remember;
or perhaps the tailor might be altering something for
him that he had to go back to try on, or perhaps——
It would be all right anyway. What did six o'clock
matter, or half-past seven, or whatever it was? It
was a fine light summer night; there was plenty of
time,—and nobody waiting for him but his mother,
that could make every allowance. And it was not as if
he had anything to do at home. He had nothing to do.
And his first day in Edinburgh after so many years.

She was glad, however, to hear the step of Janet,
so that she could call her without rising from her
seat, which somehow she felt too tired and feeble
to do.

"Janet," she said, "you will just keep back the
dinner. Mr Robert has been detained. I've been
thinking all day that perhaps he might be detained,
maybe even later than this. If we said eight o'clock
for once? It's a late hour; but better that than
giving him a bad dinner, neither one thing nor
another, neither hot nor cold. Where were you
going, my woman?" Mrs Ogilvy added abruptly,
with a suspicious glance.

"I was just gaun to take a look out. I said to
mysel' I would just look out and see if he was
coming: for it's very true, you say, a dinner in
the dead thraws, neither hot nor cauld, is just worse
than no dinner at all."

"Just bide in your kitchen," said her mistress,
peremptorily. "I'll let you know when my son
comes."

"Oh, I'll hear soon enough," Janet said. And
then the mother was left alone. But not undisturbed: for presently Andrew's slow step came
round the corner, with a clanking of waterpots and
the refreshing sounds and smell of watering—that
tranquil employment, all in accord with the summer
evening, when it was always her custom to go out
and have a talk with Andrew about the flowers.
She did not feel as if she could move to-night
—her feet were cold and like lead, her cheeks
burning, and her heart clanging in her throat.

Nevertheless the bond of custom being on her, and a strong sense that to fulfil every usual occupation was the most satisfying exercise, she presently rose and went out, the pleasant smell of the refreshed earth and thirsty plants, bringing out all the sweetest home breath of the flowers, coming to meet her as she went forth to the open door.

"It's very good for them, Andrew, after this warm day."

"Ay, it's good for them," Andrew said.

"You will mind to shut up everything as soon as my son comes home," she said.

"Oh ay," said Andrew, "there was plenty said about it yestreen."

"The sweet-williams are coming on nicely, Andrew."

"Ah," said Andrew, "they're common things; they aye thrive."

"They are very bonnie," said Mrs Ogilvy; "I like them better than your grand geraniums and things."

"There's nae accounting for tastes," Andrew said, in his gruff voice.

By this time she felt that she could not continue the conversation any longer, and went back to her chair inside. The sound of the flowing water, and even of Andrew clanking as he moved, was sweet to her. The little jar and clang fell sweetly into the evening, and they were so glad of that refreshing

shower, the silly flowers! though maybe it would
rain before the morning, and they would not need
it. Then Andrew—though nobody could say he was
quick, honest man!—finished his task and went in.
And there was a great quiet, the quiet of the falling
night, though the long light remained the same.
And the time passed for the next train. Janet came
to the door again with her heavy step. "He will no
be coming till the nine train," she said; "will you
have the dinner up?" "Oh no," cried Mrs Ogilvy;
"I'll not sit down to a big meal at this hour of the
night. Put out the beef to let it cool, and it will be
supper instead of dinner, Janet."

"But you've eaten nothing, mem, since——"

"Am I thinking of what I eat! Go ben to your
kitchen, and do what I tell you, and just leave me
alone."

Janet went away, and the long vigil began again.
She sat a long time without moving, and then she
took a turn about the house, looking into his room
for one thing, and looking at the piles of books
that he had carried up-stairs. There were few traces
of him about, for he had nothing to leave behind,
—only the big rough cloak, of a shape she had never
seen before, which was folded on a chair. She lifted
it, with a natural instinct of order, to hang it up,
and found falling from a pocket in it a big badly
printed newspaper, the same newspaper in which Mr

Somerville had showed her her son's name. She took it with her half consciously when she went down-stairs, but did not read it, being too much occupied with the dreadful whirl of her own thoughts. Nine o'clock passed too, and the colourless hours ran on. And then there was the sound all over the house of Andrew fulfilling his orders, shutting up every window and door. When he came to the parlour to shut the window by which she sat, his little mistress, always so quiet, almost flew at him. "Man, have you neither sense nor reason!" she cried. It was more than she could bear to shut and bar and bolt when nobody was there that either feared or could come to harm. No one disturbed her after that. The couple in the kitchen kept very quiet, afraid of her. Deep night came on; the last of all the trains rumbled by, making a great crash in the distance in the perfect stillness. There had been another time like this, when she had watched the whole night through. And midnight came and went again, and as yet there was no sound.

CHAPTER IX.

WHEN one struck on the big kitchen clock, with an ominous sound like a knell, Janet, trying to reduce her big step to an inaudible footfall, came "ben" again. She found her mistress sitting still idly as if she were dead, the lamp burning solemnly, not the sound even of a breath in the room. "No stocking in her hands, not even reading a book," Janet said. For a moment, indeed, with a quick impulse of fear, the woman thought that Mrs Ogilvy had died in the new catastrophe. "Oh, mem, mem!" she cried, and in an instant there was a faint stir.

"Well, Janet," Mrs Ogilvy said in a stifled voice.

"Will ye sit up longer? A' the trains are passed, and long passed. He will be coming in the morning; he must just—have missed the last."

"I am not going to my bed just yet," the mistress said.

I

"But, mem, you will be worn out. You have just had no meat and no sleep and no rest, and you'll be weariet to death."

"And what would it matter if I was?" she answered, with a faint smile.

"Oh, dinna say that; how can we tell what may be wanted of you, and needing a' your strength?"

Mrs Ogilvy roused herself at these words. "And that's quite true," she said. "You have more sense than anybody would expect; you are a lesson to me, that have-had plenty reason to know better. But, nevertheless, I will not go to my bed yet—not just yet. I can get a good sleep in this chair."

"With the window open, mem, in the dead of the night, after all Mr Robert said!"

"Do you call that the dead of the night?" said the mistress. And the two women looked out silenced in the great hush and awe of that pause of nature between the night and the day. It was like no light that ever was on sea or land, though it *is* daily, nightly, for watchers and sleepless souls. It was lovely and awful—a light in which everything hidden in the dark came to life again, like the light alone of the watchful eyes of Him who slumbereth not nor sleeps. They felt Him contemplating them and their troubles, knowing what was to come of them, which they did not, from the skies—and their hearts were hushed within them: there was silence for a moment, the profound silence that reigned out and in, in which they were as the trees.

Then Mrs Ogilvy started and cried, " What is that ? " Was it anything at all ?   There are sounds that enhance the silence, just as there are discords that increase the harmony of music—sounds of insects stirring in their sleep, of leaves falling, of a grain of sand losing its balance and rolling over on the way.   Janet heard nothing.   She shook her head in her big white cap.   And then suddenly her mistress gripped her with a force that no one could have suspected to be in those soft old hands.   " Now, listen !   There's somebody on the road, there's somebody at the gate ! "

I will not describe the heats and chills of the moment that elapsed before the big loose figure appeared on the walk, coming on leisurely, with a perceptible air of fatigue.   " Ah, you're up still," he said, as he came within hearing.   Janet had flown to open the door for him, undoing all the useless bars, making a wonderful noise in the night.   "·I could have stepped in through the window," he said.   " You've walked from Edinburgh," cried Janet; " you must be wanting some supper."   " I would not object to a little cold meat," he said, with a laugh.   His tone was always pleasant to Janet.   His mother stood and listened to this colloquy within the parlour door.   She must have been angry, you would say, jealous that her maid should be more kindly used by her son than she, exasperated by his heedless selfishness. She was none of all those things. Her heart was like a well, a fountain of thankfulness welling up before God: her whole being over-flooded with sudden relief and sweet content.

"How imprudent with that window open—in the middle of the night; how can you tell who may be about?" were the first words he said, going up himself to the window and closing it and the shutters over it hastily. "I'm sorry I'm late," he said afterwards. "I missed the last train, and then I think I missed the road. I've been a long time getting here. These confounded light nights; you've no shelter at all, however late you walk."

"You will be tired, my dear." He had brought in an atmosphere with him that filled in a moment this little dainty old woman's room. It was greatly made up of tobacco, but there was also whisky in it and other odours indiscriminate, the smell of a man who had been smoking all day and drinking all day, though the latter process had not affected his seasoned senses. Of all things horrible to her this was the most horrible: it made her faint and sick. But he was, of course, quite unconscious of any such effect, nor did he notice the paleness that had come over her face.

"Yes, I am tired," he said ; "Janet's suggestion was

not a bad idea. I have not walked so far for years. A horse between my legs, and I would not mind a dozen times the distance; but I've got out of the use of my own feet." He spoke more naturally, with a lighter heart than he had shown yet. "I have not had a bad day. I looked up some of the old howffs. Nobody there that remembered me, but still it was a little like old times."

"Wouldn't you be better, Robbie, oh my dear, to keep away from the old howffs?" she said, trembling a little.

"It was to be expected that you would say that. If you mean for the present affair, no; if you mean for general good behaviour, perhaps yes; but it is early days. I may surely take a little licence the first days I am back. There are some of your new clothes," he added, tossing down a bundle, "and more will be ready in a day or two. I've rigged myself out from head to foot. But I wouldn't have them sent out here. I'm not too fond of an address. I promised to call for them on Saturday."

The poor mother's heart was transfixed as with a sudden arrow. This, then, would be repeated again; once more she would have to watch the day out and half the night through—and again, no doubt, and again.

"There's Janet as good as her word," he said, as the sound of her proceedings in the next room became

audible. And he ate an immense meal in the middle
of the night, the light growing stronger every moment
in the crevices of the shutters. I don't know what
there is that is wholesome, almost meritorious, in the
consumption of food. Mrs Ogilvy forgot the smell
of the tobacco and the whisky in the pleasure of
seeing the roast-beef disappear in large slices from his
plate. "It was a pleasure to see him eating," she said
afterwards to Janet. Yes, it is somehow wholesome
and meritorious. It implies a good digestion, not
spoiled by other pernicious things; it implies (almost)
an easy mind and a peaceful conscience, and something
like innocence in a man. A good meal, not voracious,
as of a creature starving, but eaten with good appetite,
with satisfaction,—it is a kind of certificate of morality
which many a poor woman has hailed with delight.
They have their own way of looking at things.

And thus the evening and the morning made a
new day.

The next day, before she left her room, Mrs Ogilvy
took the newspaper, which she had laid carefully
aside, and read for the first time—locking her door
first, which was a thing she had scarcely done all her
life before—the story of the crime which had thrown
a shadow over her son, and had made him "cut and
run," as he said, for his life. She had to read it three or
four times over before she could make out what it
meant, and even then her understanding was not very

clear. For one thing, she had not, as was natural, the remotest idea what "road agents" were. Mercifully for her: for I believe, though I know as little as she, that it means, not to put too fine a point upon it, highwaymen, neither more nor less. A party of these men —she thought it must mean some kind of travelling merchants; not perhaps a brilliant career, but no harm in it, no harm in it!—had been long about the country, a country of which she had never heard the name, in a half-settled State equally unknown, and at length had been traced to their headquarters. They had been pursued hotly by the Sheriff for some time. To Mrs Ogilvy a sheriff meant an elderly gentleman in correct legal costume, a person of serious importance, holding his courts and giving his judgments. She could not realise to herself the Sheriff-Substitute of Eskshire riding wildly over moss and moor after any man; but no doubt in America it was different. It was proved that the road agents had sworn vengeance against him, and that whoever met him first was pledged to shoot him, whether he himself could escape or not. The meeting took place by chance at a roadside shanty in the midst of the wilds, and the Sheriff was shot, before his party had perceived the other, by a premeditated well-directed bullet straight to the heart. Who had fired it? The most likely person was the leader of the band, of whom the Western journalist gave a sensational history, and to secure him was the object of the police; but there were half-a-dozen others who might have done it, and whom it was of the utmost importance to secure, if only in the hope that one of them might turn Queen's evidence. (I don't know what they call this in America, nor, indeed, anything but what I have heard vaguely reported of such matters. The better instructed will pardon and rectify for themselves.) Among these, but at the end—heaven be praised, at the end!—was the name of Robert. The band had dispersed in different directions and fled, all but one, who was killed.

When she had got all this more or less distinctly into her mind, she read the story of the captain of the band, Lewis or Lew Winterman, with a dozen aliases. He was a German by origin, though an American born. He spoke English with a slight German accent. He was large and tall and fair, of great strength, and very ingratiating manners. He had gone through a hundred adventures all told at length. He had ruined both men and women wherever he took his fatal way. He was a hero of romance, he was a monster of cruelty. Slaughter and bloodshed were his natural element. He was known to have an extraordinary ascendancy over his band, so that there was nothing they would not do while under his influence; though, when free from him, they hated and feared him. Thus every man of the party was the object of pursuit, if not for himself, yet in hopes of

finding some clue to the whereabouts of this master
ruffian, whose gifts were such that, though he would
not recoil from the most cold-blooded murder, he
could also wheedle the bird from the tree. Mrs
Ogilvy carefully locked this dreadful paper away
again with trembling hands. It took her a little
trouble to find a safe place to which there was a lock
and key, but she did so at last. And when she went
down-stairs it was with a feeling that Mr Somerville's
prayer to steek her doors, and Robbie's concern for
the fastening of all the windows, were perhaps justified; but what would bring a man like that over land
and sea—what would bring him here to the peaceful
Hewan? No, no; it was not a thing for any reasonable person to fear. There were plenty of places in
the world to take refuge in more like such a man.
What would he do here?—he could find nothing to do
here. America, Mrs Ogilvy had always heard, was a
very big place, far bigger than England and Scotland
and Ireland put together. He must have plenty of
howffs there. And if not America, there was Germany, which they said he came from, or other places
on the Continent, far; far more likely to have hiding-
holes for a criminal than the country about Edinburgh. No, no. No, no. Therefore there was no
fear.

When Robert came down-stairs, which was not till
late, he was a little improved in appearance by a new

coat, but not so much as his mother had hoped. She
was disappointed, though in face of the other things
this was such a very small matter. He was just a
backwoodsman, a bushman, whatever you call it, still.
He had not got back that air of a gentleman which
had been his in his youth—that most prized and
precious thing, which is more than beauty, far more
than fine clothes or good looks. This gave her a
pang: but then there were many things that gave her
a pang, though all subsided in the thought that he
was here, that he had come back guiltless and un-
injured from Edinburgh, notwithstanding the anxiety
he had given her. But was it not her own fault that
she was anxious, always imagining some dreadful
thing? After his breakfast (again such an excellent
breakfast, quite unaffected by his late hours or his
large supper!) he came to her into the parlour
with the 'Scotsman,' which Janet had brought
him, in his hand. "I thought you would like
to hear," he said, carefully closing the door after
him. "You remember that man I mentioned to
you?"

"Yes, Robbie,"—she had almost said the man's
name, but refrained.

"There is no word of him," he said. "That was
one thing I was anxious about. There are places
where—communications are kept up. I had an address in Edinburgh to inquire."

"What has he to do with Edinburgh?" she cried in dismay.

"Nothing; but there's a kind of a communication, everywhere. Nothing has been heard of him. So long as nothing is heard of him I can breathe free. There's no reason he should come here——"

"Come here! For what would he come here?"

"How can I tell? If you knew the man——"

"God forbid I should ever know the man," she cried with fervour.

"I say Amen to that. But if you knew him, you would know it's the place that is least likely which is the place where he appears."

"It may be so," Mrs Ogilvy said; "but a place like this—a small bit house deep in the bosom of the country, and nothing but quiet country-folk about——"

"What is that but the best of places for a hunted man? He said once that if I ever came home he would come after me—that it was just the place he wanted to lie snug in, where nobody would think of looking for him. You think me a fool to be so anxious about the bolts and the bars; but the room might be empty one moment, and the next you might look round, and he would be there."

Though it was morning, before noon, and the safety of the full day was upon the house, with its open windows, he cast a doubtful suspicious glance round, as if afraid of seeing some one behind him even now.

"Robbie," said Mrs Ogilvy, "there is no man that has to do with you, were he good or bad, that I would close my doors upon, except the shedder of blood. He shall not come here."

"There is nothing I can refuse him," cried the young man. "I would say so too. I say, Curse him; I hate his very name. He's done me more harm than I can ever get the better of. I've seen him do things that would curdle your blood in your veins; but him there and me here, standing before each other—there is nothing I can refuse him!" he cried.

"Robbie, you will think I am but a poor old woman," said his mother, with her faltering voice. "I could not stand up, you will think, to any strange man; but the shedder of blood is like nothing else. It shall never be said of me that I harboured a shedder of blood."

"Oh, mother! how can you tell—how can you tell?" he cried, "when I that know tell you that I could not refuse him anything. I am just his slave at his chariot-wheels."

"But I am not his slave," said Mrs Ogilvy, with a glitter of spirit in her eyes. "I can face him, though you may not think it. He shall never come here!"

He flung himself down into a chair, and put the

newspaper between her and himself, making a semblance of reading. But this he could not keep up: the stillness, and the peace, and the innocence about him affected the man, who, whatever he was now, had been born Robbie Ogilvy of the Hewan. He made a stifled sound in his throat once or twice as if about to speak, but brought forth no certain sound for some five minutes, when he suddenly burst forth in a high but broken voice, "What would you say if I were to tell you——?" and suddenly stopped again.

"What, Robbie?" she said, quivering like a leaf.

"Nothing," he replied, looking up with sudden defiance in her face.

And there was a silence again in the room—the silence of the sweet morning: not a sound to break the calm: the birds in the trees, the scent of the roses coming in at the window—there was no such early place for roses in all Mid-Lothian—and the house basking in the sun, and the sun shining on the house, as if there was no roof-tree so beloved in all the basking and breathing earth. Then the voice of the little old lady uplifted itself in the midst of all that peace of nature — small, like her delicate frame; low—a little sound that could have been put out so easily,—almost, you would have said, that a sudden breath of wind would have put it out.

"Robbie, my son," she said, "there is nothing you
could tell me, or that any man could tell me, that
would put bar or bolt between you and me. What
is yours is mine, if there is any trouble to bear;
and thankful will I be to take my share. There is
no question nor answer between you and me. If
you've been wild in the world, my own laddie, I've
been here on my knees for you before the Lord.
Whatever there is to tell, tell it to Him, and He will
not turn His back upon you. Then, do you think
your mother will? But that's not the question—
not the question. My house is my own house, and
I will defend it and my son, and all that is in it—
ay, if it were to the death!"

He looked at her for a moment, half impressed;
but the glamour soon went out of Robert's eyes.
The reality was a very quiet feeble old woman, with
the strength of a mouse, with a flash of high spirit
such as he knew of old his mother possessed, and a
voice that shook even while it pronounced this defiance of every evil thing. Short work would be made
with that. He could remember scenes in which other
old women had tried to protect their belongings, and
short work had been made with them. He had never,
never laid a finger on one himself. If he had ever
dared to make his penitence, and could have disen-
tangled his own story from that of those among whom
he was, it might have been seen how little real guilt

there ever was in his disorderly wretched life; but he
could not disentangle it, even to himself: he felt himself guilty of many things in which he had had no
share.   Even in the cónfusion of the remorse that
sometimes came upon him, he believed himself to
have executed orders which were never given to him.
The only thing he was not doubtful about was where
these orders came from, and that if the same voice
spoke them again suddenly at any moment, it would
be his immediate impulse to obey.

And after this he took up the 'Scotsman,'—that
honest peaceable paper, with its clever articles, and
its local records, and consciousness of the metropo-
litan dignity which has paled a little in the hurry
and flash of the times — the paper that goes to
every Scotsman's heart, whatever may be his politics, throughout the world, which everywhere, even
in busy London, compatriots will offer to each other
as something always dear.   Wild as his life had been,
and distracted as he now was, the sight and the sound
of the 'Scotsman' was grateful to Robert Ogilvy.
The paper in his hands not only shielded his face
from observation, but gradually calmed him down,
drew back his interest, and, wonder of wonders, occupied his mind.   He had himself said he could always
read.   After this scene, with its half revelation and
its overmastering dread, he in a few minutes read the
'Scotsman' as if there had been neither crime nor

punishment in the world. And Mrs Ogilvy had already taken up her knitting; but what was in her heart, still throbbing and aching with the energy of that outburst, and how much less quickly the high tide died down, I will not venture to say.

CHAPTER X.

ROBERT went in again to Edinburgh a few days later, with results very similar. Mrs Ogilvy once more waited for him half through the night: but she sat with her window closed, and with a book in her hand, reading or making believe to read, and with no longer any passion of tears or panic in her heart, but a vague misery, a thrill of expectation she knew not of what, of bad or good, of danger or safety. He came in always, sometimes a little earlier, sometimes a little later, with a kind of regularity which she had to accept, which, indeed, she accepted, without remonstrance or complaint. The atmosphere about him was always the same, tobacco and whisky, to both which things the little fragrant feminine house was getting accustomed, to which she consented with a pang indescribable, but which had no consequences to make any complaint of, as she acknowledged with thankfulness. When he did

K

not go to Edinburgh, he remained quietly enough in the house, doing nothing, saying not very much, taking his walks in the darkening, when it was quite late, and consequently keeping her in a sort of perennial uneasiness, only intensified on those occasions when he went to Edinburgh. On no evening was she sure that he might not come in, in a state of alarm, bidding her extinguish every light, and watching from the chinks of the window lest some one clandestine might be roaming round the house; or that he might not appear with another at his elbow, the man whom he hated yet would obey, the shedder of blood, as she called him; or, finally, that he might never come back at all,—that the man who had so much influence over him might sweep him away, carry him off, notwithstanding all his unwillingness. It is not to be supposed that much comfort now dwelt in the Hewan, in the constant contemplation of so many dangers. Yet everything was more or less as before. The mistress of the house gave no external sign of trouble. To anxious eyes, had there been any to inspect her, there would have appeared new lines in her countenance; but no eyes were anxious about her looks. She pursued her usual habits, as careful as always of the neatness of her house, her dress, her garden, everything surrounding her. Her visitors still came, though this was her hardest burden. To them she said nothing of her

son's return. He withdrew hurriedly to his room
whenever there was the smallest sign of any one approaching; and few of them were of his time. The
neighbourhood had changed in fifteen years, as the
face of the country changes everywhere. There were
plenty of people in the neighbourhood who knew
Robert Ogilvy, but these were not of the kind who
go out in the afternoon to tea. The habit had not
begun when he left home. There were wives of his
own contemporaries among the ladies who paid their
visits at the Hewan, but Robert was not acquainted
with them. Of those whom he had known of old,
the elder ladies were like his mother, receiving their
little company, not going forth to seek it, and the
younger ones married, bearing names with which
he was not acquainted, or perhaps gone from the
country-side altogether. " I know nobody, and nobody
would know me," he said; which was a great mistake, however, for already the rumour of his return
had flashed all over the neighbourhood, and was
hotly discussed in the parish, and half of the visitors
who came to the Hewan came with the determination
of ascertaining the truth. But they ascertained nothing. He was never visible, his mother looked "just
in her ordinary," the house seemed undisturbed and
unchanged. Sometimes a whiff of tobacco was sensible to the nostrils of some of the guests; but when
one bold woman said so, Mrs Ogilvy had answered

quietly, "There is at present a great deal of smoke about the house," with a glance, or so the visitor thought, at her rose-trees, which Andrew fumigated diligently against the greenfly in that simple way. The greenfly is a subject on which all possessors of gardens are kin. The questioner determined that she would have it tried that very evening on her own rose-bushes, for Mrs Ogilvy's buds were uncommonly vigorous and clean; and so the smell of tobacco ceased to be discussed or perceived, being accounted for.

This secrecy could not, of course, have been maintained had Mrs Ogilvy taken counsel with any one, or opened her mind on the subject. It could not have been maintained, for instance, had Mr Logan, the minister, been in his right mind. I do not know that she would have naturally consulted on such a subject her legitimate spiritual guide. But the intimacy between the families was such that it could not have been hid. Even had the boys been at home instead of going to Edinburgh every day, some large-limbed rapid lad would no doubt have darted into the house with a message from Susie at an inopportune moment, and found Robert. Susie herself was the only person now whom Mrs Ogilvy half dreaded, half hoped for. The secret could not have been kept from her—that would have been impossible; and from day to day her coming was looked for, not

without a rising of hope, not without a thrill of
fear.   In other circumstances Mrs Ogilvy would
have been moved to seek Susie, to discover how
she was bearing the complications of her own lot.
Susie was the only creature for whom Mrs Ogilvy
longed: the sight of her would have been good: the
possibility of unburdening her soul, even if she had
not done it, would have been a relief, to the imagination at least.   Her complete separation from Susie
for the time, which was entirely accidental, was one
of the most curious circumstances in this curious
and changed life.

If she did not see Susie, however, she saw the
woman who was about to change Susie's life and
circumstances still more than her own were changed,
—the lady from England who carried an indefinable
atmosphere of suspicion about with her, as Robbie
carried that whiff of tobacco.   Mrs Ainslie took upon
her an air of unwarrantable intimacy which the
mistress of the Hewan resented.   " I thought you
would have come to see me," the visitor said, in a
tone of flattering reproach.

" I go to see nobody," said Mrs Ogilvy, " except
old friends, or where I am much needed.   It's a
habit of mine that is well known."

" But you must excuse me," said the other, " for
not knowing all the habits of the people here" (as
if Mrs Ogilvy of the Hewan had been but one of

the people here!). And then she made a pause and
put her head on one side, and regarded the old lady,
now impenetrable as a stone wall, with cajoling sweetness. "He has told you!" she said.

"If you are meaning the minister——"

"Oh, why should we play at hide-and-seek, when
I am dying for your sympathy, and you know very
well whom I mean? Who could I mean but——
And oh, dear Mrs Ogilvy, do wish me joy, and say
you think I have done well——"

"Upon your marriage with the minister?"

"Oh," cried the lady, holding up her hands, "don't
crush me with your minister! I think it's pretty.
I have no objections to it: but still you do call him
Mr Logan when you speak to him. Poor man! he
has been so lonely ever since his poor wife died.
And I—I have been very lonely too. Can any one
ever take the same place as a wife or a husband?
We are two lonely people——"

"Not him," said Mrs Ogilvy; "I can say nothing
for you. Very good company he has had, better
than most of the wives I see. His own daughter,
just the best and the kindest—and that has kept
his house in such order—as it will take any strange
woman no little trouble to do."

"Oh, don't think I shall attempt that," said the
visitor. "I have promised to be his wife, but not to
be his drudge. Poor Susan has been his drudge. Not

much wonder, therefore, that she could not be much of a companion to him. One can't, my dear Mrs Ogilvy, be busy with a set of children, and teaching the a b c, all day, and then be lively and amusing to a man when he comes in tired at night."

"I have nothing to say to it one way or another," said Mrs Ogilvy. "I wish you may never rue it, neither him nor you, and that is just all that will come to my lips. If she is a lively companion or not, I cannot say, but my poor Susie has been a mother to these bairns; and what he will do with the little ones turned out of the house, and Susie turned out of his house——"

"You are so prejudiced! The little girls will be far better at school—and Susie is going to marry, which she should have done ten years ago. Her father has no right to keep a girl from making a happy marriage and securing the man of her heart."

"And where is she to get," said Mrs Ogilvy, with a slight choke in her throat, "what you call the man of her heart?"

"Oh, my dear lady, you that have known Susie all through, how can you ask? He proposed to her when she was twenty, and I believe he has asked her every year since——"

"So he has told you that old story; but he had not the courage, knowing a little more than you do, to speak to me of the man of her heart. Oh no,

he had not the boldness to do that! And is Susie
aware of the happiness you are preparing for her,
her father and you?" the old lady said, grimly.

"Mr Logan," said the lady, "has a timidity about
that which I don't understand. I tell him he is
frightened for his daughter. It is as if he felt he
had jilted her."

"Indeed, and it is very like that," Mrs Ogilvy
said.

"He thought you, perhaps, dear Mrs Ogilvy, as
such a very old friend, would tell her,—and then,
when he found that you were disinclined to do it,
he—well, I fear he has shirked it again. Nothing
so cowardly as a man in certain circumstances. I
believe at the last I will have to do it myself."

"Nobody could be better qualified——"

"Do you really think so? I'm so glad you are
learning to do me justice. It's all for her good—
you know it is. To marry and have children of
her own is better than acting mother to another
person's children. Oh yes, they are her own brothers
and sisters *now;* but they will grow up, and if Susie
does not marry, what prospect has she? Those who
really love her should take all these things into
account."

Mrs Ainslie spoke these sensible words with many
little gestures and airs, which exasperated the older
woman perhaps all the more that there was nothing

to be said against the utterance itself. But at that moment she heard a step that she knew well upon the gravel outside, and of all people in the world to meet and divine who Robert was, and publish it abroad, this interloper, this stranger, who had awakened a warmer feeling of hostility in Mrs Ogilvy's bosom than any one had done before, was the last. She sat breathless, making no answer, while she heard him enter the house: he had been in the garden with his pipe and his newspaper—for it was still morning, and not an hour when the Hewan was on guard against visitors. His large step, so distinctly a man's step, paused in the hall. Mrs Ogilvy raised her voice a little, to warn him, as she made an abstract reply.

"It's rare," she said, "that we're so thankful as we ought to be—to them that deal with us for our good."

"Do you hear that step in the passage?" cried Mrs Ainslie. "Ah, I know who it is. It is dear James — it is Mr Logan, I mean. I felt sure he would not be long behind me. Mayn't I let him in?"

She rose in a flutter, and rushing to the door threw it open, with an air of eager welcome and arch discovery; but recoiled a step before the unknown personage, large, silent, with his big beard and watchful aspect, who stood listening and uncer-

tain outside. "Oh!" she cried, and fell back, not
without a start of dismay.

Mrs Ogilvy's pride did not tolerate any denial of
her son, who stood there, making signs to her which
she declined to notice. "This is my son," she said,
"the master of the house. He has just come back
after a long time away."

"Oh — Mr Ogilvy!" the lady faltered. She was
anxious to please everybody, but she was evidently frightened, though it was difficult to tell why.
"How pleased you must be to have your son come
back at last!"

He paused disconcerted on the threshold. "I did
not mean to—disturb you, mother—I did not know
there was anybody here."

"Don't upbraid me, please, with coming at such
untimely hours," she cried. Mrs Ainslie was in a
flutter of consciousness, rubbing her gloved hands,
laughing a little hysterically, but more than ever
anxious to please, and instinctively putting on her
little panoply of airs and graces. "I had business.
I had indeed. It was not a mere call meaning
nothing. Your mother will tell you, Mr Ogilvy——"
She let her veil drop over her face, with a tremulous
movement, and almost cringed while she flattered
him, with little flutterings and glances of incompre-
hensible meaning.

The woman was trying to cast her spells over

Robbie! There flew through Mrs Ogilvy's mind
a sensation which was not all disagreeable. "The
woman" was odious to her; but she was a well-
looking woman, and not an ignorant one, knowing
something of the world; and Robert, with his big
beard and his rough clothes, had given Mrs Ogilvy
the profoundly humiliating consciousness that he had
ceased to look like a gentleman; but the woman did
not think so. The woman made her little coquettish
advances to him as if he had been a prince. This
was how his mother interpreted her visitor's looks:
she thought no better of her for this, but yet the
sensation was soothing, and raised her spirits,—
even though she scorned the woman for it, and her
son for the hesitating smile which after a moment
began to light up his face.

"However," said the lady, hurriedly, "unless you
wish for the minister on my heels, perhaps I had
better go now. No? you will not be persuaded,
indeed? You are more hard-hearted than I expected.
So then there is nothing for it but that I must do
it myself. There, Mr Ogilvy! You see we have
secrets after all—mysteries! Two women can't meet
together, can they, without having something tremendous, some conspiracy or other, for each other's
ears?"

"I did not say so," said Robert, not unresponsive,
though taken by surprise.

"Oh no, you did not say so; but you were think-ing so all the same. They always do, don't they? Gentlemen have such fixed ideas about women." She had overcome her little tremor, but was more coquet-tish than ever. While she held his mother's hand in hers, she held up a forefinger of the other archly at Robert. "Oh, I've had a great deal of experience. I know what to expect from men."

She led him out after her to the door talking thus, and down towards the gate; while Mrs Ogilvy stood gazing, wondering. It was one of her tenets, too, that no man can resist such arts; but the anger of a woman who sees them thus exerted in her very presence was still softened by the sensation that this woman, so experienced, still thought Robbie worth her while. He came back again in a few minutes, having accompanied the visitor to the gate, with a smile faintly visible in his beard. "Who is that woman?" he said. "She is not one of your neigh-bours here?"

"What made you go with her, Robbie?"

"Oh, she seemed to expect it, and it was only civil. Where has she come from? and how did you pick such a person up?"

"She is a person that will soon be—a neighbour, as you say, and a person of importance here. She is go-ing to be married upon the minister, Robbie."

"The minister!" he gave a low whistle—"that will

be a curious couple; but I hope it's a new minister, and not poor old Logan, whom I—whom I remember so well. I've seen women like that, but not among ministers. I almost think I've—seen her somewhere. Old Logan! But he has a wife," Robert said.

"He had one; but she's been dead these ten years, and this lady is new come to the parish, and he has what you call fallen in love with her. There are no fules like old fules, Robbie. I like little to hear of falling in love at that age."

"Old Logan!" said Robert again. There were thoughts in his eyes which seemed to come to sudden life, but which his mother did not dare investigate too closely. She dreaded to awaken them further; she feared to drive them away. What memories did the name of Logan bring? or were there any of sufficient force to keep him musing, as he seemed to do, for a few minutes after. But at the end of that time he burst into a sudden laugh. "Old Logan!" he said; "poor old fellow! I remember him very well. The model of a Scotch minister, steady-going, but pawky too, and some fun in him. Where has he picked up a woman like that? and what will he do with her when he has got her? I have seen the like of her before."

"But, Robbie, she is just a very personable, well-put-on woman, and well-looking, and no ill-mannered. She is not one I like,—but I am maybe prejudiced, considering the changes she will make; and there is no harm in her, so far as we have ever heard here."

"Oh, very likely there is no harm in her; but what has she to do in a place like this? and with old Logan!" He laughed again, and then, growing suddenly grave, asked, "What changes is she going to make?"

"There are always changes," said Mrs Ogilvy, evasively, "when a man marries that has a family, and everything settled on another foundation. They are perhaps more in a woman's eyes than in a man's; I will tell you about that another time. But you that wanted to be private, Robbie—there will be no more of that, I'm thinking, now."

"Well, it cannot be helped," he said, crossly; "what could I do? Could I refuse to answer her? Private! —how can you be private in a place like this, where every fellow knew you in your cradle? Two or three have spoken to me already on the road——"

"I never thought we could keep it to ourselves— and why should we?" his mother said.

He answered with a sort of snort only, which expressed nothing, and then fell a-musing, stretched out in the big chair, his legs half away across the room, his beard filling up all the rest of the space. His mother looked at him with mingled sensations of pride and humiliation—a half-admiration and a half-shame. He was a big buirdly man, as Janet said; and he had his new clothes, which were at least clean and fresh: but

they had not made any transformation in his appearance, as she had hoped. Was there any look of a
gentleman left in that large bulk of a man? The
involuntary question went cold to Mrs Ogilvy's heart.
It still gave her a faint elation, however, to remember
that Mrs Ainslie had quite changed her aspect at the
sight of him, quite acknowledged him as one of the
persons whom it was her mission in the world to
attract. It was a small comfort, and yet it was a
comfort. She took up her stocking and composed
herself to wait his pleasure, till he should have finished
his thoughts, whatever they were, and be disposed to
talk again.

But when his voice came finally out of his beard
and out of the silence, it was with a startling question:
"What do you mean to do with me, mother, now I am
here?"

CHAPTER XI.

THEY sat and looked at each other across the little area of the peaceful room. He, stretching half across it, too big almost for the little place. She, in her white shawl and her white cap, its natural occupant and mistress. Her stocking had dropped into her lap, and she looked at him with a pathos and wistfulness in her eyes which were scarcely concealed by the anxious smile which she turned upon him. They were not equal in anything, in this less than in other particulars—for he was indifferent, asking her the question without much care for the answer, while she was moved to her finger-ends with anxiety on the subject, thrilling with emotion and fear. She looked at him for her inspiration, to endeavour to read in his eyes what answer would suit him best, what she could say to follow his mood, to please him or to guide him as might be. Mrs Ogilvy had not many experiences that were encouraging. She had little confidence in her power to influence and to lead. If she could know what he would like her to say, that would be something. She had in her heart a feeling which, though very quiet, was in reality despair. She did not know what to do with him—she had no hope that it would matter anything what she wanted to do. He would do what he liked, what he chose, and not anything she could say.

"My dear," she said, "when this calamity is over-past, and you have got settled a little, there will be plenty of things that you could do."

"That's very doubtful," he said; "and you have not much faith in it yourself. I've been used to do nothing. I don't know what work is like. Do you think I'm fit for it? I had to work on board ship, and how I hated it words could never tell. I was too much of a duffer, they said, to do seaman's work. They made me help the cook—fancy, your son helping the cook!"

"It is quite honest work," she said, with a little quiver in her voice—"quite honest work."

He laughed a little. "That's like you," he said; "and now you will want me to do more honest work. I will need to, I suppose." He paused here, and gave her a keen look, which, fortunately, she did not understand. "But the thing is, I'm good for nothing. I cannot dig, and to beg I am ashamed. I've done many things, but I've not worked much all my life. I will be left on your hands—and what will you do with

L

me?" He was not so indifferent, after all, as when he
began. He was almost in earnest, keeping his eye
upon her, to read her face as well as her words. But
somehow she, who was so anxious to divine him, to
discover what he wished her to say—she had no notion,
notwithstanding all her anxiety, what it was he desired
to know.

"My bonnie man!" she said, "it's a hard question
to answer. What could I wish to do with you but
what would be best for yourself? I have made no
plan for you, Robbie. Whatever you can think of
that you would like—or whatever we can think of,
putting our two heads together—but just, my dear,
what would suit you best——"

"But suppose there is nothing I would like—and
suppose I was just on your hands a helpless lump——"

"I will suppose no such thing," she said, with the
tears coming to her eyes; "why should I suppose that
of *my* son? No, no! no, no! You are young yet, and
in all your strength, the Lord be praised! You might
have come back to me with the life crushed out of you,
like Willie Miller; or worn with that weary India,
and the heat and the work, like Mrs Allender's son in
the Glen. But you, Robbie——"

"What would you have done with me," he repeated,
insisting, though with a half smile on his face, "if it
had been as bad as that—if I had come to you like
them?"

"Why should we think of that that is not, nor is like to be? Oh! my dear, I would have done the best I could with a sore heart. I would just have done my best, and pinched a little and scraped a little, and put forth my little skill to make you comfortable on what there was."

"You have every air of being very comfortable yourself," he said, looking round the room. "I thought so when I came first. You are like the man in the proverb—the parable, I mean—whose very servants had enough and to spare, while his son perished with hunger."

She was a little surprised by what he said, but did not yet attach any very serious meaning to it. "I am better off," she said, "than when you went away. Some things that I've been mixed up in have done very well, so they tell me. I never have spent what came in like that. I have saved it all up for you, Robbie."

"Not for me, mother," he said; "to please yourself with the thought that there was more money in the bank."

"Robbie," she said, "you cannot be thinking what you are saying. That was never my character. There is nobody that does not try to save for their bairns. I have saved for you, when I knew not where you were, nor if I would ever see you more. The money in the bank was never what I was thinking of. There would be enough to give you, perhaps, a good begin-ning—whatever you might settle to do."

"Set me up in business, in fact," he said, with a laugh. "That is what would please you best."

"The thing that would please me best would be what was the best for you," she said, with self-restraint. She was a little wounded by his inquiries, but even now had not penetrated his meaning. He wanted more distinct information than he had got. Her gentle ease of living, her readiness to supply his wants, to forestall them even—the luxury, as it seemed to him after his wild and wandering career, of the long-settled house, the carefully kept gardens, the little carriage, all the modest abundance of the humble establishment, had surprised him. He had believed that his mother was all but poor—not in want of any-thing essential to comfort, but yet very careful about her expenditure, and certainly not allowing him in the days of his youth, as he had often reflected with bitterness, the indulgences to which, if she had been as well off as she seemed now, he would have had, he thought, a right. What had she now? Had she grown rich? Was there plenty for him after her, enough to exempt him from that necessity of work-ing, which he had always feared and hated? It was, perhaps, not unreasonable that he should wish to know.

"I told you," he said, after a short interval, "that I

was good for nothing. If I had stayed at home, what should I have been now? A Writer to the Signet with an office in Edinburgh, and, perhaps, who can tell, clients that would have come to consult me about where to place their money and other such things." He laughed at the thought. "I can never be that now."

"No," she said, in tender sympathy with what she was quick to think a regret on his part. "No, Robbie, my dear; I fear it's too late for that now."

"Well! it's perhaps all the better: for how could I tell them what to do with their money, who never had any of my own? No; what I shall do is this: be a dependent on you, mother, all my life; with a few pounds to buy my clothes, and a few shillings to get my tobacco and a daily paper, now that the 'Scotsman' comes out daily—and some wretched old library of novels, where I can change my books three or four times a-week: and that's how Rob Ogilvy will end, that was once a terror in his way—no, it was never I that was the terror, but those I was with," he added, in an undertone.

Mrs Ogilvy's heart was wrung with that keen anguish of helplessness which is as the bitterness of death to those who can do nothing to help or deliver those they love. "Oh, my dear, my dear," she said, "why should that be so? It is all yours whatever is mine. It's not a fortune, but you shall be no

dependent—you shall have your own: and better
thoughts will come—and you will want more than a
library of foolish books or a daily paper. You will
want your own honest life, like them that went before
you, and your place in the world—and oh, Robbie!
God grant it! a good wife and a family of your own."

He got up and walked about, with large steps that
made the boards creak, and with the laugh which she
liked least of all his utterances. "No, mother, that
will never be," he said. "I'm not one to be caught
like that. You will not find me putting myself in
prison and rolling the stone to the mouth of the
cave."

"Robbie!" she cried, with a sense of something profane in what he said, though she could scarcely have
told what. But the conversation was interrupted here
by Janet coming to announce the early dinner, to
which Robert as usual did the fullest justice. Whatever he might have done or said to shock her, the
sight of his abundant meal always brought Mrs
Ogilvy's mind, more or less, back to a certain con-
tentment, a sort of approval. He was not too particular nor dainty about his food: he never gave himself airs, as if it were not good enough, nor looked
contemptuous of Janet's good dishes, as a man who
has been for years away from home so often does. He
ate heartily, innocently, like one who had nothing on
his conscience, a good digestion, and a clean record.

It was not credible even that a man who ate his
dinner like that should not be one who would work
as well as eat, and earn his meal with pleasure.   It
uplifted her heart a little, and eased it, only to see
him eat.

Afterwards it could scarcely be said that the conversation was resumed; but that day he was in a
mood for talk.   He told her scraps of his adventures,
sitting with the 'Scotsman' in his hand, which he did
not read — taking pleasure in frightening her, she
thought; but yet, after leading her to a point of
breathless interest, breaking off with a half jest—"It
was not me, it was him."   She got used to this conclusion, and almost to feel as if this man unknown,
who was always in her son's mind, was in a manner
the soul of Robert's large passive body, moving that at
his will.   Then her son returned with a sudden spring
to the visitor of the morning, and to poor old Logan
and the strangeness of his fate.   "She's like a woman
I once saw out yonder"—with a jerk of his thumb
over his shoulder—"a singer, or something of that sort,
—a woman that was up to anything."

"Don't say that, my dear, of a woman that will soon
be the minister's wife."

"The minister's wife!" he said, with a great ex-
plosion of laughter.   And then he grew suddenly
grave.   "Old Logan," he said, with a sort of hesitation, "had—a daughter, if I remember right."

" If you remember right! Susie Logan, that you played with when you were both bairns—that grew up with you—that I once thought——a daughter! Well I wot, and you too, that he had a daughter."

"Well, mother," he said, subdued, " I remember very well, if that will please you better. Susie: yes, that was her name. And Susie—I suppose she is married long ago ? "

"They are meaning," said Mrs Ogilvy, with an intonation of scorn, "to marry her now."

"What does that mean—to marry her now? Do you mean she has never married—Susie ? And why ? She must be old now," he said, with a half laugh. " I suppose she has lost her looks. And had no man the sense to see she was—well, a pretty girl—when she was a pretty girl ? "

"If that was all you thought she was!" said Mrs Ogilvy—even her son was not exempted from her disapproval where Susie was concerned. She paused again, however, and said, more softly, "It has not been for want of opportunity. The man that wants her now wanted her at twenty. She·has had her reasons, no doubt."

"Reasons — against taking a husband? I never heard there were any—in a woman's mind."

" There are maybe more things in heaven and earth —than you just have the best information upon," she said.

She thought it expedient after this to go up-stairs a little, to look for something Janet wanted, she explained. Sometimes there were small matters which affected her more than the greater ones. The early terrible impression of him was wearing a little away. She had got used to his new aspect, to his new voice, to the changed and altered being he was. The bitterness of the discovery was over. She knew more or less what to expect of him now, as she had known what to expect of the boyish Robbie of old; and, indeed, this man who was made up of so many things that were new to her had thrown a strange and painful light on the Robbie of old, whom during so many years she had made into an ideal of all that was hopeful and beautiful in youth. She remembered now, yet was so unwilling to remember. She was very patient, but patient as she was, there were some things, some little things, which she found hard to bear; as for instance about Susie—Susie: that she was a pretty girl, but must be old now, and had probably lost her looks,—was that all that Robert Ogilvy knew of Susie? It gave her a sharp pang of anger, in spite of her great patience, in spite of herself.

It took her some time to find what Janet wanted. She was not very sure what it was. She opened two or three cupboards, and with a vague look went over their contents, trying to remember. Perhaps it was

nothing of importance after all.   She went down
again to the parlour at last, to resume any conversation he pleased, or to listen to whatever he might tell
her, or to be silent and wait till he might again be
disposed to talk; passing by the kitchen on her way
first to tell Janet that she had forgotten what it was
she had promised to get for her: but if she would
wait a little, the first time she went up-stairs,—and
then the mistress returned to her drawing-room by
the other way, coming through the back passage.
She had not heard any one come to the front door.

But when she went into the room she saw a strange
sight.   In the doorway opposite to her stood a familiar
figure, which had always been to Mrs Ogilvy like
sunshine and the cheerful day, always welcome,
always bringing a little brightness with her—Susie
Logan, in her light summer dress, a soft transparent
shadow on her face from the large brim of her hat,
every line of her figure expressing the sudden pause,
the arrested movement of a great surprise and wonder,—nothing but wonder as yet.   She stood with
her lips apart, one foot advanced to come in, her
hand upon the door as she had opened it, her eyes large
with astonishment.   She was gazing at him, where he
half sat, half lay, in the great chair, his long legs
stretched half across the room, his head laid back.
He had fallen asleep in the drowsy afternoon, after
the early dinner, with the newspaper spread out upon

his knee. He had nothing to do, there was not much in the paper: there was nothing to wonder at in the fact that he had fallen asleep. His mother, to whom it always gave a pang to see him do so, had explained it to herself as many times as it happened in this way; and there sprang up into her eyes the ready challenge, the instant defence. Why should he not sleep? He had had plenty, oh plenty, to weary him; he was but new come home, where he could rest at his pleasure. But this warlike explanation died out of her as she watched Susie's face, who as yet saw nobody but this strange sleeper in possession of the room. The wonder in it changed from moment to moment; it changed into a gleam of joy, it clouded over with a sudden trouble: there came a quiver to her soft lip, and something liquid to her eyes, more liquid, more soft than their usual lucid light, which was like the dew. There rose in Susie's face a look of infinite pity, of a tenderness like that of a mother at the sight of a suffering child. Oh, more tender than me, more like a mother than me! said to herself the mother who was looking on. And then there came from Susie's bosom a long deep sigh, and the tears brimmed over from her eyes. She stepped back noiselessly from the door and closed it behind her; but stood outside, making no further movement, unable in her great surprise and emotion to do more.

There Mrs Ogilvy found her a moment after, when,

closing softly, as Susie had done, the other door upon
the sleeper, she went round trembling to the little
hall, in which Susie stood trembling too, with her
hand upon her breast, where her heart was beating so
high and loud.   They took each other's hands, but for
a moment said nothing.   Then Susie, with the tears
coming fast, said under her breath, " You never
told me ! " in an indescribable tone of reproach and
tenderness.

Mrs Ogilvy led her into the other room, where they
sat down together.   " You knew him, Susie, you knew
him ? " she said.

" Knew him !—what would hinder me to know
him ? " Susie replied, with the same air of that
offence and grievance which was more tender than
love itself.

" Oh, me ! I was not like that," the mother cried.
She remembered her first horror of him, with horror
at herself.   She that was his mother, flesh of his
flesh, and bone of his bone.   And here was Susie, that
had neither trouble nor doubt.

" To think I should come in thinking about nothing—thinking about my own small concerns—and
find him there as innocent ! like a tired bairn.   And
me perhaps the only one," said Susie, " never to have
heard a word ! though the oldest friend—I do not
mind the time I did not know Robbie," she cried, with
that keen tone of injury ; " it began with our life."

Here was the difference. He too had admitted that he remembered her very well—a pretty girl; but she must be old now, and have lost her looks. Susie had not lost her looks; it was he who had lost his looks. Mrs Ogilvy's heart sank, as she thought how completely those looks were lost, and of the unfavourable aspect of that heavy sleep, and the attitude of drowsy abandonment in the middle of the busy day. But Susie was conscious of none of these things.

CHAPTER XII.

THE day after this was one of the days on which Robert chose to go to Edinburgh, which were days his mother dreaded, though no harm that she could specify came of them. He had not seen Susie on that afternoon, but was angry and put out when he heard of her visit, and that she had seen him asleep in his chair. " You might have saved me from that," he said, angrily ; " you need not have made an exhibition of me." " I did not know, Robbie, that she was there." " It is the same thing," he cried : " you keep all your doors and windows open, in spite of everything I say. What's that but making an exhibition of me, that am something new, that anybody that likes may come and stare at ? " She thought he had reason for his annoyance, though it was no fault of hers : and it pleased her that he should be angry at having been seen by Susie in circumstances so unfavourable. Was not that the best thing for him to be

roused to a desire to appear at his best, not his worse?
He went to Edinburgh next day in the afternoon, after
the early dinner. There was no question put to him
now as to when he should be back.

During that afternoon Susie came again, and was
much disappointed and cast down not to see him.
Perhaps it was well that Susie's first sight of him
had been at a moment when he could say or do nothing to diminish or spoil her tender recollection. None
of those things that vexed the soul of his mother
affected Susie. The maturity of the man, so different
from the boy; the changed tone; the different way of
regarding all around him; the indifference to everything,—all these were hidden from her. The only
thing unfavourable she had seen of him was his personal appearance, and that had not struck Susie as
unfavourable. The long, soft, brown beard, so abundant and well grown, had been beautiful to her; his
size, the large development of manhood, had filled her
with a half pride, half respect. Pride! for did not
Robbie, her oldest friend, more or less belong to Susie
too. She had dreamt already of walking about Eskholm with him, happy and proud in his return, in the
falsification of all malicious prophecies to the contrary. He was her oldest friend, her playfellow from
her first recollection. There was nothing more wanted
to justify Susie's happy excitement—her satisfaction
in his return.

"And he is away to Edinburgh, and has never come to see us! That is not like Robbie," she cried, with a trace of vexation in her eyes.

"Susie, I will tell you and no other the secret, if it is a secret still. He had fallen into ill company, as I always feared, in that weary, far America."

"How could he help it?" cried Susie, ready to face the world in his defence, "young as he was, and nobody to guide him."

"That is true; and we that live in a quiet country, and much favoured and defended on every side, we know nothing of the lawlessness that is there. You will read even in the very papers, Susie: they think no more of drawing a pistol than a gentleman here does of taking his stick when he goes out for a walk."

Susie nodded her head in acquiescence, and Mrs Ogilvy went on: "Where that's the custom, harm will come. Men with pistols in their hands like that, that sometimes go off, even when it's not intended, as you may also read in the papers every day——. Oh, Susie! it happened that there was an accident. How can we tell at this long distance, and so little as we know their manners and their ways, the rights of it all, and what meaning there was in it, or if there was any meaning! But a shot went off, and a man was killed. I am used to it now," said Mrs Ogilvy, her lip quivering, her face appealing in every line to the younger woman at her side not—oh! not—to condemn him; "but at the first moment I was as one that had no more life. The stain of blood may be upon my son's hand."

"No, no!" cried Susie. "No, I will not believe it —not him, of all that are in the world!"

"God bless you, my bonnie dear, that is just the truth! But the shot came out of the band, he among them. There is another man that was at the head who is likely the man. And he is like Robbie, the same height, and so forth. And he has kept hold of him, and kept fast to him, and never let him go."

"I am not surprised," said Susie, very pale, and with her head high. "For Robbie would never betray him. He would never fail one that trusted in him."

"And the terror in his heart is—oh, he says little to me, but I can divine it!—the terror in his heart is that this man will come after him here."

"From America!" said Susie; "so far, so far away."

"It is not so far but that you can come in a week or a fortnight," said Mrs Ogilvy; "you or me would say, impossible: but naturally he is the one that knows best. And he does not think it is impossible. He makes us bolt all the windows and lock the doors as soon as the sun goes down. Susie, this is what is hanging over us. How can he go and see his friends, or let them know he is here, or take the good of coming home—with this hanging over him night and day?"

M

The colour had all gone out of Susie's face. She
put an arm round her old friend, and gave her a trembling almost convulsive embrace. "And you to have
this to bear after all the rest!"

"Me!" said Mrs Ogilvy; "who is thinking of me?
It is an ease to my mind to have said it out. You
were the only one I could speak to, Susie, for you will
think of him just as I do. You will excuse him and
forgive him, and explain it all within yourself——as
I do, as I must do."

"Excuse him!" cried Susie; "that will I not! but
be proud of him, because he's faithful to the man in
trouble, whoever he may be!"

Mrs Ogilvy did not say, even to Susie, that it was
not faithfulness but panic that moved Robert, and
that all his anxiety was to keep the man in trouble
at arm's - length. Even in confessing what was his
problematical guilt and danger, it was still the first
thing in her thoughts that Robbie should have the
best of it whatever the position might be. They were
walking up and down together on the level path in
front of the house — now skirting the holly hedges,
now brushing the boxwood border that made a green
edge to the flowers. Susie had come with perplexities
of her own to lay before her friend, but they all fled
from her mind in face of this greater revelation. What
did it matter about Susie? Whatever came to her, it
would be but she who was in question, and she could

bear it—but Robbie! Me! who is thinking of me?
she said to herself, as Mrs Ogilvy had said it, with a
proud contempt of any such petty subject. It was
not the spirit of self-sacrifice, the instinct of unselfish-
ness, as people are pleased to call such sentiments. I
am afraid there was perhaps a little pride in it, perhaps a subtle self-confidence that whatever one had
to fear in one's own person, what did it matter? one
would be equal to it. But Robbie—— What blood
could be shed, what ordeal dared to keep it from
him!

"You will feel now that I am always ready," said
Susie, "to do anything, if there is anything to do.
You will send for me at any moment. If it were to
take a message, if it were to send a letter, if it were
to go to Edinburgh for any news, if it were to—hide
the man——"

"Susie.!"

"And wherefore not? it's not ours to punish. I
know nothing about him: but to save Robbie and you,
or only to help you, what am I caring? I would put
my arm through the place of the bolt, like Katherine
Douglas for King James. And why should I not hide
a man in trouble? Them that went before us have
done that, and more than that, for folk in trouble,
many a day."

"But not for the shedder of blood," said Mrs
Ogilvy.

"They were all shedders of blood," cried Susie; "there was not one side nor the other with clean hands—and our fore-mothers helped them all, whichever were the ones that were pursued: and so would I any man that stood between you and peace. If he were as bad a man as ever lived, I would help him to get away."

"We must not go so far as that, Susie. We will hope that nothing will need to be done. Robbie and me, we will just keep very quiet till all this trouble blows over. I have a confidence that it will blow over," said Mrs Ogilvy, with a shadow in her eyes which belied her words.

"Certainly it will," cried Susie, with an intensity of assent which, though she knew so little, yet comforted the elder woman's heart.

And Susie once more left her friend without saying a word of the anxieties which were becoming more and more urgent in her own life. She had not yet been told what was the true state of the case, but many alarms had filled her mind, terrors which she would not acknowledge to herself. It did not seem credible that she should be dethroned from her own household place, which she had filled so long, to make way for a stranger, "a strange woman," as Susie, like Mrs Ogilvy, said; nor that the children should be taken out of her hands, and her home be no longer hers. But all other apprehensions and alarms had

been confusedly deepened and increased, she could
scarcely tell how, by the sudden interference of her
father in behalf of an old lover long ago rejected,
whose repeated proposals had become the jest of the
family, a man whom nobody for years had taken
seriously. Mr Logan had suddenly taken up his
cause, and pressed it hotly and injudiciously, filling
Susie with consternation and indignant distress. The
minister had naturally employed the most unpalatable
arguments. He had bidden her to remember that her
time was running short, that she had probably out-
stayed her market, that a wooer was not to be found
by every dykeside, and that at her age it was no longer
possible to pick and choose, but to take what you
could get. Exasperated by all this, Susie had rushed
to her friend to ask what was the interpretation of it.
But the appearance of Robert had driven every other
thought out of her mind, and now again, more than
ever, his story, the danger he was in, the reason why
his return was not published abroad and rejoiced in.
To Susie's simple and straightforward mind this was
the only point in the whole matter that was to be
deplored. She found no fault with Robbie's appearance, with his mid-day sleep, with the failure of his
career—even with the ill company and dreadful associations of which Mrs Ogilvy's faltering story had told
her. She was ready to wipe all that record out with
one tear of tenderness and pity. He had been led

away; he had come back. That he had come back
was enough to atone for all the rest. But there
should be no secret, no concealing of him, no silence
as to this great event. She accepted the bond, but it
was heavy on her soul, and went home, her mind full
of Robert, only vexed and discouraged that she must
not speak of Robert, forgetting every other trouble
and all the changes that seemed to threaten herself.
Me! who is caring about me? Susie said to herself
proudly, as Mrs Ogilvy said it. These women scorned
fate when it was but themselves that were threatened
by it.

When she was gone, Mrs Ogilvy continued for a
while to walk quietly up and down the little platform
before the door of her peaceful house. She had almost
given up her evenings out of doors since Robert's
return, but to-night her heart was soothed, her fears
were calmed. Susie could do nothing to clear up the
situation. Yet to have unbosomed herself to Susie
had done her good. The burden which was so heavy
on herself, which was Robbie in his own person, the
most intimate of all, did not affect Susie. She was
willing to take him back as at the same point where
he had dropped from her ken. There was no criticism
in her eyes or her mind,—nothing like that dreadful
criticism, that anguish of consciousness which perceived all his shortcomings, all the loss that had happened to him in his dismal way through the world,

which was in his mother's mind. - That Susie did not
perceive these things was a precious balm to Mrs
Ogilvy's wounds. It was her exacting imagination
that was in fault, perhaps nothing else or little else.
If Susie were pleased, why should she, who ought to
be less clear-sighted than Susie, be so far from pleased?
Nothing could have so comforted her as did this. She
was calmed to the bottom of her heart. Robbie would
be very late to-night, she knew; but what harm was
there in that, if it was an amusement to him, poor
laddie? He had no variety now in his life, he that
had been accustomed to so much. She heard Andrew
come clanking round from the back-garden with his
pails and his watering-pots. She had not assisted at
the watering of the flowers, not since the day of
Robbie's return, but she did so this calm evening in
the causeless relief of her spirit. "But I would not
be so particular," she said, "Andrew; for it will rain
before the morning, or else I am mistaken." "It's
very easy, mem, to be mistaken in the weather," said
Andrew; "I've thought that for a week past." "That
is true; it has been a by-ordinary dry season," his
mistress said. "Just the ruin of the country," said
the man. "Oh," cried she, "you are never content!"

But she was content that night, or as nearly content
as it was possible to be with such a profound disturbance and trouble in her being. She had her chair

brought out, and her cushion and footstool, her stocking and her book, as in the old days, which had been
so short a time before and yet seemed so far off.
It was not so fine a night as it had usually been,
she thought *then*. The light had not that opal tint,
that silvery pearl-like radiance. There was a shadow
as of a cloud in it, and the sky, though showing
no broken lines of vapour, was grey and a little
heavy, charged with the rain which seemed gathering
after long drought over the longing country. Esk,
running low, wanted the rain, and so did the thirsty
trees, too great to be watered like the flowers, which
had begun to have a dusty look. But in the meantime the evening was warm, very warm and very
still, waiting for the opening up of the fountains
in the skies. Mrs Ogilvy sat there musing, almost
as she had mused of old: only instead of the wistful longing and desire in her heart then, she had
now an ever-present ache, the sense of a deep wound,
the only partially stilled and always quivering tremor
of a great fear. Considering that these things were,
however, and could not be put away, she was very
calm.

She had been sitting here for some time, reading
a little of her book, knitting a great deal of her
stocking, which did not interfere with her reading,
thinking a great deal, sometimes dropping the knitting
into her lap to think the more, to pray a little—

one running into the other almost unconsciously
—when she suddenly heard behind her a movement
in the hedge. It was a high holly hedge, as has
been already said, very well trimmed, and impenetrable, almost as high as a man. When a man
walked up the slope from the road, only his hat,
or if he were a tall man, his head, could be seen
over it. The hedge ran round on the right-hand
side to the wall of the house, shutting out the
garden, which lay on the other slope, as on the
left it encircled the little platform, with its grass-
plot and flower-borders and modest carriage-drive
in front of the Hewan. It was in the garden behind
that green wall that the sound was, which a month
ago would not have disturbed her, which was probably only Janet going to the well or Andrew putting
his watering-cans away. Mrs Ogilvy, however, more
easily startled now, looked round quickly, but saw
nothing. The light was stealing away, the rain was
near; it was that rather than the evening which
made the atmosphere so dim. The noise had made
her heart beat a little, though she felt sure it was
nothing; it made her think of going in, though she
could still with a slight effort see to read. It was
foolish to be disturbed by such a trifle. She had
never been frightened before: a step, a sound at
the gate, had been used, before Robert came back,
to awaken her to life and expectation, to a con-

stantly disappointed but never extinguished hope.
That, however, was all over now: but at this noise
and rustle among the bushes, which was not a footstep or like any one coming, her heart stirred in
her, like a bird in the dark, with terror. She was
frightened for any noise. This was one of the great
differences that had arisen in herself.

She turned, however, again, with some resolution,
to her former occupations. It was not light enough
to see the page with the book lying open on her
knee. She took it in her hand, and read a little.
It was one of those books which, for my own part,
I do not relish, of which you are supposed to be
able to read a little bit at a time. She addressed
herself to it with more attention than usual, in order
to dissipate her own foolish thrill of excitement and
the disturbance within her. She read the words carefully, but I fear that, as is usual in such cases, the
meaning did not enter very clearly into her mind.
Her attention was busy, behind her back as it were,
listening, listening for a renewal of the sound. But
there was none. Then through her reading she began
to think that, as soon as she had quite mastered
herself, she would go in at her leisure, and quite
quietly, crying upon Janet to bring in her chair
and her footstool; and then would call Andrew to
shut the windows and bar the door, as Robbie wished.
Perhaps a man understood the dangers better, and

it was well in any case to do what he wished. She would have liked to rise from her seat at once, and go in hurriedly and do this, but would not allow herself, partly because she felt it would be foolish, as there could be no danger, and partly because she would not allow herself to be supposed to be afraid, supposing that there was. She sat on, therefore, and read, with less and less consciousness of anything but the words that were before her eyes.

When suddenly there came almost close by her side, immediately behind her, the sound as of some one suddenly alighting with feet close together, with wonderfully little noise, yet a slight sound of the gravel disturbed: and turning suddenly round, she saw a tall figure against the waning light, which had evidently vaulted over the hedge, in which there was a slight thrill of movement from the shock. He was looking at his finger, which seemed, from the action, to have been pricked with the holly. Her heart gave a great leap, and then became quiet again. There was something unfamiliar, somehow, in the attitude and air; but yet no doubt it was her son —who else could it be ?—who had made a short cut by the garden, as he had done many a time in his boyhood. Nobody but he could have known of this short cut. All this ran through her mind, the terror and the reassurance in one breath, as she started up hastily from her chair, crying, "Robbie! my dear,

what a fright you have given me.   What made you
come that way?"

He came towards her slowly, examining his finger,
on which she saw a drop of blood; then enveloping
it leisurely in the handkerchief which he took from
his pocket, "I've got a devil of a prick from that
dashed holly," he said.

And then she saw that he was not her son.   Taller,
straighter, of a colourless fairness, a strange voice,
a strange aspect.   Not Robbie, not Robbie! whoever
he was.

CHAPTER XIII.

For a moment Mrs Ogilvy's heart sank within her.
There was something in the moment, in the hour, in
that sudden appearance like a ghost, only with a noise
and energy which were not ghost-like, of this man
whom at the first glance she had taken for Robbie,
which chilled her blood. Then she reminded herself
that a similar incident had befallen her before now.
A tramp had more than once made his way into the
garden, and, but for her own lion mien, and her call
upon Andrew, might have robbed the house or done
some other unspeakable harm. It was chiefly her own
aspect as of a queen, protected by unseen battalions,
and only conscious of the extraordinary temerity of the
intruder, that had gained her the victory. She had not
felt then as she felt now : the danger had only quickened her blood, not chilled it. She had been dauntless
as she looked : but now a secret horror stole her
strength away.

"I think," she said, with a little catching of the breath, "you have made a mistake. This is no public place, it is my garden; but if you have strayed from the road, I will cry upon my man to show you the right way—to Edinburgh, or wherever you may be going."

"Edinburgh's not good for my health. I like your garden," he said, strolling easily towards her; "but look here, mother, give me something for my scratch. I've got a thorn in my hand."

"You will just go away, sir," said Mrs Ogilvy. "Whoever you may be, I permit no visitor here at this late hour of the night. I will cry upon my man."

"I'm glad you've got a man about the place," said the stranger, sitting down calmly upon the bench and regarding her little figure as she stood before him, with an air half of mockery, half of kindness. "It's a little lonely for an old lady. But then you're all settled and civilised here. None the better for that," he continued, easily; "snakes in the grass, thieves behind the door."

"I have told you, sir," said Mrs Ogilvy, trembling more and more, yet holding her ground, "that I let nobody come in here, at this hour. You look like—like a gentleman:" her voice trembled on the noiseless colourless air, in which there was not a breath to disturb anything: "you will therefore not, I am sure, do anything to disturb a woman—who lives alone, but for her faithful servants—at this hour of the night."

"You are a very plucky old lady," he said, "and you pay me a compliment. I'm not sure that I'm a gentleman in your meaning, but I'm proud that you think I look like one. Sit down and let us talk. There's no pleasure in sitting at one's ease when a lady's standing: and, to tell the truth, I'm too tired to budge."

"I will cry upon my man Andrew——"

"Not if you're wise, as I'm sure you are." The stranger's hand made a movement to his pocket, which had no significance for Mrs Ogilvy. She was totally unacquainted with the habits of people who carry weapons; and if she had thought there was a revolver within a mile of her, would have felt herself and the whole household to be lost. "It will be a great deal better for Andrew," said this man, with his easy air, "if you let him stay where he is. Sit down and let's have our talk out."

Mrs Ogilvy did not sit down, but she leant trembling upon the back of her chair. "You're not a tramp on the roads," she said, "that I could fee with a supper and a little money—nor a gentleman, you say, that will take a telling, and refrain from disturbing a woman's house. Who are you then, man, that will not go away,—that sit there and smile in my face?"

"I'm a man that has always smiled in everybody's face,—if it were the whole posse, if it were Death himself," he replied. "Mother, sit down and take things quietly. I'm a man in danger of my life."

A shriek came to her lips, but she kept it in by main force. In a moment the vague terror which had enveloped her became clear, and she knew what she had been afraid of. Here was the man who was like Robbie, who was Robbie's leader, his tyrant, whose influence he could not resist—provided only that Robbie did not come back and find him here!

"Sir," she said, trembling so that the chair trembled too under the touch of her hand, but standing firm, "you are trying to frighten me—but I am not feared. If it is true you say (though I cannot believe it is true), what can I do for you? I am a peaceable person, with a peaceable house, as you see. I have no hiding-places, nor secret chambers. Where could I put you that all that wanted could not see? Oh, for the love of God, go away! I know nothing about you. I could not betray you if—if I desired to do so."

"You would never betray anybody," he said, quite calmly. "I know what is in a face. If you thought it would be to my harm, though you hate me and fear me, you would die before you would say a word."

"God forbid I should hate you!" cried Mrs Ogilvy, with trembling white lips. "Why should I hate you? —but oh, it is late at night, and you will get no bed any place if you do not hurry and go away."

"That's what I ask myself," he said, unmoved.

"Why should you hate me, if you know nothing about me?—that is what surprises me. You know something about me, eh?—you have a guess who I am? you are not terrified to death when a tramp comes in to your grounds, or a gentleman strays: eh? You call for Andrew. But you haven't called for Andrew—you know who I am?"

"I know what you are not," she cried, with the energy of despair. "You are no vagrant, nor yet a gentleman astray. You would have gone away when I bid you, either for fear or for right feeling, if you had been the one or the other. I know you not. But go, for God's sake go, and I will say no word to your hurt, if all the world were clamouring after you. Oh, man, will ye go?"

She thought she heard that well-known click of the gate,—the sound which she had listened for, for years —the sound most unwished and unlooked for now—of Robbie coming home. He saw her momentary pause and the holding of her breath, the almost impercep-tible turn of her head as she listened. It had now become almost dark, and she was not much more than a shadow to him, as he was to her; but the white-ness of her shawl and cap made her outline more dis-tinct underneath the faintly waving shadows of the surrounding trees. The stranger settled himself into the corner of the bench. He watched her repressed movements and signs of agitation with amusement, as

N

one watches a child. She would not betray him—but even in the dimness of the evening air she betrayed herself. Her eagerness, her agitation, were far more, he judged rightly, being a man accustomed to study the human race and its ways, than any chance accident would have brought about. She was a plucky old lady. A vagrant would have had no terrors for her, still less a gentleman—a gentleman! that name that the English give such weight to. Her appeal to him as being like one had gone deep into his soul.

"I will do better," he said, "mother, than seek a bed in any strange place; you will give me one here."

"I hope you will not force me—to take strong measures," she said, with consternation which she could scarcely conceal. "There is a constable—not far off. I will have to send for him, loath, loath though I would be to do so, if ye will not go away."

The stranger laughed, and made again that movement towards his pocket. "You will have to provide then for his widow and his orphans: and a country constable has always a large family," he said.

"Man," cried the little lady with passion, "will ye mock both at the law and at what is right? Then you shall not mock at me. I will put you forth from my door with my own hands."

"Ah," he said, startled, "that's a different thing."

He was moved by this extraordinary threat. Even
in her agitation Mrs Ogilvy felt there must be some
good in him, for he was visibly moved. And she
felt her power. She went forward undaunted to take
him by the arm. When she was close to him he put
out his hand, and smiled in her face, not with a smile
of ridicule but of appeal. "Mother," he said, "is it
the act of a mother to turn a man out of doors to the
wild beasts that seek his life—even if he has deserved
it, and if he is not her son?"

There came from her strained bosom a faint cry. A
mother, what is that? The tigress that owns one cub,
and would murder and slay a thousand for it, as men
sometimes say—or something that is pity and help
and love, the mother of all sons through her own?
Her hand dropped from his shoulder. The sensation
that she would have done what she threatened, that
he would not have resisted her, made her incapable
even of a touch after that.

"Besides," he said in another tone, having, as he
perceived, gained the victory, "I have come to tell
you of your son."

A swift and sudden change came over Mrs Ogilvy's
mind. He did not know, then, that Robbie had come
back. He had come in ignorance, not meaning any
harm, meaning to appeal to her for help for Robbie's
sake. And she was in no danger from him, though
Robbie was. She might even help him secretly, and

do her son no harm.   If only a good Providence would
keep Robbie late to-night.

" Sir," she said, " I can do nothing against you with
my son's name on your lips ; but if you are in danger
as you say, there is no safety for you here.   I have
friends coming to see me that would wonder at you,
and find out about you, and would not be held back
like me.   I cannot undertake for what times they
might come, morning or night : and their first question
would be, Who is that you have in your house ? and,
What is he doing here ?   You would not be safe.   I
have a number of friends—more than I want, more
than I want—if there was anything to hide.   But
if you will trust yourself to me, I will find a good
bed for you, and a safe place, where my word will
be enough.   I will send my woman-servant with you.
That will carry no suspicion : and I will come myself
in the morning to see what I can do for you—what
you want, if it is clothes or if it is money, or——
Ah ! I think I heard the click of that gate,—that
will be somebody coming.   There is a road by the
back of the house—oh, come with me and I will
show you the way ! "

For a moment he seemed inclined to yield ; but
he saw her extreme agitation, and his quick percep-
tion divined something more than alarm for him
behind.

" I think," he said, stretching himself out on the

bench, "that I prefer to take the risks and to stay.
If I cannot take in a parcel of your country-folks, I
am not good for much. You can say I am a friend
of Rob's. And that is true, and I bring you news of
him—eh? Don't you want to hear news of your
son?"

She heard a step on the gravel coming up the
slope, slow as it was now, not springy and swift as
Robbie's once was, and her anguish grew. She took
hold of his arm again, of his hand. "Come with
me, come with me," she cried, scarcely able to get
out the words, "before you are seen! Come with
me before you are seen!"

He was so carried away by her passion, of which
all the same he was very suspicious, that he permitted
her to raise him to his feet, following her impulse
with a curious smile on his face, perhaps touched by
the feeling of the small old soft hand that laid hold
upon his—when Janet with her large solid figure filling
the whole framework of the door suddenly appeared
behind him. "Will I bring in the supper, mem?"
Janet said in her tranquil tones, "for I hear Mr
Robert coming up the road: and you're ower lang
out in the night and the falling dew."

The stranger threw himself back on the bench with
a loud laugh that seemed to tear the silence and rend
it. "So that's how it is!" he said. "You've got Rob
here—that's how it is! I thought you knew more

than you said. Dash you, old woman, I was beginning to believe in you! And all the time it was for
your precious son!"

Mrs Ogilvy took hold of the back of her chair again
to support her. Here was this strange man now in possession of her poor little fortress. And Robbie would
be here also in a moment. Two lawless broken men,
and only she between them, a small old woman, to
restrain them, to conceal them, to feed and care for
them, to save their lives it might be. She felt that
if the little support of the chair were taken from
her she would drop. And yet she must stand for
them, fight for them, face the world as their champion.
She felt the stranger's reproach, too, thrill through
her with a pang of compunction over all. Yes, it
had been not for his sake, not for pity or the love of
God, but for her son's sake, for the love of Robbie.
She was the tigress with her cub, after all. Her
heart spoke a word faintly in her own defence, that
it was not to betray this strange man that she had
intended, but to save him too : only also to get him
out of her way, out of Robbie's way; to save her
son from the danger of his company, and from those
still more apparent dangers which might arise from
his mere presence here. She did not say a word,
however, except faintly, with a little nod of her
head to Janet, "Ay,—and put another place." The
words were so little distinct that, but for her mistress's

look towards the equally indistinct figure on the bench, Janet would not have understood. With a little start of surprise and alarm she disappeared into the house, troubled in her mind, she knew not why. " Andrew," she said to her husband when she returned to the kitchen, " I would just take a turn about the doors, if I were you, in case ye should be wanted." " Wha would want me ? and what for should I turn about the doors at this hour of the nicht ? " " Oh, I was just thinking——" said Janet: but she added no more. After all, so long as Mr Robert was there, nothing could happen to his mother, whoever the strange man might be.

There was silence between the two outside the door of the Hewan — silence through which the sound of Robbie's slow advancing step sounded with strange significance. He walked slowly nowadays— at least heavily, with the step of a man who has lost the spring of youth: and to-night he was tired, no doubt by the long day in Edinburgh, and going from place to place seeking news which, alas! he would only find very distinct, very positive, at home. While Mrs Ogilvy, in this suspense, almost counted her son's steps as he drew near, the other watcher on the bench, almost invisible as the soft dimness grew darker and darker, listened too. He said " Groggy ? " with a slight laugh, which was like a knife in her breast. She thought she smelt the sickening atmos-

phere of the whisky and tobacco come into the pure
night air, but said half aloud, " No, no," with a sense
of the intolerable.   No, no, he had never given her
that to bear.

And then Robbie appeared another shadow in the
opening of the road.   He did not quicken his pace,
even when he saw his mother waiting for him: his
foot was like lead—not life enough in it to disturb
the gravel on the path.

" You're late, Robbie."

" I might have been later and no harm done," he
said, sulkily.   " Yes, I'm late, and tired, and with bad
news which is the worst of all."

" What bad news ? " she cried.

Robbie did not see the vague figure, another shadow,
in grey indistinguishable garments like the night,
which lay on the bench.   He came up to her heavily
with his slow steps, and then stopped and said, with
an unconscious dramatic distinctness, " That fellow—
has come home.   He's in England, or perhaps even in
Scotland, by now: and the peace of my life's gone."

" Oh, Robbie," cried his mother in anguish, wring-
ing her hands; and then she put her hands on his
shoulders, trying to impart her information by the
thrill of their trembling, which gave a shake to his
heavy figure too.   " Be silent, be silent; say no
more ! "

" Why should I say no more ?   I expected you

would feel it as I do: home was coming over me, the feeling of being here—and you—and Susie. But now that's all over. You cannot get away from your fate. That man's my fate. He will turn me round his little finger,—he will make me do, not what I like, but what he likes. It's my fault. I have put myself in his power. I would go away again, but I know I would meet him, round the first corner, outside the door." And Robert Ogilvy sighed—a profound, deep breath of hopelessness which seemed to come from the bottom of his heart. He put his heavy hand on the chair which had supported his mother. She now stood alone, unsupported even by that slight prop.

"You will come in now, my dear, and rest. You have had a hard day: and everything is worse when you are tired. Janet has laid your supper ready; and when you have rested, then we'll hear all that has happened—and think," she said, with a tremor in her voice, " what to do."

She did not dare to look at the stranger directly, lest Robbie should discover him; but she gave a glance, a movement, in his direction, an appeal—which that close observer understood well enough. She had the thought that her son might escape him yet—at which the other smiled in his heart, but humoured her so far that he did not say anything yet.

" It is easy for you," said Robbie, with another pro-

found sigh, "to think what you will do—you neither
know the man, nor his cleverness, nor the weak deevil
I am. I'll not go in. That craze of yours for all
your windows open—they're not shut yet, by George!
and it's ten o'clock and more—takes off any feeling of
safety there might be in the house. I shall sit here
and watch for him. At least I can see him coming,
here."

"Robbie, oh Robbie! come in, come in, if you
would not kill me!"

"Don't take so much trouble, old lady," said the
stranger from the bench, at the sound of whose voice
Robbie started so violently, taking up the chair in his
hand, that his mother made a spring and placed herself between them. "I see what you want to do, but
you can't do it. It's fate, as he says; and he'll calm
down when he knows I am here. So, Bob, you stole
a march on me," he said, raising himself up. He was
the taller man, but Robbie was the heavier. They
stood for a moment—two dark shadows in the night
—so near that the whiteness of Mrs Ogilvy's shawl
brushed them on either side.

"You're here, then, already!" Robbie held the chair
for a moment like a weapon of offence, and then
pitched it from him. "What's the good? I might
have known, if there was an unlikely spot on the
earth, that's where you would be found."

"You thought this an unlikely spot? Why, you've

told me of it often enough, old fellow: safety itself
and quiet; and your mother that would feed us like
fighting cocks. Where else did you think I would
come? The t'other places are too hot for us both.
But I say, old lady, I should not mind having a look
at that supper now: we've only been waiting for Rob,
don't you know?"

Mrs Ogilvy, in her anguish, made still another
appeal. She said, "For one moment listen to me. I
don't even know your name; but there's one thing I
know—that you two are safest apart. I am not, sir,
meaning my son alone," she said with severity, for the
stranger had given vent to a short laugh, "nor for the
evil company that I have heard you are. I am speaking just of your safety. You are in more danger than
he is, and there's more chance they will look for you
here than elsewhere. If it was to save your life," she
added, after a pause to recover her voice, "even for
Robbie, no, I would not give up a young man like you
to what you call your fate. But you're safest apart:
if you think a moment you will see that. I will,"
cried the little indistinguishable whiteness between
the two men, "take it in my hands. You shall have
meat, you shall have rest, you shall have whatever
you need to take you—wherever may be best; not for
him, but for you. Young man, in the name of God
listen to me—it's not that I would harm you! The
farther off you are from each other the safer you are—

both.   And I'll help — I'll help you with all my
heart."

"There's reason in what she says, Bob," said the
stranger, in an easy voice, as if of a quite indifferent
matter. "The old lady has a great deal of sense.
You would have been wise to take her advice long
ago while there was time for it."

She stood between them, her hands clasped, with a
forlorn hope in the new-comer, who was not contemptuous of her, like Robbie—who listened so civilly to all
she said.

"But," he added, with a laugh, "what's safety after
all?   It's death alive; it's not for you and me.   The
time for a meal and a sleep, and then to face the world
again—eh, Bob? that's all a man wants. Let's see that
supper.   I am half dead for want of food."

CHAPTER XIV.

Robert had led the way sullenly into the dining-room. He had made as though he would not sit down at table, where the other placed himself at once unceremoniously, pulling towards him the dish which Janet had just placed on the table, and helping himself eagerly—waiting for no grace, giving no thanks, nor even the tribute of civility to his entertainers, as Mrs Ogilvy remarked in passing, though her mind was full of other and more important things. "I'm too tired, I think, to eat; I'll go to bed, mother," Robbie said. Mrs Ogilvy seized the chance of separating him from the other with rapture. She ventured—it was not always she could do so—to give him a good-night kiss on his cheek, and whispered, "I will send you up something," unwilling that he should suffer by so much as a spoilt meal.

"What! are you going to leave me in the lurch, Bob? steal another march on me, now I've thrown

myself like an innocent on your good faith? That's
not like a *bon camarade*. I thought we were to stick
to each other for life or death."

"I never bargained—you were to come here and
frighten my mother."

"No, no," she cried; "no, no," with her hand on his
arm patting it softly, endeavouring to lead him away.

"Your mother's not frightened, old boy. She's full
of pluck, and we're the best of friends. It's you
that are frightened. You think I've got hold of you
again. So I have, and you're not going to give me the
slip so soon. Sit down and don't be uncivil. I never
yet got the good of a dinner by myself."

Mrs Ogilvy held her son's arm with her hand. She
felt the thrill in him turning towards his old comrade,
though he did not move. Perhaps the pressure of her
hand was too strong on his arm. A woman does not
know exactly how far to go. An added hair's-breadth
is sometimes too much.

"I don't want to be uncivil," said Robbie, after a
moment's hesitation. "After all, I think I'll try to
eat a morsel, mother; I'm in my own place. And you
asked him in, I suppose; he's in a manner your
guest——"

"If you think so, Robbie——" Her hand loosened
from his arm. Perhaps if she had been firm at that
moment,—but she had already been fighting for a long
time; and when a woman is old she gets tired. Her

legs were trembling under her.   She did not feel as if
she could stand many minutes longer.   She did, however; while Robbie, with an air of much sullenness
and reluctance, took his place at the table, and secured
the remains of the dish which his friend had nearly
emptied.   Robert held his place as host with an air of
offended dignity, which would have touched his mother
with amusement had her mind been more free.   But
there was no strength in him; already he was yielding to the stronger personality; and as he ate and
listened, though in spite of himself, it was clear that
one by one the reluctances gave way.   Mrs Ogilvy did
not pretend to take part in the meal.   It was prepared
for Robbie, as was always the case when he went to
Edinburgh and returned late.   She remained in the
room for a time, sometimes going to the kitchen to see
what more could be found to replenish the table,—for
the stranger ate as if he had fasted for a twelvemonth,
and Robbie on his part had always an excellent appetite.   How it did not choke them even to swallow a
morsel in the situation of danger in which they were,
bewildered her.   And greater wonders still arose.   As
she went and came, the conversation quickened between them; and when she came back the second
time from the kitchen, Robbie was leaning back in his
chair, his mouth open in a great peal of laughter, his
countenance so brightened and smoothed out, that for
the first time since his return Mrs Ogilvy's heart

bounded with a recognition of her bright-faced smiling boy as he had been, but was no more. His face overcast again for a moment at the sight of her, as if that was enough to damp all pleasurable emotion ; and when she had again looked round the table to see if anything was wanted, the mother, with a little movement of wounded pride, left them. She went into her parlour, and sat down in the dark, in the silence, to rest a little. If her overstrained nerves and the quick sensation of the wound of the moment brought a tear or two to her eyes, that was nothing. Her mind immediately began to plan and arrange how this dangerous stranger could be got away, how his safety could be secured. I presume that Mrs Ogilvy had forgotten what his crime was. Is it not impossible to believe that a man who is under your own roof, who is like other men, who has smiled and spoken, and shown no barbarous tendency, should be a murderer ? The consciousness of that had gone out of her mind. She thought, on the contrary, that there was good in him : that he was not without understanding, even of herself, an old woman, which was, Mrs Ogilvy was aware, unusual among young men. He had no contempt for her, which was what they generally had, even Robbie : perhaps—it was at least within the bounds of possibility—he might be got to do what she suggested. She searched into all the depths to find out what would be the best. To provide a place for him more

private than the Hewan, a room in a cottage which
she knew, where he would be made quite comfortable;
and then, after great thought taken, where would be
the best and safest refuge, to get him to depart thither,
with money enough—money which, with a faint pang
to lose it for Robbie, she felt would be well-spent
money to free him for ever from that dangerous companion. Mrs Ogilvy thought, and better thought, as
she herself described the process: where would be the
safest place for him to go? How would one of the
Highland isles do, or the Isle of Man, or perhaps these
other islands which she believed were French, though
that would most likely make no difference—Guernsey
or Jersey, or some of these? She was strongly, in her
mind, in favour of an island. It was not so easy to
get at, and yet it was easy to escape from should there
be any pursuit. She thought, and better thought, sitting there in the dark, with the window still open, and
the air of the night blowing in. The wind was cold
rather; but her mind was so taken up that she scarcely
felt it. It is when the mind is quite free that you
have time to think of all these little things.

While she was sitting so quiet the conversation
evidently warmed in the other room, the voices grew
louder, there were peals of laughter, sounds of gaiety
which had not been heard there for many a day.
Mrs Ogilvy's heart rose in spite of herself. She had
not heard Robbie laugh like that—not since he was

o

a boy. God bless him! And, oh, might she not say, God bless the other too, that made him laugh so hearty? He could not be all bad, that other one: certainly there was good in him. It was not possible that he could laugh like that, a man hunted for his life, if he had his conscience against him too. She began to think that there must be some mistake. And so great are the inconsistencies of human nature, that this mother who had repulsed the stranger with almost tragic passion so short a time ago, sat in the dark soothed and almost happy in his presence— almost glad that her Robbie had a friend. She heard Janet come and go, with a cheerful word addressed to her, and giving cheerful words in return and advice to the young men to go to their beds and not sit up till all the hours of the night. After one of these colloquies Robbie came into the room where Mrs Ogilvy was. "Are you here, mother?" he said, "sitting in the dark without a candle — and the window still open. I think it is your craze to keep these windows open, whatever I may say."

"It can matter little now, Robbie — since he's here."

"Oh, since he's here! and how about those that may come after him? But you never will see what I mean. There is more need than ever to bar the doors." He closed the window himself with vehemence, and the shutters, leaving her in total darkness. "I will tell Janet to bring you a light," he said.

"You need not do that: I will maybe go up-stairs."

"To your bed—as Janet has been bidding us to do."

"I'll not promise," said Mrs Ogilvy; "I've many things to think of."

"Never mind to-night; but there's one thing I want of you,—your keys. Janet says the mistress locks everything up but just what is going. There is next to nothing in the bottle."

" Oh, Robbie, my man, it's neither good for him nor for you! It would be far better, as Janet says, to go to your beds."

"It is a pretty thing," said Robbie, "that I cannot entertain a friend, not for once, and he a stranger that has heard me boast of my home; and that you should grudge me the first pleasant night I have had in this miserable dull place."

"Oh, Robbie!" she cried, as if he had given her a blow. And then trembling she put her keys into his hand, groping to find it in the dark. He went away with a murmur, whether of thanks or grumbling she could not tell, and left her thus to feel the full force of that flying stroke. Then she picked herself up again, and allowed to herself that it was a dull place for a young man that had been out in the world and had seen much. And it was natural that he should

be pleased and excited, with a man to talk to. Almost
all women are humble on this point. They do not
hope that their men can be satisfied with their company, but are glad that they should have other men
to add salt and savour to their life. It gave Mrs
Ogilvy a pang to hear her gardevin unlocked, and the
bottles sounding as they were taken out: but yet that
he should make merry with his friend, was not that
sanctioned by the very Scripture itself? She sat there
a while trying to resume the course of her thoughts;
but the sound of the talk, the laughing, the clinking
of the glasses, filled the air and disordered all these
thoughts. She went softly up-stairs after a while;
but the sounds pursued her there almost more distinctly, for her room was over the dining-room,—the
two voices in endless conversation, the laughter, the
smell of their tobacco. You would have said two
light-hearted laddies to hear them, Mrs Ogilvy said
to herself: and one of them a hunted man, in danger
of his life! She did not sleep much that night, nor
even go to bed, but sat up fully dressed, the early
daylight finding her out suddenly in her white shawl
and cap when it came in, oh! so early, revealing the
whole familiar world about,—giving her a surprise,
too, to see herself in the glass, with her candle flicker-
ing on the table beside her. It was broad daylight—
but they would not see it, their shutters being closed
—before the sounds ceased, and she heard them stum-

bling up-stairs, still talking and making a great noise in the silence, to their rooms; and then after a while everything was still. And then she could think.

Then she could think! Oh, her plan was a very simple one, involving little thought,—first that house down the water, on the very edge of the river, where Andrew's brother lived. It was as quiet a place as heart could desire, and a very nice room, where in her good days, in Robbie's boyhood, in the time when there were often visitors at the Hewan, she had sent any guest she had not room for. Down the steep bank behind on which the Hewan stood, you could almost have slid down to the little house in the glen. There would be very little risk there. Robbie and he could see each other, and nobody the wiser; and then, after he was well rested, he would see the danger of staying in a place like the Hewan, where anybody at any moment might walk up to the door. And then the place must be chosen where he should go. If he would but go quiet to one of the islands, and be out of danger! Mrs Ogilvy's mind was very much set on one of the islands; I cannot tell why. It seemed to her so much safer to be surrounded by the sea on every side. If he would consent to go to St Kilda or some place like that, where he would be as safe as a bird in its nest. Ah! but St Kilda—among the poor fisher-folk, where he would have no one to speak to. A chill came over her heart in the middle of her plans.

Would he not laugh in her face if she proposed it? Would he go, however safe it might be? Did he care so much for his safety as that? She wrung her hands with a sense of impotence, and that all her fine plans, when she had made them, would come to nothing. She might plan and plan; but if he would not do it, what would her planning matter? If she planned for Robbie in the same way, would he do it? And she had no power over this strange man. Then after demonstrating to herself the folly of it, she began her planning all over again.

In the morning there were the usual pleasant sounds in the house of natural awakening and new beginning, and Mrs Ogilvy got up at her usual hour and dressed herself with her usual care. She saw, when she looked at herself in the glass, that she was paler than usual. But what did that matter for an old woman? She was not tired—she did not feel her body at all. She was all life and force and energy, thrilling to her finger-points with the desire of doing something—the ability to do whatever might be wanted. She would have gone off to St Kilda straight without the loss of a moment, if her doing so could have been of any avail. But of what avail could that have been? The early morning passed over in its usual occupations, and grew to noon before there was any stirring up-stairs. Then Janet, who had no responsibility, who had always kept her old footing with

Robbie as his old nurse who might say anything and do anything—without gravity, laughing with him at herself and her old domineering ways, yet sometimes influencing him with her domineering more than his mother's anxious love could do—Janet went boldly up-stairs with her jugs of hot water, and knocked at one door after another. Mrs Ogilvy then heard various stirrings, shouts to know what was wanted, openings of doors, Robbie, large and heavy, though with slippered feet, going into his companion's room, and the loud talk of last night resumed. Nearly one o'clock, the middle of the day. Alas for that journey to St Kilda, or anywhere! When the day was half over, how was any such enterprise to be undertaken? And if the police were after him—the police! in her honourable, honest, stainless house—how was he to get away, to have a chance of escape? in his bed and undefended, sleeping and insensible to any danger, till one of the clock. It must have been two before Robbie showed down-stairs. He was a little abashed, not facing his mother—looking, she thought, as if his eyes had been boiled.

"We were a little late last night," he said. "I'm sorry, but it's nothing to look so serious about. Lew's first night."

"Robbie," she said, "it's nothing. I'm old-fashioned. I have my prejudices. But it was not that I was thinking of. Is he in danger of his life or no?"

Robbie blanched a little at this, but shook himself
with nervous impatience. "That's a big word to use,"
he said.

"It was the word he used to me when he came
upon me last night. If he is in danger of his life, he
is not safe for a moment here."

"Rubbish!" said Robbie; "why is he not safe? It
is as out of the way as anything can be. Not a soul
about but your village people, who don't know him
from Adam, nor anything about us, good or bad. I
am just your son to them, and he is just my friend."

"If that were so! It is not a thing I know about:
it is only what you have told me, him and you. He
said he was in danger of his life."

"He was a fool for his pains; but he always liked
a sensation, and to talk big——"

"Then it is not true?"

She looked at him, and he at her. He was pale,
too, with the doings of last night, but a quick colour
flashed over his face under her eyes. "I am not going
to be cross-examined," he said. Then after a pause:
"It may be true, and it mayn't be true—if they're on
his track. But he doesn't think now that they are on
his track."

"He thought so last night, Robbie."

"What does it matter about last night? You're insufferable—you can imagine nothing. There is a difference between a man when he's tired and fasting,

and when he's had a good rest and a square meal.
He doesn't think so now. He's quite happy about us
both. He says we'll pull along here famously for a
time. You so motherly (he likes you), and Janet such
a good cook, and the whisky very decent. He's a con-
noisseur, I can tell you!—and nobody here that has
half an idea in their heads——"

"You may be deceived, there," said Mrs Ogilvy,
suddenly resenting what he said—"you may be deceived in that, both him and you——"

"Not about the cook and the whisky," said Robbie,
with a laugh. "In short, we think we can lie on our
oars a little and watch events. We can cut and run
at any moment if danger appears."

"You say 'we,' Robbie?"

"Yes," he said, with a momentary scowl, "I said
'we.' Of course, I'm in with Lew as soon as he turns
up. I always said I was. You forget the nonsense
I've talked about him. That's all being out of sight
that corrupts the mind. Lord, what a difference it
makes to have him here!"

She looked a little wistfully at the young man to
whom her own love and devotion mattered nothing.
He calculated on it freely, took advantage of it, and
thought no more of it—which was "quite natural":
she quieted all possibilities of rebellion in her own
mind by this. "But, Robbie," she said, "if he is in
danger. I'm not one to advise you to be unfaithful to

a friend—oh, not even if—— But his welfare goes before all. If it's true all I've heard—if there's been wild work out yonder in America, and he's blamed for it——"

"Who told you that?"

"Partly Mr Somerville before you came, Robbie, and partly yourself—and partly it was in a newspaper I read."

"A newspaper!" he cried, almost with a shout. "If it has been in the newspapers here——"

"I did not say it was a newspaper here."

"I know what it was," said Robbie, with a scornful laugh. "You've been at a woman's tricks. I thought you were above them. You've searched my pockets, and you've found it there."

"I found it lying with your coat, in no pocket: and I had seen it before in Mr Somerville's hands. You go too far—you go too far!" she said.

"Well," he said with bravado, "what does a Yankee paper matter?—nobody reads them here. Anyhow," he added, "Lew and I, we're going to face it out. We'll stay where we are, and make ourselves as comfortable as we can. Danger at present there's none. Oh, you need not answer me with supposing this or that; I know."

Mrs Ogilvy opened her lips to speak, but said no word. She was perhaps tempted to suggest that it was her house, her money, her life and comfort, of which these two men were disposing so calmly; but she did not. After all, she said to herself, it was not hers, but Robbie's; everything that was hers was his. She had saved the money which he might have been spending had he been at home—which he might have been extravagant with, who could tell?—for him. And should she grudge him the use of it now? If he was right, if all was safe, if there was no need for alarm, why, then—— Her peace was gone; but had she not all these years been ready to sacrifice peace, comfort, life itself—everything in the world—for Robbie's sake? And now that he had been brought back to her as if it were out of the grave,—"this thy son was dead, and is alive again; he was lost, and is found,"—what was there more to say? That father who ran out to meet his son, who fell upon his neck, and clothed him in the best garment, and would not even listen to his confession and penitence—perhaps when the prodigal had settled back again into the monotony of home, was not so happy in him as he had hoped to be.

CHAPTER XV.

THERE followed after this a period which was the most terrible of Mrs Ogilvy's life. It had not the anguish of that previous time when Robert had disappeared from his home; but in pain and active distress, and the horrors of fear and anxiety, it was sometimes almost as bad—sometimes worse than that. When she looked back on it after, it seemed to her like a nightmare, the dream of a long fever too dreadful to be true. The happiness of having her son under her own roof was turned into torture, though still remaining in its way a kind of terrible happiness; for did not she see him day by day falling into all that was to her mind most appalling—the habits of such a life as was odious and terrible to the poor lady, with all her traditions of decent living, all her prejudices and delicacies? His very voice had changed; it was more gay and lively at times than she had ever known, and this gave her a pang of

pleasure often in the midst of her trouble. Indeed
there were times when even the noise of the two
young men in the house affected her mind with a
certain pleasure and elation, and gratitude to God
that she was there to make their life possible, to make
it comfortable, to give them occasion for the light-
heartedness, though she could not understand it,
which they showed. But these were evanescent
moments, and her life day by day was a kind of
horror to her, as if she were herself affected by the
careless ways, the profane words, the self-indulgence,
and disregard of everything lovely and honest and of
good report, which she seemed to be encouraging and
keeping up while she looked on and suffered.

The situation is too poignant to be easily recorded.
One has heard of a wife oppressed and disgusted by a
dissipated husband; one has heard of the horrors of
a drunkard's home. But this was a different thing.
So far as any one in the house was aware, these
young men were not drunkards. There were no
dreadful scenes in which they lost control of themselves or the possession of their senses. Was it
almost worse than that? Mrs Ogilvy felt as if she
were being put through the treatment which some
people suppose to be a cure for that terrible weakness,
the mixture of intoxicating spirit with every meal
and every dish. Her very cup of tea, the old lady's
modest indulgence, seemed to be flavoured from the

eternal whisky-bottle which was always there, the
smell and the sight of which made her sick, made her
frantic with suppressed misery. They meant no
harm, she tried to explain to herself. It was a habit
of their rough life, and the much exercise and fatigue
to which they subjected themselves, for good or for
evil, in the far-away place from which they had come,
the outskirts of civilisation. They were not capable
of understanding what it was to her to see her trim
dining-room always made disorderly (as she felt) by
that bottle, the atmosphere flavoured with it, its presence always manifest. The pipes, too: her mantelpiece, always so nicely arranged with its clock, its
flower-vases, its shells and ornaments, was now en-
cumbered and dusty with pipes, with ashes of cigars,
with cans and papers of tobacco: how they would
have laughed had they known what a vexation this
was! or rather Robbie would have been angry—he
would have said it was one of her ridiculous ways—
and only the other would have laughed. It is a little
hard to have your son speak of your ridiculous ways
before another man who is indulgent and laughs. But
still the pipes were nothing in comparison with that
other thing — the bottle of whisky always there.
What would the grocer in Eskholm think, from whom
she got her supplies, when, instead of the small discreet bottle at long intervals—for not to have whisky
in the house, the old-fashioned Scotch remedy for so

many things, would have seemed to Mrs Ogilvy almost a crime—there were gallon jars, she did not like to ask Andrew how many, supplied to the Hewan? The idea that it was not respectable cut into her like a knife. And it would be thought that it was Robbie who consumed all that,—Robbie, who was known to be there, yet never had been seen in Eskholm, or taking his walks like other sober folk on Eskside.

And they turned life upside down altogether, both in and out of the house. They rarely went out in daylight, but would take long walks, scouring the country in the late evening, and come home very late to sit down to a supper specially prepared for them, as on the first day of the stranger's appearance. He had affected to think it was the ordinary habit of the house, and approved of it much, he said. And they sat late after it, always with a new bottle of whisky, and went to bed in the daylight of the early summer morning, with the natural consequence that they did not get up till the middle of the day, lacerating Mrs Ogilvy's mind, doing everything that she thought most disorderly and wrong. She never went to bed until they had come in and she had seen them safely established at their supper. And then she would go quietly up-stairs, but not to rest—for her room was over the dining-room, as has been said, and the noise of their talk, their jokes and laughter, kept sleep from her eyes. She was not a very good sleeper at the best. It could scarcely, she said to herself, be considered their fault. And sometimes the sound of their cheerful voices brought a sudden sense of strange happiness with it. Men that are ill men, that have done dreadful things, could not laugh like that, she would sometimes feel confident—and Robbie gay and loud, though all that she had once hoped to be refinement had gone out of his voice: this had something in it that went to her heart. If he was happy after all, what did anything else matter? His voice rang like a trumpet. There was no sound in it of depression or dejection. He had recovered his spirits, his confidence, his freedom. The heavy dulness, which was his prevailing mood before the stranger appeared, was gone. Then he had been discontented and miserable, notwithstanding the thankfulness he expressed to have escaped from the dominion of his former leader. But now he was, or appeared to be, happy, hugging his chains, delighted, as it seemed, to return to his bondage. It was not likely that this change could be a subject of gratification to his mother; and yet his altered tone, his brightened aspect, the sound of his laughter, gave her something that was almost like happiness. But for this, perhaps, she could not have borne as she did the transformation of her life.

The two young men sometimes went to Edinburgh, as Robbie had been in the habit of doing before the other's arrival. They went in the morning and re-

turned late at night, the much disturbed and troubled
household sitting up for them to give them their meal
and secure their perfect comfort.   After the first time
Mrs Ogilvy, though her heart was always full of anxiety
for their safety, thought it best not to appear when they
returned.   They had both gibed at her anxiety, at the
absurdity and impossibility of her sitting up for them,
and her desire to tie her son to her apron-strings.
Robbie was angry, indignantly accusing her of making
him ridiculous by her foolish anxiety.   Poor Mrs
Ogilvy had no desire to tie him to her apron-strings.
It was not foolish fondness, but terror, that was in
her heart.   She had a fear—almost a certainty—that
one time or other they would not come back,—that
they would hear bad news and not return at all, but
depart again into the unknown, leaving her on the
rack.

But though she did not appear, she sat up in her room
at the window, watching for the click of the gate, the
sound of their steps on the path, the dark figures in the
half dark of the summer night.   They had means of getting news, she knew not how, and came back sometimes
elated and noisy, sometimes more quiet, according as
these were bad or good.   And then she heard Janet
bustling below bringing their supper, asking, in the
peremptory tones which amused them in her, if they
wanted anything more, if they could not just get what
they wanted themselves, and let a poor woman, that

P

had to be up in the morning to her work, get to her
bed. Sometimes Janet held forth to them while she
put their supper on the table. "It's fine for you twa
strong buirdly young men, without a hand's turn to
do, to turn day into nicht and nicht into day—though,
losh me! how ye can pit up with it, just jabbering and
reading idle books a' the day, and good for nothing, is
mair than I can tell. But me, I'm a hard-working
woman. I've my man's breakfast to get ready at
seeven, and the house to clean up, and to keep the
whole place like a new pin. Bless me, if ye were to
take a turn at the garden and save Andrew's auld
bones, that are often very bad with the rheumatism,
or carry in a bucket of coals or a pail of water for me
that am old enough to be your mother, it would set
you better. Just twa strong young men, and never
doing a hand's turn—no a hand's turn from morning
to nicht."

"There's truth in what she says, Bob—we are a
couple of lazy dogs."

"I was not just made," said Robbie, who was less
good-humoured than his friend, "to hew wood and to
draw water in my own house."

"It would be an honour and a credit to you to do
something, Mr Robert," said Janet, with a touch of
sternness. "Eh, laddie! the thing that's maist unbe-
coming in this world is to eat somebody's bread and
do nothing for it—no even in the way of civeelity—

for here's the mistress put out of everything. She has
no peace by night or by day. Do you think she is
sleepin', with you making a' that fracaw coming in
in the middle of the nicht, and your muckle voices
and your muckle steps just making a babel o' the
house? She's no more sleepin' than I am: and my
opinion is that she never sleeps—just lies and ponders
and ponders, and thinks what's to become of ye. Eh,
Mr Robert, if you canna exerceese your ain business,
whatever it may be——"

Then there was a big laugh from both of the young
men. "We have not got our tools with us, Janet,"
said the stranger.

"I'm no one that holds very much with tools, Mr
Lewis," said Janet. "Losh! I would take up just the
first thing that came, and try if I couldna do a day's
work with that, if it were me."

Mr Lewis was what the household had taken to
calling the visitor. He had never been credited with
any name, and Robert spoke to him as Lew. It was
Janet who had first changed this into Mr Lewis.
Whether it was his surname or his Christian name
nobody inquired, nor did he give any information, but
answered to Mr Lewis quite pleasantly, as indeed he
did everything. He was, as a matter of fact, far more
agreeable in the house than Robbie, who, quiet enough
before he came, was now disposed to be somewhat
imperious and exacting, and show that he was master.

The old servants, it need scarcely be said, were much aggrieved by this. "He would just like to be cock o' the walk, our Robbie," Andrew said.

"And if he is, it's his ain mother's house, and he has the best right," said Janet, not disposed to have Robert objected to by any one but herself. "He was aye one that likit his ain way," she added on her own account.

"That's the worst o' weemen wi' sons," said Andrew; "they're spoilt and pettit till they canna tell if they're on their heels or their head."

"A bonnie one you are to say a word against the mistress," cried Janet; "and weemen, says he! I would just like to ken what would have become of ye, that were just as bad as ony in your young days, if it hadna been for the mistress and me?"

But on the particular evening on which Janet had bestowed her advice on the young men in the dining-room, they continued their conversation after she was gone in another tone. "That good woman would be a little startled if she knew what work we had been up to," said Lewis; "and our tools, eh, Bob?" They both laughed again, and then he became suddenly serious. "All the same, there's justice in what she says. We'll have to be doing something to get a little money. Suppose we had to cut and run all of a sudden, as may happen any day, where should we get the needful, eh?"

"There's my mother," said Robert; "she'll give me whatever I want."

"She's a brick of an old woman; but I don't suppose, eh, Bob? she's what you would call a millionaire." Lew gave his friend a keen glance under his eyelids. His eyes were keen and bright, always alive and watchful like the eyes of a wild animal; whereas Robbie's were a little heavy and veiled, rather furtive than watchful, perhaps afraid of approaching danger, but not keeping a keen look-out for it, like the other's, on every side.

"No," said Robert, with a curious brag and pride, "not a millionaire—just what you see—no splendour, but everything comfortable. She must have saved a lot of money while I was away. A woman has no expenses. And I'm all she has; she'll give me whatever I want."

"You are all she has, and she'll give you—whatever you want."

"Yes; is there anything wonderful in that? You say it in a tone——"

"We're not on such terms as to question each other's tones, are we?" said Lew. "Though I'm idle, as Janet says, I have always an eye to business, Bob. Never mind your mother; isn't there some old buffer in the country that could spare us some of his gold? The nights are pretty dark now, though they don't last long—eh, Bob?"

There was more a great deal than was open to a
listening ear in the tone of the question. And Robert
Ogilvy grew red to his hair. "For God's sake," he
cried, "not a word of that here—in my own place,
Lew! If there's anything in the world you care
for——"

"Is there anything in the world I care for?" said
the other. "Not very much, except myself. I've
always had a robust regard for that person. Well—
I'm not fond of doing nothing, though your folks
think me a lazy dog. Janet's eyes are well open,
but she's not so clever as she thinks. I'm beginning
to get very tired, I can tell you, of this do-nothing
life. I'd like to put a little money in my pocket,
Rob. I'd like to feel a little excitement again. We'll
take root like potatoes if we go on like this."

Mr Lewis's talk was sprinkled with words of a more
energetic description, but they waste a good deal of
type and a great many marks of admiration. The
instructed can fill them in for themselves.

"I don't think we could be much better off," said
Robbie, with a certain offence; "plenty of grub, and
good of its kind—you said that yourself—and a safe
place to lie low in. I thought that was what you
wanted most."

"So it was, if a man happened always to be in the
same mind. I want a little excitement, Bob. I want
a good beast under me, and the wind in my face. I

want a little fun—which perhaps wouldn't be just
fun, don't you know, for the men we might have the
pleasure of meeting——"

"If those detective fellows get on the trail you'll
have fun enough," Robert said.

"I—both of us, if you please, old fellow: we're in
the same box. The captain—and one of the chief
members of the gang. That's how they've got us
down, recollect. You never knew you were a chief
member before—eh, Rob? But I don't like that sort
of fun. I like to hunt, not to be hunted, my boy.
And I'm very tired of lying low. Let's make a run
somewhere—eh? I like the feeling of the money
that should be in another man's pocket tumbling
into my own."

"It'll not do—it'll not do, Lew, here; I won't have
it," cried Robbie, getting up from his supper and
pacing about the room. "I never could bear that
part of it, you know. It seems something different in a
wild country, where you never know whose the money
may be—got by gambling, and cheating, and all that,
and kind of lawful to take it back again. No, not
here. I'll give myself up, and you too, before I
consent to that."

"I've got a bit of a toy here that will have something to say to it if any fellow turns out a sneak,"
said Lew, with that movement towards his pocket
which Mrs Ogilvy did not understand.

"Does this look like turning out a sneak?" said Robbie, looking round with a wave of his hand. "You've been here nearly a month: has any one ever said you were not welcome? Keep your toys to yourself, Lew. Two can play at that game; but toys or no toys, I'm not with you, and I won't follow you here. Oh, d—— it, *here!* where there's such a thing as honesty, and a man's money is his own!"

"My good fellow," said the other, "but for information which you haven't to give, and which I could get at any little tavern I turned into, what good are you? You never were any that I know of. You were always shaking your head. You didn't mind, so far as I can remember, taking a share of the profits; but as for doing anything to secure them! I can work without you, thank you, if I take it into my head."

"I hope you won't take it into your head," said Robbie, coming back to the table and resuming his chair. "Why should you, when I tell you I can get anything out of my mother? And with right too," he continued, "for I should have been sure to spend it all had I been at home; and she only saved it because I was not here. Therefore the money's justly mine by all rules. It isn't that I should like to see you start without me, Lew, or that I wouldn't take my share, whatever—whatever you might wish to do. But what's the good, when you can get it, and begged to accept it, all straight and square close at hand?"

" For a squeamish fellow you've got a good stiff conscience, Bob," said Lew, with a laugh. "I like that idea,—that though it's bad with an old fogey trotting home from market, it ain't the same with your mother. In that way it would be less of a privilege than folks would think to be near relations to you and me, eh? I've got none, heaven be praised! so I can't practise upon 'em. But you, my chicken! that the good lady waits up for at nights, that she would like to tie to her apron-strings——"

" It's my own money," said Rob; " I should have spent it twice over if I had been at home."

And presently they fell into their usual topics of conversation, and this case of conscience was forgotten.

Meanwhile Mrs Ogilvy fought and struggled with her thoughts up-stairs. She had all but divined that there had been a quarrel, and had many thoughts of going down, for she was still dressed, to clear it up. For if they quarrelled, what could be done? She could not turn Lewis out of her house—and indeed her heart inclined towards that soft-spoken ruffian with a most foolish softness. He might perhaps scoff a little now and then, but he was not unkind. He was always ready to receive her with a smile when she appeared, which was more than her son was, and had a way of seeming grateful and deferential whether he was really so or not, and sometimes said a word to soothe feelings which Robbie had ruffled, without ap-

pearing to see, which would have spoiled all, that
Robbie had wounded them.   Of the two, I am afraid
that Mrs Ogilvy in her secret heart, so far down that
she was herself unconscious of it, was most indulgent
to Lew.   Who could tell how he had been brought up,
how he had been led astray ?   He might have been
an orphan without any one to look after him, whereas
Robbie——   Her heart bled to think how few ex-
cuses Robbie had, and yet excused him with innumer-
able eager pleas.   But the chief thing was, that life
was intolerable under these conditions : and what
could she do, what could she propose, to mend them ?
—life turned upside down, a constant panic hanging
over it, a terror of she knew not what, a sensation as
of very existence in danger.   What could be done,
what could any one do ?   Nothing, for she dared not
trust any one with the secret.   It was heavy upon her
own being, but she dared not share it with any other.
She dared not even reveal to Janet anything of the
special misery that overwhelmed her : that it was
possible the police might come — the police ! — and
watch the innocent house, and bring a warrant, as if
it were a nest of criminals.   It made Mrs Ogilvy jump
up from her seat, spring from her bed, whenever this
thought came back to her.   And in the meantime she
could do nothing, but only sit still and bear it until
some dreadful climax came.

She had a long struggle with herself before she

permitted herself the indulgence of going in to Edinburgh to see Mr Somerville, who was the only other person who knew anything about it. After many questions
with herself, and much determined endurance of her
burden, it came upon her like an inspiration that this
was the thing to do. It would be a comfort to be able
to speak to some one, to have the support of somebody else's judgment. It is true that she was afraid
of leaving her own house even for the little time that
was necessary ; but she decided that by doing this
early in the morning before the young men were up,
she might do it without risk. She gave Janet great
charges to admit no one while she was away. "Nobody—I would like nobody to come in. Mr Robert is
up so late at night that we cannot expect him to get
up early *too ;* but I would not like strange folk who do
not know how late he has to sit up with his friend, to
come in and find him still in his bed at twelve o'clock
in the day. There's no harm in it ; but we have all
our prejudices, and I cannot bide it to be known.
You will just make the best excuse you can——"

"You may make your mind easy, mem," said Janet;
" I will no be wanting for an excuse."

"So long as you just let nobody in," said her mistress. Mrs Ogilvy had never in her life availed herself even of the common and well-understood fiction,
" Not at home," to turn away an unwelcome visitor;
but she did not inquire now what it was that Janet

meant to say. She went away with a little lightening
of her heavy heart. To be able to speak to somebody
who was beyond all doubt, and incapable of betraying
her, of perhaps having something suggested to her,
some plan that would afford succour, was for the
moment almost as if she had attained a certain relief.
It was July now, the very heat and climax of the year.
The favoured fields of Mid-Lothian were beginning to
whiten to the harvest; the people about were in light
dresses, in their summer moods and ways, saying to
each other, " What a beautiful day—was there ever
such fine weather ? "—for indeed it was a happy year
without rain, without clouds. To see everybody as
usual going about their honest work was at once a
pang and a relief to Mrs Ogilvy. The world, then,
was just as before—it was not turned upside down ;
most people were busy doing something; there was no
suspension of the usual laws. And yet all the more
for this universal reign of law and order, which it was
a refreshment to see—all the more was it terrible to
think of Robbie, lawless, careless of all rules, wasting
his life—of the two young men whom she had left behind her, both in the strength of their manhood, doing
nothing, good for nothing. These two sensations,
which were so different, tore Mrs Ogilvy's heart in
two.

CHAPTER XVI.

MR SOMERVILLE was engaged with another client, and
it was a long time before Mrs Ogilvy could see him.
She had to wait, trembling with impatience, and dis-
mayed by the passage of time, following the hands of
the clock with her eyes, wondering what perhaps
might be happening at home. She was not, perhaps,
on the face of things, a very strong defensive force,
but she had got by degrees into the habit of feeling
that safety depended more or less upon her presence.
She might have perhaps a little tendency that way by
nature, to think that her little world depended upon
her, and that nothing went quite right when she was
away; but this feeling was doubly strong now. She
felt that the little house was quite undefended in her
absence, that all the doors and windows which she
could not bear to have shut were now standing wide
open to let misfortune come in.

When she did at last succeed in seeing Mr Somer-

ville, however, he was very comforting to her. It was
not that he did not see the gravity of the situation. He
was very grave indeed upon the whole matter. He did
not conceal from her his conviction that Robert stood
a much worse chance if he were found in the company
of the other man. "Which is no doubt unjust," he
said, " for I understood you to say that your son had a
great repugnance to this scoundrel who had led him
astray." Mrs Ogilvy responded to this by a very faltering and doubtful "Yes." Yes indeed—Robbie had
said he hated the man; but there was very little
appearance on his part of hating him now—and Mrs
Ogilvy herself did not hate Lew. She hated nobody,
so that this perhaps was not wonderful, but her feeling
towards the scoundrel, as Mr Somerville called him,
was more than that abstract one. She felt herself his
defender, too, as well as her son's. She was eager
to save him as well as her son. To ransom Robbie by
giving up his companion was not what she thought of.

I do not know whether she succeeded in conveying
this impression to Mr Somerville's mind. But yet it
was a relief to her to pour out her heart, to tell all
her trouble; and the old lawyer had a sympathetic
ear. They sat long together, going over the case, and
he insisted that she should share his lunch with him,
and not go back to the Hewan fasting after the long
agitating morning. Even that was a relief to Mrs
Ogilvy, though she was scarcely aware of it, and in

her heart believed that she was very impatient to get away. But the quiet meal was grateful to her, with her kind old friend taking an interest in her, persuading her to eat, pouring out a modest glass of wine, paying all the attention possible in his old-fashioned old-world way. She was very anxious to get back, and yet the tranquil reflection gave her a sense of peace and comfort to which she had been long a stranger. There were still people in the world who were kind, who were willing to help her, who would listen and understand what she had to bear, who believed everything that was good about Robbie,—that he had been " led away," but was now anxious, very anxious, to return to righteous ways. Mrs Ogilvy's heart grew lighter in spite of herself, even though the news was not good—though she ascertained that there was certainly an American officer in Edinburgh whose mission was to track out the fugitives. "He must not stay at the Hewan—it would be most dangerous for Robert: you must get him to go away," the old gentleman said.

"If I could but get him to do that! but, oh, you know by yourself how hard it is for the like of me, that never shut my doors in my life to a stranger, to say to a man, Go!—a man that is a well-spoken man, and has a great deal of good in him, and has no parents of his own, and never has had instruction nor even kindness to keep him right.'

"Mrs Ogilvy, he is a murderer," said Mr Somerville, severely.

"Oh, but are you sure of that? If I were sure! But a man that sits at your table, that you see every day of his life, that does no harm, nor is unkind to any one—how is it possible to think he has done anything like that?"

"But, my dear lady," said Mr Somerville, "it is true."

"Oh," cried Mrs Ogilvy, "how little do we know, when it comes to that, what's true and what's not true! He's not what you would call a hardened criminal," she said, with a pleading look.

"It's not a small matter," said the lawyer, "to kill a man."

"Oh, it is terrible! I am not excusing him," said Mrs Ogilvy, humbly.

These young men had disturbed all the quiet order of her life. They had turned her house into something like the taverns which, without knowing them, were Mrs Ogilvy's horror. Nobody could tell what a depth of shame and misery there was to her in the noisy nights, the long summer mornings wasted in sleep; nor how much she suffered from the careless contempt of the one, the angry criticism of the other. It was her own boy who was angrily critical, treating her as if she knew nothing, and made the other laugh. One of these scenes sprang up in her mind as she spoke, with all its accessories of despair. But yet she could not but excuse the stranger, who had some good in him, who was not a hardened criminal, and make her fancy picture of Robert, who had been "led astray." The sudden realisation of that scene, and the terror lest something might have happened in the meantime, something from which she might have protected them, seized upon her once more after her moment of repose. She accepted with trembling Mr Somerville's proposal to come out to the Hewan to see Robbie, and to endeavour to persuade him that his friend must be got away. "It is just some romantic notion of being faithful to a friend," said the old gentleman, "and the prejudice which is in your mind too, my dear mem, in favour of one that has taken refuge in your house—but you must get over that, in this case, both him and you. It is too serious a matter for any sentiment," said Mr Somerville, very gravely.

In the meantime things had been following their usual routine at the Hewan. The late breakfast had been served; the three o'clock dinner, arranged at that amazing hour in order to divide the day more or less satisfactorily for the two young men, had followed. That the mistress should not have come home was a great trouble and anxiety to Janet, but not to them, who were perhaps relieved in their turn not to have her anxious face, trying so hard to approve of them, to laugh at their jests and mix in their conversation, superintending their meal. "Where's your mother having her little spree?" said the stranger. "In Edinburgh, I suppose," said Robbie. "Eh! Edinburgh? that's not very good for our health, Bob. She might drop a word——" "She will never drop any word that would involve me," said Robert. "Well, she's a brick of an old girl, and pluck for anything," said the other. And then the conversation came to a stop. Their talk was almost unintelligible to Janet, who was of opinion that Mr Lewis's speech was too "high English" for any honest sober faculties to understand. Mrs Ogilvy's presence, though all that she felt was their general contempt for her, had in fact a subduing influence upon them, and the mid-day meal was generally a comparatively quiet one. But when that little restraint was withdrawn, the afternoon stillness became as noisy as the night, and their voices and laughter rose high.

It was while they were in full enjoyment of their meal that certain visitors arrived at the Hewan— not unusual or unfamiliar visitors, for one of them was Susan Logan, whose visits had lately been very few. Susie had been more wounded than words could say by Robbie's indifference. He had been now more than a month at home, but he had never once found his way to the manse, or showed the slightest inclination to renew his "friendship," as she called it, with his old playfellow. Susie, whose fortunes and spirits were very low, who was now aware of what was in store for her, and whose mind was painfully occupied with the consideration of what her own life was to be when her father's second marriage took place, was more than usually susceptible to such an unkindness and affront, and she had deserted the Hewan and her dearest friend his mother, though it was the moment in her life when she wanted support and sympathy most. "He shall never think I am coming after him, if he does not choose to come after me," poor Susie had said proudly to herself. And Mrs Ogilvy, without at all inquiring into it, was glad and thankful beyond measure that Susan, whom next to her son she loved best in the world, did not come. She, too, wanted sympathy and support more than she had ever done in her life, but in her present fever of existence she was afraid lest the secrets of her house should be betrayed even to the kindest eye.

Susie was accompanied on this occasion by Mrs Ainslie, her future stepmother, a very uncongenial companion. It was not with her own will, indeed, that she made the visit. It had been forced upon her by this lady, who thought it "most unnatural" that Susie should see so little of her friends, and who was anxious in her own person to secure Mrs

Ogilvy's countenance. They did not approach the house in the usual way, but went up the brae through the garden behind, which was a familiarity granted to Susie all her life, and which Mrs Ainslie eagerly desired to share. The way was steep, though it was shorter than the other, and the elder lady paused when they reached the level of the house to take breath. "Dear! the old lady must have company to-day. Listen! there must be half-a-dozen people to make so much noise as that. I never knew she entertained in this way."

"She does not at all entertain, as you call it, Mrs Ainslie: though it may be some of Robbie's friends." Susie spoke with a deeper offence than ever in her voice; for if Robbie was amusing himself with friends, it was more marked than ever that he did not come to the manse.

"Entertain is a very good word, Miss Susie, let me tell you, and I shall entertain and show you what it means as soon as your dear father brings me home."

"I shall not be there to see, Mrs Ainslie," said Susie, glad to have something which justified the irritation and discomfort in her mind.

"Oh yes, you will," said the lady. "You shan't make a stolen match to get rid of me. I have set my heart on marrying you, my dear, like a daughter of my own."

To this Susie made no reply; and Mrs Ainslie

having recovered her breath, they walked together round the corner, which was the dining-room corner, with one window opening upon the shrubbery that sheltered that side of the house. Susie's rapid glance distinguished only that there were two figures at table, one of which she knew to be Robbie; but her companion, who was not shy or proud like Susie, took a more deliberate view, and received a much stronger sensation. Immediately opposite that side window, receiving its light full on his face, sat the mysterious inmate of Mrs Ogilvy's house, the visitor of whom the gossips in the village had heard, but who never was seen anywhere nor introduced to any visitor. Mrs Ainslie uttered a suppressed exclamation and clutched Susie's arm; but at the same time hurried her along to the front of the house, where she dropped upon one of the garden benches with a face deeply flushed, and panting for breath. The dining-room had another window on this side, but the blinds were drawn down to keep out the sunshine. This did not, however, keep out the sound of the voices, to which she listened with the profoundest attention, still clutching Susie's arm. "My goodness gracious! my merciful goodness gracious!" Mrs Ainslie said.

Susie was not, it is to be feared, sympathetic or interested. She pulled her arm away. "Have you lost your breath again?" she said.

Mrs Ainslie remained on the bench for some time, panting and listening. The voices were quite loud and unrestrained. One of them was telling stories with names freely mentioned, at which the other laughed, and at which this lady sitting outside clenched her fist in her light glove. After a minute Susie left her, saying, " I will go and find Mrs Ogilvy," and she remained there alone, with the most extraordinary expressions going over her face. Her usual little affectations and fine-ladyism were gone. It must have been an expressive face by nature; for the power with which it expressed deadly panic, then hatred, then a rising fierceness of anger, was extraordinary. There came upon her countenance, which was that of a well-looking, not unamiable, but affected, middle-aged woman in ordinary life, something of that snarl of mingled terror and ferocity which one sees in an outraged dog not yet wound up to a spring upon his offender. She sat and panted, and by some curious gift which belongs to highly-strained feeling heard every word.

This would not have happened had. Mrs Ogilvy been at home—the voices would not have been loud enough to be audible so clearly out of doors; for the respect of things out of doors and of possible listeners, and all the safeguards of decorum, were always involved in her presence. Also, that story would not have been told; there was a woman in it who was not a good woman, nor well treated by Lew's strong speech: therefore everything that happened afterwards no doubt sprang from that visit of Mrs Ogilvy's to Edinburgh; and, indeed, she herself had foreseen, if not this harm, which she could not have divined, at least harm of some kind proceeding from the self-indulgence to which for one afternoon she gave way.

"No, Miss Susie, the mistress is no in, and I canna understand it. She went to Edinburgh to see her man of business, but was to be back long before the dinner. The gentlemen—that is, Mr Robert and his friend—are just at the end o't, as ye may hear them talking. I'll just run ben and tell Mr Robert you are here."

"Don't do that on any account, Janet. Mrs Ainslie is with me, sitting on the bench outside, and she has lost her breath coming up the hill. Probably she would like a glass of water or something. Don't disturb Mr Robert. It is of no consequence. I'll come and see Mrs Ogilvy another day."

"You are a sight for sore een as it is. The mistress misses ye awfu', Miss Susie: you're no kind to her, and her in trouble."

"In trouble, Janet! now that Robbie has come home!"

"Oh, Miss Susie, wherever there are men folk there is trouble; but I'll get a glass of wine for the lady."

Janet's passage into the dining-room to get the wine was signalised by an immediate lowering of the tone

of the conversation going on within. She came out
carrying a glass of sherry, and was reluctantly followed by Robert, who came into the drawing-room,
somewhat down - looked and shamefaced, to see his
old companion and playmate. Janet, for her part,
took the sherry to Mrs Ainslie, who had drawn her
veil, a white one, over her face, concealing a little her
agitated and excited countenance. The lady was pro-
fuse in her thanks, swallowed the wine hastily, and
gave back the glass to Janet, almost pushing her away.
"Thanks, thanks very much; that will do. Now leave
me quiet a little to recover myself."

"Maybe you would like to lie down on the sofa in
the drawing-room out of the sun. The mistress is no
in, but Mr Robert is there with Miss Susie."

"No, thanks; I am very well where I am," said
Mrs Ainslie, with a wave of her hand. The conversation inside had ceased, and from the other side of
the house there came a small murmur of voices. Mrs
Ainslie waited until Janet had disappeared, and then
she moved cautiously, making no sound with her feet
upon the gravel, round the corner once more to the
end window. Cautiously she stooped down to the
window ledge and looked in. He was still seated
opposite to the window, stretching out his long legs,
and laying back his head as if after his dinner he was
inclined for a nap. His eyes were closed. He was
most perfectly at the mercy of the spy, who gazed in

upon him with a fierce eagerness, noting his dress, his thickly grown beard, all the peculiarities of his appearance. She even noticed with an experienced eye the heaviness of his pocket, betraying something within that pocket to which he had moved his hand without conveying any knowledge to Mrs Ogilvy. All of these things this woman knew. She devoured his face with her keen eyes, and there came from her a little unconscious sound of excitement which, though it was not loud, conveyed itself to his watchful ear. He opened his eyes drowsily, said something, and then closed them again, taking no more notice. Lew had dined well and drank well; he was very nearly asleep.

She crept round again to the front and took her seat on the bench, again pulling down and arranging the white veil, which was almost like a mask over her face. Susie and Robert came out to her a few minutes after, she leading, he following. "If you will come in and rest," said Robert, "my mother will probably be back very soon."

"Oh no, it is best for us to get home," said Mrs Ainslie. "Tell your dear mother we were so sorry to miss her. You were very merry with your friend, Mr Robert, when we came up to the house."

"My friend?" said Robbie, startled. "Yes—I have a friend in the house."

"All the village knows that," said the lady, "but

not who he is. Now I have the advantage of the rest,
for I saw him through the window."

Robert was still more startled and disturbed.
"We're—not fond of society—neither he nor I. I
was trying to explain to Susie; but it sounds disagreeable. I—can't leave him, and he knows nobody,
so he won't come with me."

"Tell him he has an acquaintance now. You will
come to see me, won't you? I've been a great deal
about the world, and I've met almost everybody—
perhaps you, Mr Robert, I thought so the other day,
and certainly—most other people: you can come to
see me when you go out for your night walks that
people talk of so. Oh, I like night walks. I might
perhaps go out a bit with you. Dark is very long of
coming these Scotch nights, ain't it? But one of these
evenings I'll look out for you." She paused here, and
gave him a malicious look through her veil. "I'll
look for you, Mr Robert—and Lew."

Robert stood thunderstruck as the ladies went away.
Susie's eyes had sought his with a wistful look, a sort
of appeal for a word to herself, a something to be said
which should not be merely formal. But Robbie was
far too much concerned to have a thought to spare for
Susie. She had not heard Mrs Ainslie's last words:
if she had heard them, she would have cared nothing,
nor thought anything of them. What could this
woman be to Robbie? was she trying to charm him

as she had charmed the innocent unconscious minister? Susie turned away indignantly, and with a sore heart. She saw that she was nothing to her old comrade, her early lover; but yet she did not know how entirely she was nothing to him, and how full his mind was of another interest. He hurried back into the dining-room with panic in his soul. Lew lay stretched out on his chair as Mrs Ainslie had seen him; the warm afternoon and the heavy meal had overcome him; his long legs stretched half across the room; his head was thrown back on the high back of his chair. His eyes were shut, his mouth a little open. More complete rest never enveloped and soothed any fat and greasy citizen after dinner. Robert looked at him with mingled irritation and admiration. It is true that there was no thought of peril in the outlaw's mind —this long interval of quiet had put all his alarms to sleep—but he would have been equally reckless, equally ready to take his rest and his pleasure, had he been consciously in the midst of his foes.

"Lew," said Robert, shaking him by the shoulder, and speaking in a subdued voice very different from the noisy tones which had betrayed them,—"Lew, wake up — there's spies about — there's danger at hand."

"Eh!" cried the other. He regarded his friend for an instant with the half-conscious smile of an abruptly awakened sleeper. The next moment he had shaken

himself, and sat up in his chair awake and intelligent
to his very finger-points. "Spies—danger—what did
you say?"

His hand stole to his pocket instinctively once more.

"Oh, there's no occasion for that," said Robert. "All
that has happened is this,—there is a woman here—
that knows you, Lew——"

"A woman—that knows me!" Perhaps it was
genuine relief, perhaps only bravado to reassure his
comrade—"Well, Bob, the question is, is she a pretty
one?"

"For heaven's sake," cried Robert, "be done with
nonsense—this is serious. She's—not a young woman.
I've heard of her: she's a stranger, but has got some
influence in the place. She saw you as she passed
that window."

"I thought I saw some one pass that window—it's
a devil of a window, a complete spy-hole."

"And she must have recognised you. She invited
me to come to see her when we were out on one of our
night walks,—and to bring Lew."

Lew gave a long whistle: the colour rose slightly
on his cheek. "We'll take her challenge, Bob, my fine
fellow, and see what she knows. Jove! I've been
getting bored with all this quiet. A start's a fine
thing. We'll go and look after her to-night."

CHAPTER XVII.

IF Mrs Ogilvy had been at home, it is almost certain
that none of these things could have happened—if
she had not been kept so long, if Mr Somerville's
other client had not detained him, and, worst of all,
if she had not been beguiled by the unaccustomed
relief of a sympathetic listener, a friendly hand held
out to help her, to waste that precious hour in taking
her luncheon with her old friend. That was pure
waste—to please him, and in a foolish yielding to
those claims of nature which Mrs Ogilvy, like so
many women, thought she could defy. To-day, in
the temporary relief of her mind after pouring out
all her troubles—a process which for the moment
felt almost like the removal of them—she had become
aware of her own exhaustion and need of refreshment
and rest. And thus she had thrown away voluntarily
a precious hour.

She met Susie and Mrs Ainslie at her own gate,

and though tired with her walk from the station, stopped to speak to them. "We found the gentlemen at their dinner," Mrs Ainslie said, her usual jaunty air increased by a sort of triumphant excitement, "and therefore of course we did not go in; but I rested a little outside, and the sound of their jolly voices quite did me good. They don't speak between their teeth, like all you people here."

"My son—has a friend with him,—for a very short time," Mrs Ogilvy said.

"Oh yes, I know—the friend with whom he takes long walks late in the evening. I have often heard of them in the village," Mrs Ainslie said.

"His visit is almost over—he is just going away," said Mrs Ogilvy, faintly. "I am just a little tired with my walk. Susie, you would perhaps see—my son?"

"I saw Robbie—for a minute. We had no time to say anything. I—could not keep him from his dinner —and his friend," Susie said, with a flush. It hurt her to speak of Robbie, who had not cared to see her, who had nothing to say to her. "We are keeping you, and you are tired: and me, I have much to do —and perhaps soon going away altogether," said Susie, not able to keep a complaint which was almost an appeal out of her voice.

"She will go to her own house, I hope," cried Mrs Ainslie; "and I hope you who are a friend of the family will advise her for her good, Mrs Ogilvy. A good husband waiting for her—and she threatens to go away altogether, as if we were driving her out. Was there ever anything so silly—and cruel to her father—not to speak of me——"

"Oh, my dear Susie! if I were not so faint—and tired," Mrs Ogilvy said.

And Susie, full of tender compunction and interest, but daring to ask nothing except with her eyes, hurried her companion away.

Mrs Ogilvy went up with a slow step to her own house. She was in haste to get there—yet would have liked to linger, to leave herself a little more time before she confronted again those two who were so strong against her in their combination, so careless of what she said or felt. She thought, with a sickness at her heart, of those "jolly voices" which that woman had heard. She knew exactly what they were—the noise, the laughter, which at first she had been so glad to hear as a sign that Robbie's heart had recovered the cheerfulness of youth, but which sometimes made her sick with misery and the sense of helplessness. She would find them so now, rattling away with their disjointed talk, and in her fatigue and trouble it would "turn her heart." She went up slowly, saying to herself, as a sort of excuse, that she could not walk as she once could, that her breath was short and her foot uncertain and tremulous, so that she could not be sure of not stumbling even in the approach to her own house.

It was a great surprise to her to see that Robbie was looking out for her at the door. Her alarm jumped at once to the other side. Something had happened. She was wanted. The fact that she was being looked for, instead of pleasing her, as it might have done in other circumstances, alarmed her now. She hurried on, not lingering any more, and reached the door out of breath. "Is anything wrong? has anything happened?" she cried.

"What should have happened?" he answered, fretfully; "only that you have been so long away. What have you been doing in Edinburgh? We thought, of course, you would be back for dinner."

"I could not help it, Robbie. I had to wait till I saw—the person I went to see."

"And who was the person you went to see?" he said, in that tone half-contemptuous, as if no one she wished to see could be of the slightest importance, and yet with an excited curiosity lest she might have been doing something prejudicial and was not to be trusted. These inferences of voice jarred on Mrs Ogilvy's nerves in the weariness and over-strain.

"It is of no consequence," she said. "Let me in, Robbie—let me come in at my own door: I am so wearied that I must rest."

"Who was keeping you out of your own door?"

he cried, making way for her resentfully. "You tell me one moment that everything is mine—and then you remind me for ever that it's yours and not mine, with this talk about your own door."

Mrs Ogilvy looked up at him for a moment in dismay, feeling as if there was justice, something she had not thought of, in his remark; and then, being overwhelmed with fatigue and the conflict of so many feelings, went into her parlour, and sat down to recover herself in her chair. There were no "jolly voices" about, no sound of the other whose movements were always noisier than those of Robbie; and Robbie himself, as he hung about, had less colour and energy than usual — or perhaps it was only because she was tired, and everything around took colour from her own mood.

"Is he not with you to-day?" she said faintly.

"Is he not with me?—you mean Lew, I suppose: where else should he be? He's up-stairs, I think, in his room."

"You say where else should he be, Robbie? Is he always to be here? I'm wishing him no harm—far, far from that; but it would be better for himself as well as for you if he were not here. Where you are, oh Robbie, my dear, there's always a clue to him: and they will come looking for him—and they will find him—and you too—and you too!"

R

"What's the meaning of all this fuss, mother—me too, as you say?"

"Well," said Mrs Ogilvy, "it is perhaps not extraordinary—my only son; but I've no wish that harm should come to him—oh, not in this house, not in this house! If he would but take warning and go away where he would be safer than here! I've been in Edinburgh to ask my old friend, and your father's friend, and your friend too, Robbie, what could be done—if there was anything that could be done."

"You have gone and betrayed us, mother!"

"I have done no such thing!" cried Mrs Ogilvy, raising herself up with a flush of indignation—"no such thing! It was Mr Somerville who brought me the news first, before you appeared at all. He was to hurry out to that weary America to defend you—or send a better than himself: that was before you came back, when we thought you were there still, and to be tried for your life. I was going—myself," she said, suddenly faltering and breaking down.

"You would not have gone, mother," said Robbie, with a certain flash of self-appreciation and bitter consciousness.

"Ay, that I would to the ends of the earth! You are my Robbie, my son, whatever you are—and oh, laddie, you might be yet—everything that you might have been."

"Not very likely," he said, with a half groan and

half sneer. "And what might I have been? A respectable clod, tramping to kirk and market—not a thought in my head nor a feeling in my heart—all just habit and jog-trot. I'm better as I am."

"You are not better as you are. You are just good for nothing in this bonnie world that God has made—except to put good meat into you that other folk have laboured to get ready, and to kill the blessed days He has given you to serve Him in, with your old books, and your cards, and any silly things that come into your head. I have seen you throwing sticks at a bit of wood for hours together, and been thankful sometimes that you were diverting yourselves like two bairns, and no just lying and lounging about like two dogs in the warmth of the fire. Oh, Robbie, what it is to me to say that to my son! and all the time the sword hanging over your heads that any day, any day may come down!"

"By Jove, the old girl's right, Bob!" said a voice behind. Lew had become curious as to the soft murmur of Mrs Ogilvy's voice, which he could hear running on faintly, not much interrupted by Robbie's deeper tones. It was not often she "preached," as they said—indeed she had seldom been allowed to go further than the mildest beginning; but Rob had been this time caught unprepared, and his mother had taken the advantage. Lew came in softly, with his lips framed to whistle, and his hands in his pockets. He had already picked his comrade out of a sudden Slough of Despond, caused by alarm at the declaration of the visitor, which, to tell the truth, had made himself very uneasy. It would not do to let the mother complete the discouragement: but this adventurer from the wilds had a candid soul; and while Robert stood sullen, beat down by what his mother said, yet resisting it, the other came in with a look and word of acquiescence. "Yes, by Jove, she was right!" It did not cost him much to acknowledge this theoretical justice of reproof.

"The difficulty is," he added calmly, "to know what to do in strange diggings like these. They're out of our line, don't you know. I was talking seriously to him there the other day about doing a stroke of work: but he wouldn't hear of it—not here, he said, not in his own country. Ask him; he'll tell you. I don't understand the reason why."

Mrs Ogilvy, startled, looked from one to another: she did not know what to think. What was the stroke of work which the leader had proposed, which the follower would not consent to? Was it something for which to applaud Robbie, or to blame him? Her heart longed to believe that it was the first—that he had done well to refuse: but she could only look blankly from one to another, uninformed by the malicious gleam in Lew's eyes, or by the spark of

indignant alarm in those of Robbie. Their meaning
was quite beyond her ken.

"If you will sit down," she said, "both of you, and
have a moment's patience while I speak. Mr Lew, I
am in no way your unfriend."

"I never thought so," he said: "on the contrary,
mother. You have always been very good to me."

He called her mother, as another man might have
called her madam, as a simple title of courtesy; and
sometimes it made her angry, and sometimes touched
her heart.

"But I have something to say that maybe I have
said before, and something else that is new that you
must both hear. This is not a safe place for you, Mr
Lew—it is not safe for you both. For Robbie, I am
told nobody would meddle with him—alone; but his
home here gives a clue, and is a danger to you—and
to have you here is a danger for him, who would not
be meddled with by himself, but who would be taken
(alack, that I should have to say it!) with you."

"I think, Bob," said Lew, "that we have heard
something like this, though perhaps not so clearly
stated, before."

He had seated himself quite comfortably in the
great chair which had been brought to the parlour for
Robbie on his first arrival,—and was, as he always
was, perfectly calm, unruffled, and smiling. Robbie
stood opposite in no such amiable mood. His shaggy

eyebrows were drawn down over his eyes: his whole
attitude, down-looking, shifting from one foot to the
other, with his shoulders up to his ears, betrayed his
perturbation and disquiet. Robbie had been brought
to a sudden stop in the fascination of careless and
reckless life which swept his slower nature along in
its strong current. Such a thing had happened to him
before in his intercourse with Lew, and always came
uppermost the moment they were parted. It was the
sudden shock of Mrs Ainslie's announcement, and his
friend's apparently careless reception of it, which had
jarred him first: and then there was something in the
name of mother, addressed to his own mother by a
stranger—which he had heard often with quite different feelings, sometimes half flattered by it—which
added to his troubled sense of awakening resistance
and disgust. Was he to endure this man for ever, to
give up everything for him, even his closest relation-
ship? All rebellious, all unquiet and miserable in the
sudden strain against his bonds, he stood listening
sullenly, shuffling now and then as he changed from
one foot to another, otherwise quite silent, meeting no
one's eye.

"Well," said Mrs Ogilvy, her voice trembling a
little, "I am perhaps not so very clear; but this other
thing I have to say is something that is clear enough
and new too, and you will know the meaning of it
better than me. I have been to-day to the gentleman

who was the first to tell me about all this—and who was to have sent out—to defend my son, and clear him, if it was possible he should be cleared. Listen to me, Robbie! That gentleman has told me to-day —that there is an American officer come over express to inquire—— It will not be about Robbie—they will leave him quiet—think, Mr Lew!—it will be for——"

"For me, of course," he said, lightly. "Well! if there's danger we'll meet it. I like it, on the whole— it stirs a fellow's blood. We were getting too comfortable, Bob, settling down, making ourselves too much at home. The next step would have been to be bored—eh? won't say that process hadn't begun."

"Sir," said Mrs Ogilvy, "you will not say I have been inhospitable, or grudged you whatever I could give——"

"Never, mother," he said. "You've been as good as gold." He had risen from his seat, and begun to walk about with an alert light step. The news had roused him; it had stirred his blood, as he said. "We must see about this exit of yours—subterraneous is it? —out of the Castle of Giant Despair—no, no, out of the good fairy's castle, down into the wilds. You must show me this at once, Bob. If there's a Yank on the trail there's no time to be lost."

"There is perhaps no time to be lost—but not for him, only for you. My words are not kind, but my meaning is," cried Mrs Ogilvy. "It is safest for you not to be with him, and for him not to be with you. Oh, do not wait here till you're traced to the house, till ye have to run and break your neck down that terrible road, but go while everything is peaceable! Mr Lew, you shall have whatever money you want, and what clothes we can furnish, and—and my blessing—God's blessing."

"Don't you think," he said, turning upon her, "you are undertaking a little too much? God's blessing upon a fellow like me—that has committed every sin and repented of none, that have sent other sinners to their account, and wronged the orphan, and all that. God's blessing——!"

He was standing in the middle of the room, in which he was so inappropriate a figure, with his back to the end window, which was towards the west. It was now late in the afternoon, and the level rays pouring in made a broad bar across the carpet, and fell upon one side of his form, which partially intercepted its light and cut it with his tall outline. Mrs Ogilvy put her hands together with a cry.

"What is that? What is it? Is it not just the blessed sun that He sends upon the just and the unjust—never stopping, whatever you have done—His sign held out to you that He has all His blessings in His hand, ready to give, more ready than me, that am a poor creature, no fit to judge? Oh, laddie—for you're little more — see to Him holding out His hand!"

He had turned round, with a vague disturbed motion, not knowing what he did, and stood for a moment looking at the sunshine on the carpet, and his own figure which intercepted it and received the glory instead. For a moment his lip quivered; the lines of his face moved as if a wind had blown over them; his eyes fixed on the light, as if he expected to see some miraculous sight. And then he gave a harsh laugh, and turned round with a shrug of his shoulders. "It's pretty," he said, "mother, as you put it : but there's no time to enter into all that. I've perhaps got too much to clear up with God, don't you know, to do it at a sitting; but I'll remember, for your sake, when I've time. Eh? where were we before this little picturesque incident? You were saying I should have money—to pay my fare, &c. Well, that's fair enough. Make it enough for two, and we'll be off, eh, Bob? and trouble her no more."

But Robbie did not say a word. It was not any wise resolution taken; it was rather a fit of temper, which the other, used to his moods, knew would pass away. Lew gave another shrug of his shoulders, and even a glance of confidential criticism to the mother, as if she were in the secret too. "One of his moods," he said, nodding at her. "But, bless you! when one knows how to take him, they don't last." He touched

her shoulder with a half caress. "You go and lie
down a bit and rest. You're too tired for any more.
We'll have it all out to-night, or at another time."

"I am quite ready now—I am quite ready," she
cried, terrified to let the opportunity slip. He nodded
at her again, and waved his hand with a smile. "Come
along, Bob, come along; let us leave her in quiet. To-
night will be soon enough to settle all that—to-night
or—another time." He took Rob by the arm, and
pushed his reluctant and half-resisting figure out of
the room. Robert was sullen and indisposed to his
usual submission.

"Let me go," he said, shaking off the hand on his
arm; "do you think I'm going to be pushed about like
a go-cart?"

"If you're a go-cart, I wish you'd let me slip into
you," said the other. It was not a very great joke,
but Robert at another moment would have hailed it
with a shout of laughter. He received it only with a
shrug of his shoulders now.

"I wish you'd make up your mind and do something," he said.

"I have: the first thing is to see who that woman
is——"

"A woman! when you've got to run for your life."

"Do you think I mean any nonsense, you fool?
She's not a woman, she's a danger. Man alive, can't
you see? She'll have to be squared somehow. And

look here, Bob," he said suddenly, putting his arm through that of his friend's, who retained his reluctant attitude—"don't sulk, you ass: ain't we in the same boat—get all you can out of the old girl. We'll have to make tracks, I suppose—and a lot of money runs away in that. Get everything you can out of her. She may cool down and repent, don't you see? Strike, Bob, while the iron's hot. The old girl——"

"Look here, I'll not have her called names; neither mother, as if you had any right to her—nor—nor any other. We've had enough of that. I'll not take any more of it from you, Lew!"

"Oh, that's how it is!" said the other coolly, with a sneer. "Then I beg to suggest to you, my friend Bob, that the respectable lady we're talking of may repent; and that if you're not a fool, and won't take more energetic measures, you'll strike, don't you see, while the iron is hot."

Rob gave his friend a look of sullen wrath, and then disengaged his arm and turned away.

"You'll find me in Andrew's bower, among the flower-pots," Lew called after him, and whistling a tune, went off behind the house to the garden, where in the shade Andrew kept his tools and all the accessories of his calling. He had no good of his ain tool-house, since thae two were about, Andrew complained every day.

CHAPTER XVIII.

THE Hewan was very quiet and silent that afternoon. Mrs Ogilvy perhaps would not have recognised the crisis of exhaustion at which she had
arrived, had it not been for the remarks of the
stranger within her doors, the unwelcome guest
whom she was so anxious to send away, and who
yet had an eye for the changes of her countenance
which her son had not. He took more interest in
her fatigue than Robbie, who did not remark it
even now, and to whom it had not at all occurred
that his mother should want care or tenderness.
She had always given it, in his experience; it did
not come into his mind. But, tutored by Lew, Mrs
Ogilvy felt that she could do no more. She went
to her room, and even, for a wonder, lay down on
her bed, half apologising to herself that it was just
for once, and only for half an hour. But the house
was very quiet. There was no noise below to keep

her watchful. If there were any voices at all, they came in a subdued murmur from the garden behind, where perhaps Robbie was showing to his friend the breakneck path down the brae to the Esk, which nobody had remembered during the many years of his absence. It had been his little mystery which he had delighted in as a boy. There was no gate opening on it, nor visible mode of getting at it. The little gap in the hedge through which as a boy he had squeezed himself so often was all concealed by subsequent growth, but Robert's eyes could still distinguish it. Mrs Ogilvy said to herself, " He will be showing him that awful road—and how to push himself through." She felt herself repeat vaguely "to push himself through, to push himself through," and then she ceased to go on with her thoughts. She had fallen asleep; so many times she had not got her rest at night—and she was very tired. She fell asleep. She would never have permitted herself to do so but for these words of Lew. He was not at all bad. They said he had taken away a man's life—God forgive him!—but he saw when a woman was tired—an old woman—that was not his mother: may be—if he had ever had a mother—— And here even these broken half-words, that floated through her brain, failed. She fell asleep — more soundly than she had slept perhaps for years.

The thoughts that passed through the mind of

the adventurer in his retreat in Andrew's tool-house
could not have been agreeable ones, but they are
out of my power to trace or follow. Women are
perhaps more ready to see their disabilities in this
way than men. A man will sometimes set forth
in much detail, as if he knew, the fancies, evanescent and changeful as a dream, of a girl's dawning
mind, putting them all into rigid lines of black and
white. Perhaps he thinks the greater comprehends
the less: but how to tell you what was the course
of reflections and endless breaks and takings up of
thought in the mind of a man who had a career
to look back upon, such as that of Lew, is not
in my power. I might represent them as caused
by sudden pangs of remorse, by dreadful questions
whether, if he had not done this or that——! by
haunting recollections of the look of a victim, or
of the circumstances of the scenes in which a crime
had been committed: by a horrible crushing sense
that nothing could recall those moments in which
haste and passion had overcome all that was better
in him. I do not believe that Lew thought of any
of these things: he had said he repented of nothing
—he thought of nothing, I well believe, but of the
present, which was hard enough for any man, and
how he was to get through it. It was a situation
much worse than that of yesterday. Then he had still
continued to wonder at his absolute safety, at the

extraordinary, almost absurd fact, that he was in a place where nobody had ever heard of him, where his name did not convey the smallest thrill of terror to the feeblest. He had laughed at this, even when he was alone, not without a sense of injury, and conviction that the people around must be "born fools": but yet a comfortable assurance of safety all the same — safety which had half begun to bore him, as he said. But now that situation had altogether changed. There was a woman in this place, even in this place, who knew him, to whose mind it had conveyed a thrill that he should be here. And there was a man in Scotland who had arrived to hunt him down. His being had roused up to these two keen points of stimulation. They seemed to a certain degree to set him right with himself, a man not accustomed to feel himself nobody: and in the second place, they roused him to fight, to that prodigious excitement, superior perhaps to any other kind, which flames up when you have to fight for your life. I suggest with diffidence that these were probably the thoughts that went through him, broken with many admixtures which I cannot divine. I believe that at that moment less than at any other was he sorry for the crimes that he had committed. He had no time for anything in (what he would have called) the way of sentiment. He had quite enough to do thinking how to get out of this strait, to get again

into safety, and safety of a kind in which he should
be less hampered than here. There was the old
woman, for instance, who had been kind to him,
whom he did not want to shock above measure or
to get into trouble. He resolved he would not take
refuge in any place where there was an old woman
again, unless she were an old woman of a very different kind. Mrs Ogilvy was quite right in her
conviction that there was good in him. He did not
want to hurt her, even to hurt her feelings. In short,
he would not have anything done to vex her, unless
there was no other way.

But though I cannot throw much light on his
thoughts, I can tell you how he spent the afternoon,
to outward sight and consciousness. Robert Ogilvy,
before the arrival of this companion, had discovered
that he could arrange himself a rude sort of a loung-
ing-place by means of an old chair with a broken
seat, and some of the rough wooden boxes, once
filled with groceries, &c., which had been placed in
the tool-house to be out of the way, and in which
Andrew sometimes placed his seedlings, and sometimes his strips of cloth and nails and sticks for
tying up his flowers. Lew had naturally edged his
friend out of this comfortable place. The seat of the
chair was of cane-work, and still afforded support to
the sitter, though it was not in good repair; and the
boxes were of various heights, so that a variety of

levels could be procured when he tired of one. His meditations were promoted by smoke, and also by a great deal of whisky-and-water, for which he took the trouble to disarrange himself periodically to obtain a fresh supply from the bottle which it disturbed Mrs Ogilvy to see so continually on the table in the dining-room. It would have been more convenient to have it here—and it was seldom that Lew subjected himself to an inconvenience; but he did in this case, I am unable to tell why. It must be added that this constant refreshing had no more effect upon him than as much water would have had on many other people. And those little pilgrimages into the dining-room were the only sound he made in the quiet of the house.

Robbie had gone out, to chew his cud of very bitter fancy. His thoughts were not so uncomplicated, so distinguishable, as those of his stronger-minded friend. He had been seized quite suddenly, as he had been at intervals ever since he fell under Lew's influence, with a revulsion of feeling against this man, to whom he had been for this month past, as for years, with broken intervals, before, the chose, the chattel, the shadow and echo. It was perhaps the nature of poor Robbie to be the chose of somebody, of any one who would take possession of him except his natural guides: but there was a strain of the fantastic in his spirit, as well as an instinct for what was lawful and right, which

had made him insufferable among the strange com-
rades to whom he had drifted, yet never was strong
enough to sever him from their lawless company.
He had never himself done any violent or dishonest
act, though he was one of the band who did, and had
doubtless indirectly profited by their ill-gotten gains.
Perhaps refraining himself from every practical breach
of law, it gave him a pleasure, an excitement, to see the
others breaking it constantly, and to study the strange
phenomena of it? I suggest this possible explanation
to minds more philosophical than mine. Certainly
Robbie was not philosophical, and if he was moved by
so subtle a principle, was quite unaware of it. He
was in a tumult of disgust on this occasion with Lew,
and everything connected with him—with all the
trouble of hiding him, of securing his escape, of
keeping watch and ward for his sake, and of getting
money for him out of the little store which his mother
had saved for him, Robbie, and not for any stranger.
This piquant touch of personal loss perhaps did more
than anything else to intensify his sudden ill-humour,
offence, and rebellion. He strayed out to see if the
gap could be passed, if the deep precipitous gully
down the side of the hill gave shelter enough for a
hurried escape. As he wandered down towards the
little stream, his eyes suddenly became suspicious, and
he saw a pursuer behind every tree and bush. He
thought he saw a man's hat in the distance always

disappearing as he followed it: he thought even that
the little girls playing beyond in the open looked at
him with significant glances, pointing him out to each
other—and this indeed was not a fancy; but there
was nothing dangerous in the indication—"Eh, see
yon man! that's the lady's son at the Hewan "—
which these young persons, not at all conspirators,
gave.

. In the evening, as it began to grown dark, the two
men as usual went out together. It means almost
more than a deadly quarrel, and the substitution of
hate for love or liking, to break a habit even of recent
date; and Robert had hated Lew, and longed to be
delivered from him, a dozen times at least, without
anything following. They went out very silent at
first, very watchful, not missing a single living
creature that went past them, though these were not
many. They had both the highly educated eyes of
men who knew what it was to be hunted, and were
quick to discover every trace of a pursuer or an
enemy. But the innocent country road was innocent
as ever, with very few passengers, and not one of
them likely to awaken alarm in the most nervous
bosom. The silence between them, however, continued
so long, and it was so difficult to make Robbie say
anything, that his companion began at last to ask
questions, already half answered in previous conversations, about the visitor who had recognised him.

'Somebody who has not been very long here—a stranger (like myself), but likely to form permanent relations in the place (*not* like me there, alas!)," said Lew. "Not to put too fine a point upon it, she's going to marry the minister. That's so, ain't it?" Lew said.

"That's what it is, so far as I know."

"Look here," he went on, "there's several things in that to take away its importance. In the first place, it could not be in the first society of Colorado—the *crême de la crême*, you know—that she'd meet me."

To this Robert assented merely with a sort of groan.

"From which it follows, that if she is setting up here in the odour of sanctity, it's not for her interests to make a fuss about my acquaintance."

"She might give you up, to get rid of you," Robert said, curtly.

"Come now," said his companion; "human nature's bad enough, but hanged if it's so bad as that."

"Oh, I thought you were of opinion that nothing was too bad——"

"Hold hard!" said Lew. "If you mean to carry on any longer like a bear with a sore head, I propose we go home."

"It's as you like," Robert said.

"Bob," said the other, "mutual danger draws fellows together: it's drawn you and me together scores of times. We're lost, or at all events I'm lost, if it turns out different now."

"Do you think I'm going to give you up?" said Rob, almost with a sneer.

"No, I don't," said Lew, calmly. "You haven't the spirit. Your mammy would do it like a shot, if it wasn't for—other things."

"What other things?" cried Rob, fiercely.

"Well, because she's got a heart—rather bigger than her spirit, and that's saying a great deal: and because she believes like an Arab—and that's saying a great deal too—in her bread and salt."

"Look here!" cried Rob, looking about him for a reason, "I don't mean to stand any longer the way you speak of my mother. Whatever she is, she is my mother, and I'll not listen to any gibes on that subject —least of all from you."

"What gibes? I say her heart is greater even than her spirit. I might say that"—and here Lew made something like the sign of the Cross, for he had queer fragments of religion in him, and sometimes thought he was a Roman Catholic—"of the Queen of heaven."

"You call her mother," cried Bob, angrily.

"I should like to know," said his companion, whose temper was invulnerable, "where I could find a better name."

"And old girl," cried Rob, working himself into a sort of fury, "and—other names."

"I beg your pardon, old fellow; there I was wrong. It don't mean anything, you know. It means dear old lady; but I know it's an ugly style, and comes from bad breeding, and I'll never do it again."

A sort of grunt, half satisfied, half sullen, came from Rob, and his companion knew the worst was over. "Let's think a little," he said—"you're grand at describing—tell me a bit what that woman is like."

Rob hesitated for some minutes, and then his pride gave way.

"She's what you might call all in the air," he said.

"Yes?"

"But looks at you to see if you think her so."

"That's capital, Bob."

"She has a lot of fair hair—dull-looking, it might be false, but I don't think somehow it is—and no colour to speak of, but might put on some, I should say. She looks like that."

Lew put his arm within Rob's as if accidentally, and gave forth a low whistle. "If that's *her*," he said, "and she's going to marry a minister—I should just think she would like to get me out of the way."

"But why, then, should she ask you to come and see her?—for she had seen you on the sly, and that was enough."

"There's where the mystery comes in: but you never know that kind of woman. There's always a screw loose in them somewhere. She repents it, perhaps, by now. Let's make a round by her house, wherever it is, and perhaps we'll see her through a window, as she saw me."

"It's close to the village—it's dangerous—don't think of it," said Rob.

"Dangerous!" cried the other: "what's a man for but to face danger—when it comes? I'm twice the man I was last night. I smell the smell of gunpowder in the air. I feel as if I could face the worst road, ten minutes' start, and fifty mile an hour."

If this trumpet-note was intended to rouse Rob, it was successful. His duller spirit caught the spark of excitement, which moved it only to the point of exhilaration and drove the last mist away. They went on, always with caution, always watchful, through a corner of the little town where the houses were almost all closed, and the good people in bed. No two innocent persons, however observant, were they the finest naturalists or scientific observers in the world, ever saw so much in a dark road as these two broken men. They saw the very footsteps of the few people who came towards them in the darkness, darker here with the shadow of the houses than in the open country, but not important enough to have lights: and could tell what manner of people they were—honest, meaning no harm, or stealthy and prepared for mischief—though they never saw the faces that belonged to them. "There's one that means no

good," Lew said. There was no man in the world
who had a greater contempt for a petty thief. "I've
half a mind to warn some one of him."

"For goodness' sake, make no disturbance," said the
(for once) more prudent Rob.

Presently they came to Mrs Ainslie's house, a little
square house, with its door close to the road, but
a considerable garden behind. There was light in
the windows still, but no chance of seeing into the
interior behind the closed blinds. "Let's risk it, Bob;
let's go and pay our call like gentlemen," said Lew.

"You don't think of such a thing!" cried Robert,
holding him back. This was perhaps one of the
things that bound Lew's followers to him most. Sometimes the excitement of risk and daring got into his
veins like wine, and then the youngest and least
guarded of them had to change *rôles* with the captain
and restrain him. But whether Rob could have succeeded in doing so can never be known, for at the
moment there were sounds in the house, and the door
was opened, and a conversation, begun inside, was
carried on for a minute or two there. The pair who
appeared were the minister and Mrs Ainslie. He all
dark, his face shaded by his hat: she in a light dress,
and with a candle in her hand, which threw its light
upon her face. She was saying good-night, and bidding her visitor take care of the corner where it was
so dark. "There is what your people call a dub there,"

she said, with one of those shrill laughs which cut the
air—and she held the candle high to guide her visitor's
parting steps. He answered, in a voice very dull and
low-pitched after hers, that he was bound to know
every dub in the place; and so went off, bidding her, if
she went to Edinburgh in the morning, be sure to be
back in good time.

She stood there for a moment after he was gone,
and held up her candle again, as if that could pierce
instead of increasing the darkness around her, and
looked first in one direction, then in the other. Then
she stood for a second minute as if listening, and then
slightly shaking her head, turned and went in again.
If she could have seen the two set faces watching her
out of the darkness, within the deep shadow of the
opposite wall! Lew grasped Rob's arm as in a vice,
and with the other hand sought that pocket to which
he turned so naturally: while Rob followed the movement in a panic, and got his hand upon that which
already had half seized the revolver. "You wouldn't
be such an idiot, Lew!"

"If I gave her a bullet," said the other in the darkness, "it would be the least of her deserts, and the
cheapest for the world." Their voices could not have
been audible to Mrs Ainslie, turning to shut her door,
but something must have thrilled the air, for she
came out and looked up and down again. Was she
as fearless as the others, and fired with excitement

too? And then the closing of the door echoed out
into the stillness,—not the report of the revolver,
thank heaven! She had shown no signs of alarm:
but the two men, as they went away, trembled in
every limb—Rob with alarm and excitement, and the
sense that murder had been in the air; his companion
with other feelings still.

It was very late when Mrs Ogilvy woke, and then
not of herself, but by Robbie's call, whom she suddenly
roused herself to see standing in the dark by her bedside. It was quite dark, not any lingering of light in
the sky, which showed how far on in the night it was.
She sprang up from her bed, crying out, "What has
happened—what have I been doing?" with something
like shame. "Have I been sleeping all this time?"
she cried with dismay.

"Don't hurry, mother—you were tired out. I'm
very glad you have slept. Nothing's wrong. Don't
get up in a hurry. I should like to speak to you here.
I've—got something to say."

"What is it, Robbie?—whatever it is, my dear, would
you not like a light?"

"No; I like this best. I used to creep into your
room in the dark, if you remember, when I had something to confess. I had always plenty to confess,
mother."

"Oh, my Robbie, my dear, my dear!"

She stretched out her hands to him to touch his, to

draw him near: but he still hung at a little distance, a tall shadow in the dark.

"It is not for myself this time. It is Lew: he was very much touched with what you said to-day. He'll go, I believe—whether with me or not. I might see him away, and then come back. But the chief thing after all, you know, is the money. You said you would give him——"

"Oh, Robbie, God be praised!—whatever he required for his passage, and to give him a new beginning; but you'll not leave me again, not you, not you!"

"I did not say I would," he said, with a querulous tone in his voice. "His passage! He wouldn't go back to America, you know."

"No, my dear, I did not suppose he would. I thought—one of the islands," said Mrs Ogilvy, in subdued tones.

"One of the islands! I don't know what you mean" (and, indeed, neither did she), "unless it were New Zealand, perhaps—that's an island: but you would not banish him there, mother. Lew thinks he might go to India. He might begin again, and do better there."

"India—that is far, far away—and a dear passage, and all the luxuries you want there. Robbie, I would not grudge it for myself—it is for you, my dear."

"If he had plenty of money, it would be his best chance."

Mrs Ogilvy slid softly off the bed, where she had been listening. She was as generous as a princess—as princesses used to be in the time of the fairy tales; but it startled her that this stranger should expect " plenty of money " from her hands. " How could we give him that ? " she said : " and whatever went to him, it would be taken from you, Robbie. If you will fix on a sum, I will do everything I can. I do not grudge him—no, no. My heart is wae for him. But to despoil my only son, my one bairn, for a stranger. It is not just, it is not what I should do——"

" Would you give him a thousand pounds, mother ? "

" A thousand pounds ! " she cried with a shriek. " Laddie, are ye wild ?—the greatest part of what you will have—the half, or near the half, of all. I think one of us is out of our senses, either you or me ! "

CHAPTER XIX.

MRS AINSLIE, who is a person with whom this history is little concerned, and whose character and antecedents I have no desire to set forth, had been moved, by the suddenness and unexpectedness of her vision through the dining-room window of the Hewan, to commit what she afterwards felt to be a great mistake. Hitherto, after the experience gained in a hundred adventures, she had found the *rôle* which she had chosen to play in the rustic innocence of Eskholm not a difficult one. No one suspected her of anything but a little affectation, a little absurdity, and a desire to be believed a fine lady, which, if it did not deceive the better instructed, yet harmed nobody. Society, even in its most obscure developments — and especially village society—is suspicious, people say. If so—of which I am doubtful—then it is generally suspicious in the wrong way; and there was nobody in Eskholm who had the least suspicion of Mrs Ainslie's ante-

cedents, or imagined that she could be anything but
what she professed to be, an officer's widow. Military
ladies are allowed to be like their profession, a little
pushing and forward, not meek and mild like the
model woman. She knew herself, of course, how much
cause for suspicion there was; and she saw discovery
in people's eyes who had never even supposed any
inquiry into the truth of her statements to be called
for: and thus she was usually very much on her guard,
notwithstanding the apparent freedom of her manners
and lightness of her heart. But the sudden sight of
an old comrade in the very midst of this changed and
wonderful life of respectability which she was living,
had startled her quite out of herself. Lew! in the
midst of respectability even greater than her own, in
the Hewan, the abode of all that was most looked up
to and esteemed! The surprise took away her breath;
and with the surprise there came a flood of recollections, of remembered scenes—oh! very much more
piquant than anything known on Eskside; of gay
revelry, movement, and adventure, fun and freedom.
That life which is called "wild" and "gay" and "fast,"
and so many other misnomers, and which looks in
general so miserable to the lookers-on, has no doubt
its charms like another, and the excitements of the
past look all pure dash and delight to the people who
have forgotten what deadliest of all *ennui* lay behind
them. There flashed upon this woman a sudden

thought of a gay meeting like those of old, full of reminiscence, and mutual inquiry, what has become of Jack and what has happened to Jill, and of laughter over many a sport and feat that were past. It did not occur to her at the moment that to hear what had happened to Jack and Jill would probably be dismal enough. She thought only, amid the restraints of the present life in which no fun was, what fun to see one of the old set again, and to ask after everybody, and hear all that had been going on, all at her ease, and without fear of discovery in the middle of the night. She divined without difficulty that Lew was here in hiding for no innocent cause, and that Mrs Ogilvy's long-vanished son, who was mysteriously known to have returned, but who had never showed himself openly, was in some compromising way involved with him, and keeping him out of sight. She understood now the stories about the long night-walks of the two gentlemen at the Hewan of which she had heard : and her well-worn heart gave a jump to think of a jovial meeting so unexpected, so refreshing, in which she could renew her spirit a little more than with all the preparations necessary for her future part of the minister's wife. It would be a farewell to the past which she could never have dared to anticipate, and the thought gave an extraordinary exhilaration, as well as half-panic which was part of the exhilaration, to her mind. It was as if a stream of life had been poured into her veins — life, which was not always enjoyable, but yet was living, according to the formula of those to whom life has probably more moments of complete dulness and self-disgust than to the dullest of those half-lives which they despise.

But when Mrs Ainslie got home, and began to reflect on the matter, she saw how great a mistake she had made. If she knew him, so did he also know her and all her antecedents. It had given her a thrill of pleasure to think of meeting him, and talking over the past; but it was equally possible to her to betray him, in her new *rôle* as a respectable member of society: and she knew that she would not hesitate to do so, should it prove necessary. But it was equally possible that he might betray her. It did not take her more than five minutes' serious thinking, when the first excitement of the discovery was over, to show her that to disclose herself to Lew, and put in his hands a means of ruining her, or of holding her in terror at least, was the last thing that was to be desired. Lew in Colorado, or as a chance exile from that paradise, ready to disappear again into the unknown, was little dangerous, and a chance meeting with him the most amusing accident that was likely to befall her. But Lew in England, or, still worse, Scotland, at her very door, ready on any occasion to inform her new friends who she was or had been, was a very different matter. She owned to herself that she had never done anything so mad or foolish in her life. On the eve of becoming Mr Logan's wife, of being provided for for the rest of her life, of being looked up to and respected, and an authority in the place—and by one foolish word to throw all this, which was almost certainty, into the chaos of risk and daily danger, at the mercy of a man who could spoil everything if he pleased, or could at least hold the sword over her head and make her existence a burden to her! What a thing was this which she had done! When she saw Mr Logan to the door on that evening, her aspect was more animated and bright than ever, but her heart in reality was quaking. It was foolish of her to take the candle; but it was her habit, and it would have been remarked, she thought in her terror, if she had not done it: and then she stood and looked up and down, still with that light in her hand —thankful that at least the minister was gone, that he would not meet these visitors if they came: then with relief making up her mind that they would not come—that Lew, if he were in hiding, would be as much afraid of her as she of him.

She had a disturbed night, full of alarm and much planning and thinking, sitting up till it was almost daylight, in terror that the visit which she had been so foolish as to invite might be paid at any unlawful hour. And when the next morning came, it was apparent to her that she must do something at once

T

to provide against such a danger, to save herself from
the consequences of her foolishness. How it had been
that an adventuress like this had managed to secure
for her daughter the most respectable of marriages in
respectable Edinburgh, is a question into which I
cannot enter. It had not been, indeed, Mrs Ainslie's
doing at all. The girl, who knew none of her
mother's disreputable secrets, had made acquaintance
in a foreign hotel with some girls of her own age, who
had afterwards invited her to visit them in Edinburgh.
Such things are done every day, and come to harm so
seldom that it is scarcely worth taking the adverse
chances into consideration. And there, in the shelter
of a most respectable family, the most respectable of
men had fallen in love with Sophie. It was all so
rapid that examination into the position of the Ainslies
was impossible. Sophie had no money : her father had
been killed in some campaign in India which happened to coincide with the date of her birth. She was
pretty, and not anything but good so far as her up-
bringing had permitted. I give this brief sketch in
hot haste, as indeed the matter was done—for Mrs
Ainslie had announced that she had only come to
Eskholm for a few weeks, and was going "abroad"
again immediately. Perhaps it was the acquisition
of a son-in-law so absolutely correct as Mr Thomas
Blair—dear Tom, as his mother-in-law always called
him—that put into her head the possibility of becom-

ing herself an exceptionable member of society, furnished with all possible certificates by marrying Mr
Logan. At all events, it was her son-in-law to whom
she now betook herself after many thoughts, with that
skill of the long-experienced schemer which is capable
of using truth as an instrument often more effectual
than falsehood. She went to him (he was a lawyer)
with all the candour of a woman who has made, with
grief for her neighbour, a dreadful discovery, and who
in the interests of her neighbour, not in her own—for
what could she have to do with anything so wicked
and terrible ?—thinks it necessary to reveal what she
has seen. In this way she made Mr Blair aware of
the circumstances of her visit at the Hewan, and the
man she had seen there. She told him that she had
been present at the trial of this man in America—it
was one of her frank and simple statements, which were
so perfectly candid and above board, that she had
lived in various parts of America after her husband's
death—for various terrible crimes. She had seen him
in court for days together, and could not be mistaken
in him: and the idea that so excellent a person as
Mrs Ogilvy had such a man in her house was too
dreadful to think of. What should she do ? Should
she warn Mrs Ogilvy ? But then no doubt he was in
some way mixed up with Mrs Ogilvy's son, who had
lately returned home in a mysterious and unexpected
way. Mr Blair was much interested by the story.

He sympathised fully in the dreadful dilemma in which the poor lady found herself. He, too, knew Mrs Ogilvy, and remembered Robbie in his youth perfectly well. He was always a weak fellow, ready to be led away by any one. No doubt her idea was quite right. And then he smote his hand upon his leg, and gave vent to a whistle. "What if it should turn out to be this Lew Smith or Lew Wallace or something, for whom there was a warrant out, and a detective from America on the search!"

"Lew—that is exactly the name—I had forgotten —his other name I don't remember. He was spoken of as Lew——"

"And you could swear to this fellow? You are sure you could swear to him?"

"Swear! oh, with a clear conscience! But don't ask me to, dear Tom. Think what it is for a delicate woman — the publicity, the notoriety! Oh, don't make me appear in a court: I should never, never survive it!" she cried.

"Oh, nonsense, mamma!" The respectable son-in-law was so completely innocent of all suspicion that he had adopted his wife's name for her mother. "But I allow it's not pleasant for a lady," he said: "perhaps you won't be wanted—but you could on an emergency swear to him."

"If it was of the last necessity," she said, trembling, and her trembling was very real. She said to

herself at the same moment, No! never! appear in
an open court with Lew opposite to me, — never!
never! She was one of the many people in the world
who think, after they have put the match to the gunpowder, that there is still time to do something to
make it miss fire.

Tom Blair was very sympathetic with the woman's
tremors who could not appear in a public court, and
yet would do so if it was absolutely necessary. He
bade her go home to Sophie and have some lunch, and
that he would himself return as early as he could, and
tell her if he heard anything. And Mrs Ainslie went
to the Royal Crescent, where the pair were established,
and admired the nice new furniture, and the man in
livery of whom Sophie was so proud. But she did
not wait to hear what news dear Tom would bring
home. She left all sorts of messages for him, telling
of engagements she had, and things to be done for
Mr Logan. She could not face him again: and it
began to appear a danger for her, though she had
great confidence in her powers of invention, to be
questioned too closely by any one accustomed to evidence, who might turn her inside out before she
knew. And, indeed, her mind was very busy working, now that she had put that match to the gunpowder, to prevent it going off. She went into a
stationer's shop on the way to the station, and got
paper and an envelope, and wrote, disguising her hand,

an anonymous letter to Mrs Ogilvy, bidding her get
her guest off at once, for the police were after him.
This was a work of art with which Mrs Ainslie was
not at all unacquainted, and she flattered herself that
the post-mark "Edinburgh" would quench all sug-
gestions of herself as its author. If he only could
get away safe without compromising any one, that
would be so much better. She did not want to be
hard upon him. Oh, not at all. She had been silly,
very silly, to think of a meeting: but she bore him no
malice. If he had the sense to steal away before any
one went after him, that would be far the best and
the safest of all.

She went home to her house, and there proceeded
with her preparations for her marriage, which had
been going on merrily. She spent the afternoon with
her dressmaker, an occupation which pleased her very
much. She was not a needlewoman, she could not
make anything that was wanted for herself—but she
could stand for hours like a lay figure to be "tried
on." That did not weary her at all; and this process
made the time pass as perhaps nothing else could
have done. Mr Logan once more spent the evening
with her, and she had again a time of dreadful
anxiety, in the fear that still Lew might appear,
might meet the minister at the door, and rouse a
thousand questions. For the first time it began to
appear possible to her that her marriage might not

come off after all. She might never wear these new dresses—all dove-colour and the softest semi-religious tints—as Mr Logan's wife. She might have to set out on the world again, and get her living somehow, instead of being safe for the rest of her days. Instinctively she began to scheme for that, as well as for the direct contrary of that, and in the same breath arranged, in her mind, for the packing of the new dresses and their transfer to the capacious cupboards in the manse, and for sending them back to the dressmaker if she should have to turn her back on the manse and fly. She did not feel sure now which thing would come to pass.

But once more the evening passed and nobody came. She stood for some time at her door after the minister left: but this time in the darkness, without any candle, listening earnestly for any step or movement in the night; but no one came. Had he taken fright and gone away at once? That was the thing most to be desired, but from that very fact the most unlikely to have happened. It was too good to be true; and Lew was not the man to be challenged and not to accept the challenge — unless he were arrested already! That was always possible, but that too was almost too good to be true. And then there was the chance that he might say something about her, that he might spoil her fortune without doing any good to his own. If she harmed him, it was for

good reasons, to save herself; and also, a plea not to
be despised, to save poor good old Mrs Ogilvy: but
he, if he did so, would do it only out of revenge, and
without knowing even that it was she who had betrayed him. All that night and the next day she was
in a great state of nervous excitement, not able to
keep quiet. She went to the manse, and she came
back again, and could not rest anywhere. Apparently nothing had happened; for if there had been a
raid of the police, however private, and an arrest
effected at the Hewan—and she knew Lew would
not tamely allow himself to be taken—some news of
it must have oozed out. It would be strange if it
passed off without bloodshed, she said to herself. She
would have understood very well that movement of
his hand to his pocket which Mrs Ogilvy beheld so
quietly without knowing at all what it meant. However carefully he might be entrapped, however sudden
the rush might be upon him, Lew, who always had
his wits perfectly about him, would have time to get
at his revolver. She knew so much better than any
one what must happen, and yet here she was a mile
off and knowing nothing. She fluttered out and in of
the manse in the afternoon in her excitement, very
gay to all appearance, and talking a great deal.

"You are in excellent spirits to-day, my dear,"
said the minister, who was delighted with her gaiety.
"But I hope the leddy be-na fey," was what his old

experienced cook, who, not able to tolerate a new mistress, was leaving, said.

"You used to pay visits in the evening before I came on the scene," she said to her elderly lover. "You used to go and see your ladies: now confess —I know you did."

"I don't know what you mean by my ladies," said the minister, who was, however, flattered by the imputation. "I have never had any lady, my dear, till I met you."

"That is all very well," she replied, "but we know what pastoral visits mean. You don't go and see the men like that. Now there is Mrs Ogilvy, who was, you told me, your oldest friend. You never go near her now. You used to go there at all times—in the afternoons, and in the evenings, and sometimes to supper——"

"My dear, I have wanted to see nobody but you for a couple of months past," the minister said.

"Let us go back to the old customs," she said. "I want a bit of change to-night. I have got the fidgets or something. I can't sit still. I want, if you understand what that is, or if you won't be shocked, a bit of a spree."

"Oh, I understand what it is," said Mr Logan, with a laugh; "but I am much shocked, and when you come to the manse you must not speak any more of a bit of a spree."

"I shan't want it then perhaps," she said, with a look that flattered the foolish man. "But, for the present moment, what do you say to walking up to the Hewan after supper?—and then perhaps we shall see something of Mrs Ogilvy's two mysterious men."

"You'll not do that, surely you'll not do that, papa!" cried Susie. "Mrs Ogilvy's men are just her son Robbie, whom we all know, and some friend of his. They are not mysterious—there is nothing at all to find out—and it would vex her if we tried to find out," she cried in a troubled tone.

"You shall just come too, to punish you for your objections, Susie. Come, come! I have taken one of my turns to-night. I can't keep still. Let us go. The walk will be delightful, and then it will amuse me to find out the mysterious men. I shouldn't wonder if I knew one of them. I always know somebody wherever I go. Now, are you going to humour me, James, or are you not? I shall take the last train to Edinburgh, and go to a theatre or somewhere to blow away my fidgets, if you won't come."

"We must just humour her, Susie," said the minister.

"Do so if you like, papa," said Susie; "but not me. I have plenty to do at home."

"She thinks Mr Maitland may perhaps look in,

to ask for the hundredth time if she will fix the
day. That's always amusing—a man after you like
that; but make her come, James, make her come.
I want her to come with us to-night."

"I tell you we will just have to humour her,
Susie," Mr Logan said. He was charmed, and yet
he was a little troubled too by the vivacity of his
betrothed. When she was "at the manse," as he
said, she must be made to understand that noctur-
nal expeditions like this were not in an elderly bride-
groom's way. But at all events, for once she must
be humoured to-night.

CHAPTER XX.

MRS OGILVY rose from her bed after the little conversation which had roused her more effectually than
anything else could have done, more than half ashamed
of having slept, and a little feverish with her sudden
awakening and Robbie's strange demand: and though
it was late—more like, indeed, the proper and lawful
moment for going to bed than for getting up and making an unnecessary toilet in the middle of the night—
put on her cap again, and her pretty white shawl, and
went down-stairs. She had put on one of the fine
embroidered China crape-shawls which were for the
evening, and, to correspond with that, a clean cap
with perfectly fresh ribbons, which gave her the air
of being in her best, more carefully dressed than
usual. And her long sleep had refreshed her. When
she went into the dining-room, where Janet was
removing the remains of the supper from the table,
she was like an image of peace and whiteness and

brightness coming into the room, to which, however, carefully Janet might arrange it, the two men always gave a certain aspect of disorder. Mrs Ogilvy had tried to dismiss from her face every semblance of agitation. She would not remember the request Robbie had made to her, nor think of it at all save as a sudden impulse of reckless generosity on his part to his friend. The two young men, however, were not equally successful in composing their faces. Robbie had his pipe in his hand, which he had crammed with tobacco, pushing it down with his thumb, as if to try how much it would contain; but he did not light it: and even Lew, usually so careless and smiling, looked grave. He it was who jumped up to place a chair for her. Janet had so far improved matters that the remains of the meal were all cleared away, and only the white tablecloth left on the table.

"I think shame of myself," said Mrs Ogilvy, "to have been overtaken by sleep in this way: but it is very seldom I go in to Edinburgh, and the hot streets and the glaring sun are not what I am used to. However, perhaps I am all the better of it, and my head clearer. I doubt if, when it's at its clearest, it would be of much service to you—men that both know the world better than I do, though you are but laddies to me."

"Yes; I think we know the world better than you do," said Lew. "We've been a bit more about. This is a sweet little place, but you don't see much of life;

and then you're too good, mother, to understand it if you saw it," he said.

"You are mistaken, Mr Lew, in thinking there is little life to be seen here: everywhere there is life, in every place where God's creatures are. Many a story have I seen working out, many a thing that might have been acted on the stage, many a tragedy, too, though you mightn't think it. The heart and the mind are the same wherever you find them—and love, that is the grandest and most terrible thing on this earth, and death, and trouble. Oh, I could not tell you in a long summer day the things I have seen!"

"Very different from our kind of things, mother," said Lew, with a laugh. "I don't suppose you've seen anything like the fix we're in at present, for instance: the police on our heels, and not a penny to get out of the way with—and in this blessed old country, where you've to go by the railway and pay for all your meals. These ain't the things that suit us, are they, Bob?"

Robert was standing up, leaning against the securely closed and curtained window. The night was very warm, and the windows being closed, it was hot inside. His face was completely in shade, and he made no reply, but stood like a shadow, moving only his hand occasionally, pressing down the tobacco in the overcharged pipe.

"I have told you, Mr Lew," Mrs Ogilvy said, with a slight quiver in her voice, "that whatever money you may want for your journey, and something to give you a new start wherever you go, you should have, and most welcome—oh, most welcome! I say, not for my Robbie's sake, but out of my own heart. Oh, laddie, you are but young yet! I have said it before, and I will say it again—whatever you may have done in the past, life is always your own to change it now."

"We will consider all that as said," said Lew, with the movement of concealing a slight yawn. "You've been very kind in that as in everything else, putting my duty before me; but there's something more urgent just at present. This money—we must go far, Bob and I, if we're to be safe——"

"Not Robbie, not Robbie!" she cried.

"We must go far if we're to be safe, not back where we were. It's a pity when a place becomes too hot to hold you, especially when it's the place that suits you best. We'll have to go far. I have my ideas on that point; but it's better not to tell them to you: for then when you are questioned you can't answer, don't you see."

"But Robbie — is not pursued. Robbie, Robbie! you will never leave me! Oh, you will not leave me again, and break my heart!"

Robbie did not say a word: his face was completely in the shadow, and nothing could be read there any more than from his silent lips.

"Going far means a deal of money; setting up

again means a deal of money. If we were to open a
bank, for instance," said Lew, with a short laugh—
"a most respectable profession, and just in our way.
Thàt's probably what we shall do—we shall open a
bank; but it wants money, a deal of money—a great
deal of money. You would like to see your son a
respectable banker, eh? Then, old lady, you must
draw your purse-strings."

"I do not think," said Mrs Ogilvy, "that Robbie
would do much as a banker—nor you either, Mr
Lew. You would have to be at office-desks every day
and all the day. To me it would seem natural, but to
you that have used yourselves, alack! to such different things—— And then it is not what you call
just money that is wanted. It is capital; and where
are you to find it? Oh, my dear laddies, in this you
know less, not more, than me. You must get folk
to trust in you by degrees when you have showed
yourselves trustworthy. But a bank at once, without either character—alack, that I should say it!—
or capital. Oh no, my dears, oh, not a bank, not a
bank, whatever you do!"

"You must trust us, mother—we know what we're
talking about: a bank—which is perhaps not just
exactly the kind of thing you are thinking of—is
the only thing for Bob and me; but we must have
money, money, money," he said, tapping with his
hand upon the table.

"Capital," said Mrs Ogilvy, with a confident air of having suggested something quite different.

"It's the same thing, only more of it; and as that lies with you to furnish, we shall not quarrel about the word."

"There is some mistake," said Mrs Ogilvy, with dignity. "I have never said, I have never promised. Mr Lew, I found out to-day what was the passage-money of the farthest place you could go to, and I have got the siller here in the house."

The dark figure at the window stirred a little, raising a hand as if in warning: the other listened with a sudden, eager gleam in his eyes, leaning forward. It made his face shine to hear of the money in the house.

"Yes," he said, joyfully, "that's something like speaking. I love a practical mind. You have got it here in the house?" There came a certain tigerish keenness into his look, as if he might have snatched at her, torn it from her. The shadow against the window stirred a little, but whether in sympathy with the keen desire of the one, or touched by the aspect of the other, it was impossible to tell. Meanwhile Mrs Ogilvy, suspecting nothing, saw nothing to fear.

"It is in the house. I got it even in English notes, that you might have no trouble. There will be a hundred pounds," said Mrs Ogilvy. She spoke with a

U

little pride, as of one announcing a great thing, a
donation almost unparalleled, but which yet she gave
like a princess, not grudging. "And thirty besides," she
added, with a little sigh, "that when you get there you
may not be without a pound in your pocket. I give
it you with all my heart, Mr Lew. Oh, if the money,
the poor miserable siller, might maybe be the means
of calling you back to a steady and to an honest life!"

Lew said nothing in reply: his hungry eyes, lighted
up by such a gleam of covetousness, gave one fiery
glance at Robbie standing, as it seemed, imperturb-
able, immovable, in the shade. Then he began to
beat out a tune on the table with his fingers: but he
made no other answer, to Mrs Ogilvy's great surprise.

"I believe," she said, with hesitation, "that will
pay a passage even to India; but if you should find
that it will need more——"

He went on with his tune, beating on the table,
half whistling to accompany the beats of his fingers.
Something of the aspect of a fierce animal, lashing its
tail, working itself up into fury, had come into his
usually smiling pleasant looks, though the smile was
still on his face.

"I fear," he said, with the gleam in his eyes which
she began to perceive with wonder, "that it is not
enough. They will be of no use to us, these few
shillings. I thought you would have done anything
for your son; but I find, mother, that you're like all

the mothers, good for everything in words, but for a little less in money. You will have to give us more than that——"

Mrs Ogilvy was much surprised, but would not believe her ears. She said mildly, "I have told you, Mr Lew: it is not for my son, but chiefly out of a great feeling I have for yourself, poor laddie, that have nobody to advise you or lead you in a better way."

"You may preach if you like," he said, with a laugh, "if you're ready to pay; but no preaching without paying, old lady. Come, let's look at it a little closer. Here are you rolling in money, and he there, your only son, sent out into the world——"

"Not Robbie," she cried, with a gasp, "not Robbie! I said it was for you——"

"We do not mean to be parted, however," he said. "You must double your allowance, mother, and then see how much you can add to that."

She looked at her son, clasping her hands together, her face, amid the whiteness of her dress, whiter still, its only colour the eyes, so bright and trustful by nature, looking at him with a supreme but voiceless appeal. Whether it touched him or not, could not be seen: he stirred a little, but probably only as a relief from his attitude of stillness—and his face was too deep in the shade to betray any expression for good or for evil.

Then Mrs Ogilvy rose up trembling to her feet. She said, clasping her hands again as if to strengthen herself, " I have been very wishful to do all to please you—to treat you, Mr Lew, as if you were—what can I say ?—not my own son, for he is but one—but like the son of my friend. But I have a duty—I am not my own woman, to do just what I please. I have a charge of my son before the Lord. I will give you this money to take you away, for this is not your place or your home, and you have nothing ado here. But my son: Robbie, all I have is yours— you can have it all when you like and how you like, my own boy. But not to go away with this man. If you will forsake your home, let it be well considered and at another time. To take you away with this man, fleeing before the pursuer, taking upon you a shame and a sin that is not yours—— No! I will not give you a penny of your father's money and my savings for that. No, no!—all, when you will, in sobriety and judgment, but nothing now."

Her smallness, her weakness, her trembling, were emphasised by the fact that she seemed to tower over Lew where he sat, and to stand like a rock between the two strong men."

"You're a plucky old girl," said her antagonist, with a laugh—" I always said so—game to the last: but we can't stand jabbering all night, don't you know.

Business is business. You must fork out if you were the Queen, my fine old lady. Sit down, for there's a good deal to say."

"I can hear what you have to say as I am, if it is anything reasonable," Mrs Ogilvy said. She felt, though she could scarcely keep that upright position by reason of agitation and fear, that she had an advantage over him as she stood.

He sprang to his feet before she knew what was going to happen, and with two heavy hands upon her shoulders replaced her in her chair. I will not say forced her back into it, though indeed that was how it was. She leaned back panting and astonished, and looked at him, but did not rise or subject herself to that violence again.

"I hope I did not hurt you—I didn't intend to hurt you," he said: "but you must remember, mother, though you treat us as boys, that we're a pair of not too amiable men—and could crush you with a touch, with a little finger," he added, looking half fiercely, half with a jest, into her eyes.

"No," she said very softly, "you could not crush me—not with all your power."

"Give that paper here, Bob," said his chief.

Robert scarcely moved, did not reveal himself in any way to the light, but with a faint stir of his large shadow produced a folded paper which had been within the breast of his coat. Lew took it and played with it somewhat nervously, the line of white like a wand of light in his hands.

"You are rolling in wealth," he said.

She made as if she had said "No!" shaking her head, but took no other notice of the question.

"We have reason to suppose you are well off, at least. You have got your income, which can't be touched, and you have got a lot of money well invested."

She did not make any reply, but looked at him steadily, marking every gesture.

"It is this," he said, "to which Bob has a natural right. I think we are very reasonable. We don't want to rob you, notwithstanding our great need of money: you can see that we wish to use no violence, only to set before you what you ought to do."

"I will not do it," said Mrs Ogilvy.

"We'll see about that. I have been thinking about this for some time, and I have taken my measures. Here is a list which we got from your man—the old fogey you threatened us with—or at least from *his* man. And here is a letter directing everything to be realised, and the money paid over to your son. You will sign this——"

"From my man—you are meaning Mr Somerville?" Mrs Ogilvy looked at the paper which had been thrust into her hand, bewildered. "And he never said a word of it to me!"

"Don't let us lay the blame where it isn't due," said the other, lightly :- "from his man. Probably the respectable old fogey never knew——"

"Ah!" she cried, "the clerk that was Robbie's friend! Then it was Robbie himself——"

"Robbie himself," said Lew, in the easiest tone, "as it was he who had the best, the only, right to find out. Now, mother, come! execute yourself as bravely as you have done the other things. Sign, and we'll have a glass all round, and part the best friends in the world. When you wake in the morning you'll find we've cleared out."

"It was Robbie," she said to herself, murmuring, scarcely audible to the others, "it was Robbie— Robbie himself." She took no notice of the paper which was placed before her. All her mind seemed occupied by this. "Robbie—it was Robbie, my son."

"Who should it be but Bob? Do you think that information would have been furnished to me? What did I know about it? It was Bob, of course; and don't you think he was quite right? Come! here's pen and ink ready. Sign, and then it will be all over. It goes against me, mother, to ask anything you don't like — it does, though you mayn't believe me. Now, one moment, and the thing will be done."

He spoke to her, coaxing her, as to a child, but there was a kindling devil in his eye. Robbie never

raised his head or opened his mouth, but he made
to his comrade an imperative gesture with his hand.
The tension was becoming too much to bear.

"Come, mother," said Lew, "sign—sign!"

This time she did not rise up as before. She had
a faint physical dread of provoking his touch upon
her person again; but she lifted her head, and looking
at him, said steadily, "No."

"No?—you say this to us who could—kill you with
a touch?"

"I will not do it," she said.

"Do you know what you are saying, old woman?—
tempting me, tempting him, to murder? You needn't
look to the door: there is not a soul that could hear
you—Andrew's fast asleep, and you wouldn't call him,
to bear witness against your son."

"No," she said, "I would not call him to bear witness—against—my son."

"Sign! sign! sign!" cried Lew; "do you think
we'll wait for you all night?"

"I will not sign."

"Old woman! you wretched old fool, trusting, I
suppose, to that fellow there! Better trust me than
him. Look here, no more of this. You shall sign
whether you will or not." He seized her hand as
he spoke, thrust the pen into it, and forced it upon
the paper. Her little wrist seemed to crush together
in his big hand. She gave a faint cry, but no more.

Her fingers remained motionless in his hold. He was growing red with impatience and fury, his eyes fierce, his mouth set. She looked up at him for a moment, but said not a word.

" Will you do it ? will you do it ?—at once !—when I tell you."

" No."

He let her hand go and seized her by the shoulders. He had by this time forgotten everything except that he was crossed and resisted by a feeble creature in his power. And in this state he was appalling, murder in his eye, and an ungovernable impulse in his mind. He seized her by her shoulders, the white shawl crumpling in soft folds not much less strong to resist than the flesh beneath in his hands, and shook her, violently, furiously, like a dog rather than a man.

" Do what I tell you, woman ! Sign !"

" No."

She thought that she was dead. She thought it was death, her breath going from her, her eyes turning in their sockets. Next moment a roar of rage seemed to pass over her head, she was pushed aside like a straw flung out of the fiery centre of the commotion, the grip gone from her shoulders, and she herself suddenly turned as it were into nothing, like the chair at which she clutched to support herself, not knowing what it was. She had a vision for a moment of Robbie, her son, standing where she had

stood, tearing and tearing again in a hundred pieces
a paper in his hands, while Lew against the opposite
wall, as if he too had been dashed out of the way like
herself, stood breathing hard, his eyes glaring, his arm
up. Next moment she was pushed suddenly, not
without violence, thrust out of the room, and the
door closed upon her. All was dark outside, and
she helpless, broken, bleeding she thought, a wounded,
lacerated creature, not able to stand, far more unable in the tumult and trouble of body and soul to
go away, to seek any help or shelter. She dropped
down trembling upon her knees, with her head against
that closed door.

CHAPTER XXI.

How this night passed over, this dreadful night, under the once peaceful roof of the Hewan, was never known. It must have been dawn, though it seemed to her so dark, when Mrs Ogilvy dropped on her knees by the dining-room door—and how she got to her own room she did not know. She came to herself with the brilliant summer morning pervading all things, her room full of light, her body full of pain, her mind, as soon as she was conscious, coming back with a dull spring to the knowledge of catastrophe and disaster, though for the first moment she could not tell what it was. She was lying upon her bed fully dressed, her white shawl, which she had been wearing last night, flung, all crumpled, upon the floor, but nothing else changed. A thicker shawl had been thrown over her. Who was it that had carried her upstairs? This became an awful question as her mind grew clearer. Who was it? who was it?—the victor—

perhaps the survivor—— She was aching from head
to foot, feeling as if her bones were broken, and she
could never stand on her feet again; but when this
thought entered her mind she sprang up from her bed
like a young girl. The survivor!—perhaps Robbie,
Robbie, her once innocent boy, with the stain of blood
on his hands: perhaps—— Mrs Ogilvy snatched at
the shawl on the floor, which looked almost as if something dead might lie hidden under it, and wrapped
herself in it, not knowing why, and stole down-stairs
in the brightness of that early morning before even
Janet was stirring. She hurried into the dining-room,
from which she had been shut out only a few hours
ago, with her heart leaping in her throat, not knowing what awful scene she might see. But there was
nothing there. A chair had been knocked down, and
lay in the middle of the floor in a sort of grotesque
helplessness, as if in mockery of the mother's fears.
Nothing else. She stood for a moment, rendered weak
again by sudden relief, asking herself if that awful
vision of the night had been merely a dream, until
suddenly a little heap of torn paper flung upon the
ornaments in the grate brought it back again so
vividly that all her fears awoke once more. Then she
stole away again to the bedrooms, in which, if all was
well, they should be lying asleep. There was no
sound from Robbie's, or she could hear none from the
beating of her heart. She stole in very softly, as she

had not ventured to do since the first morning after his return. There he lay, one arm over his head like a child, breathing that soft breath of absolute rest which is almost inaudible, so deep and so quiet. What fountains of love and tenderness burst forth in the old mother's breast, softening it, healing it, filling its dryness with heavenly dew. Oh, Robbie, God bless him! God bless him! who at the last had stood for his mother—who would not let her be hurt —who would rather lose everything. And she had perhaps been hard upon him! There was no blood on the hand of one who slept like *that*. She went to the other door and listened there with her heart lightened; and the breathing there was not inaudible. She retired to her own room almost with a smile on her face.

When Mrs Ogilvy came into the room in which the two young men awaited her for the only meal they shared, the early dinner, she was startled to see a person who seemed a stranger to her in Lew's place. He wore Lew's clothes, and spoke with Lew's voice, but seemed another man. He turned to Robert as she drew back bewildered, and burst into a laugh. "There's a triumph for me; she doesn't know me," he said. Then he approached her with a deprecating look. " I am the man that was so rude to you last night. Forget there was ever such a person. You see I have thrown off all semblance of him." He spoke gravely and with a sort of dignity, standing in the same place in which

Mrs Ogilvy remembered in a flash of sudden vision he
had almost shaken the life out of her last night, glaring at her with murderous eyes. There was a gleam
in them still which was not reassuring; but his aspect
was everything that was penitent and respectful. The
change in his appearance was made by the removal of
the beard which had covered his face. He had suddenly grown many degrees lighter in colour, it seemed,
by the removal of that forest of dark hair; and the man
had beautiful features, a fine mouth, that rare beauty
either in man or woman. His expression had always
been good-humoured and agreeable. It was more so,
a look in which there seemed no guile, but for that
newly awakened tigerish expression in his eyes. Mrs
Ogilvy felt a thrill of terror such as had not moved
her through all the horrors of the previous night, when
Robbie for a moment left the room. She felt that the
handsome smiling man before her would have strangled
her without a moment's hesitation had there been any
possibility of getting the money for which he had
struggled in another way, in what was for her fortunately the only possible way. She felt his grip upon
her shoulders, and a shiver ran through her in spite
of herself. She could not help a glance towards the
door, where, indeed, Janet was at the moment about
to come in, pushing it open before her. There was no
danger to-day, with everybody about—but another
night—who could tell?

When the dinner was over, Lew addressed her again.
"This," he said, putting up his hand to his chin, "is my
toilette de voyage. You are going to be free of us soon.
We shall make no flourish of trumpets, but go suddenly
as we came."

"If it doesn't prove too late," said Robert, gruffly.

"Listen to the croaker! It isn't, and it shan't be,
too late. I don't admit the possibility—so long as
your mother, to whom we behaved so badly last
night——"

"You," Mrs Ogilvy breathed forth in spite of
herself.

"Oh, he was in it just as much as I was," said
the other, lightly; "but he's a canny Scot, Bob; he
knows when to stop. I, when I am in a good way,
don't."

There was a savage meaning in the lightness of
this speech and the smile that accompanied it. Mrs
Ogilvy, terrified, felt herself again shaking like a leaf,
like a rag in these tremendous hands. And Robbie,
who only knew when to stop—oh, no, no—oh, no, no
—she would not believe that: though he had stood
still long and looked on.

"You shall see that I will keep my word," she said,
and hurried out of the room to fetch the money which
she had brought from Edinburgh with so many pre-
cautions. She who had been above all fear felt it now
penetrating to her very soul. She locked her door

when she went into her room, a precaution she had
probably never taken in her life before. She caught
a glimpse of herself in the mirror as she passed, and
saw that her countenance was blanched, and her eyes
wide with fright. Two men, perhaps—at least one
in the fulness of his strength—and she such a little
old feeble woman. Had the money she possessed been
more easily got at, she knew that she would have had
short shrift. And, indeed, if he killed her, there would
have been no need of making her sign anything first.
It would all go to Robbie naturally—provided she
could be sure that Robbie would be free of any share
of the guilt. Oh, he would be free! he would not
stand by and see her ill-used—he had not been able
to bear it last night. Robbie would stand by her
whatever happened. But her bosom panted and her
heart beat in her very throat. She had to go down
again into the room where red murder was in the
thoughts of one, and perhaps—God forbid it! God
forbid it! Oh, no, no, no!—it was not in nature:
not on his mother, not on any one to kill or hurt
would Robbie ever lay a hand.

She went down-stairs after a very short interval,
and as she reached the dining-room door heard the
voice of Lew talking to Janet in the most genial
tones. He was so cheerful, so friendly, that it was
a pleasure to hear so pleasant a voice; and Robbie,
very silent behind backs, was altogether eclipsed·by

his friend, although to Janet too that often sullen
Robbie was " my ain laddie," dear in spite of all.
But there was no drawback in her opinion of Mr
Lewis, as she called him, "Aye canty and pleasant,
aye with a good word in his head; no pride about
him; just as pleasant with me as if I were the
Duchess hersel'." She held up her hands in expressive horror as she met her mistress at the door. "He
carries it off wi' his pleasant ways; but oh, he has just
made an objeck of himself," Janet said.

Mrs Ogilvy went in, feeling as if she were going to
her doom. She took her little packet to the table, and
put it down before him. The room was filled with
clouds of smoke; and that bottle, which was so great
a trial to her, stood on the table; but these details
had sunk into absolute insignificance. She had taken
the trouble to get the money in English notes and gold
—the latter an unusual sight in the Hewan, where
one-pound notes were the circulating medium. In
the tremor of her nerves and commotion of her feelings she had added twenty pounds which were in the
house, of what she called "her own money," the money
for the housekeeping, to the sum which she had told
him was to be for him. It was thus a hundred and
fifty pounds which she put before him—hastily laying
it down as if it burned her, and yet with a certain
reluctance too.

"Ah!" he said, and threw a look across the table to

X

Robbie; "another twenty pounds — and more where
that came from, mother, eh?"

"I have no more—not a farthing," she said, hastily;
"this was my money for my house. I thought I would
add it to the other: since you were not pleased—last
night."

It was evidently an unfortunate movement on her
part. "You will perhaps find some more still," he
said, with a laugh, "before this night. It's not very
much for two, and one your only son; but there will
be plenty of time to settle that to-night."

"Robbie," she said, breathlessly, "is not going—he
is not going: it is for you."

"Are you not going, Bob?"

Robert said not a word in reply—he sat with his
head supported on his hands, his elbows on the table:
and his countenance was invisible—he made no movement or indication of what he meant to do.

"I have no more," said Mrs Ogilvy, with a trembling voice; for she was afraid of the look, half fierce,
half mocking, with which he met her eyes. "It would
perhaps have been better if I had—money in the bank,
and could draw a cheque like most people now; but I
have always followed the old-fashioned way, and all
I have is in the hands of——"

She broke off with a quavering, broken sound—
seeing over again the scene of last night, and the
paper with Mr Somerville's name upon it,—she re-

membered now, suddenly, that Mr Somerville's name
was upon the paper which they had wanted her to
sign. What had become of Mr Somerville that he
had not come, as he promised, to speak to Robbie, to
persuade the other one to go away? It was difficult
to recall to herself the fact that it was only two days
since she had gone to Edinburgh and poured her
trouble into his sympathetic ears. Perhaps it would
have been better if she had not done this, or opened
her heart to any one. Mr Somerville would never
betray them, he would not betray Robbie; but still it
seemed that something had happened between that
time and this, a greater sense of insecurity, the feeling
that something was going to happen. Things had
been better before, when that strange life which she
had felt to be insupportable was going on: now it was
more than insupportable, it was almost over, and
after—— ? A great chasm seemed to have opened
at her feet, and she felt herself hurrying towards it,
but could not tell what was below. After? what was
to happen after, if Robbie drifted away again, and she
saw his face no more?

He avoided her all day, while she watched for him
at every corner, eager only to get a word, to ask a
question, to put forth a single prayer. The afternoon
was terribly long: it went over, one sunny hour after
another, hot, breathless, terrible. It was clear by all
those signs that a thunderstorm was coming, and the

most appalling roll of thunder would have been a
relief; but even that delayed its coming, and a dead
stillness hung over heaven and earth. There was not
a breath of air, the flowers languished in the borders,
the leaves hung their heads, and all was still indoors.
She did not know what the young men were doing,
but they made no sound. Perhaps the weather affected
them too—perhaps, another storm coming, which they
had been long looking for, had overcome their spirits.
Perhaps they were making preparations for their de-
parture. But what preparations could they make,
unless it were a bundle on the end of a stick like the
tramps? She said to herself *they*, and then with
anguish changed it in her mind to *he*, but did not
believe it even while she did so. No! she had a conviction in her heart that Robbie would go. What was
there to keep him back? Nothing but dulness and
the society of an old woman. What was that to keep
a man at home? She was not angry with him, nor
intolerant, but simply miserable. What was there in
her to make a young man happy at home? to keep
him contented without society or any amusement?
No, no, she could not blame Robbie. He wanted
movement, he wanted life at his age. He was not
even like a young lad who sometimes has a great
feeling for his mother. She could not expect it of
him that he should stay here for his mother. Even
the flight, the excitement of being pursued, the diffi-

culty of getting away—Mrs Ogilvy had heard that
such things were more attractive than quietness and
safety at home. It was natural—and, what was the
chief thing above all other, Robbie was not so much,
not so very much, to blame.

She was still wandering about when the day began
to wane into evening, like an unquiet soul. Where
were they? what were they doing? The quiet of the
house became dreadful to her. She who had loved her
quiet so, who had felt it so insupportable to have her
calm solitude so spoiled and broken!—but now she
would have given much only to hear the scuffle of
their feet, the roar of their loud laughter. She went
about the house from one room to another, avoiding
only the bedrooms where she supposed they were.
She would not drive them out of that last refuge. She
would not interfere there, be importunate, disturb
them, if, perhaps, it was the last day.

And then she went outside and gazed right and left
for she knew not what. She was looking for no one—
or was it the storm she was looking for? Everything
was grey, the sky, like some deep solid lid for the
panting breathless world, stealing down upon the
earth, closely hiding the heavens: it seemed to come
closer and closer down, as if to smother the universe
and all the terrified creatures on it. The birds flew
low, making little agitated flights, as if they thought
the end of the world was at hand. So did she, to

whom, as far as she knew, everything was hastening
to a conclusion—her son about to disappear again into
the unknown, if he had not already done so, and her
life about to be wound up for ever.   For she knew
well there would be no second coming back.   Oh!
never, never again would she sit at her door, and listen
and hope for his step on the path.   If he left her now,
it would be for ever.   It might be that for the sake of
the money he would have seen some violence done to
his mother; but no money, if it were ten times as
much, would bring him back again—none! none! not
if it were ten times as much.   If he went now, he
would never come back; and how could she keep him
from going now ?

About seven o'clock the windows of heaven were
opened, and torrents of rain fell—not the storm for
which everybody had been looking, but only the tail
of the storm, which sounded all round the horizon in
distant dull reports, like a battle going on a dozen
miles away, and the tremendous downpour of rain.
She said to herself, "In such a night they can never
go," with a mingled happiness and despair—happiness
to put off the inevitable, to gain perhaps a propitious
moment, and supplicate her son not to go; and despair
in the prospect of another twenty-four hours of misery
like this, the dreadful suspense, the terror of she knew
not what.   When the first darkening of the twilight
began, Mrs Ogilvy began to think of another night to

go through, and Lew's laughing threats, and the devil
in his eyes. He had said there would be time to talk
of that to-night. Perhaps he would murder her to-
night; and all the country-side would believe it was
her son, and curse him, though it would not be Robbie
—not Robbie, who had saved her once, but perhaps
might not again. She asked herself whether it would
not be better to go away somewhere, to save herself
and, above all, them, from such a dreadful temptation.
But where could she go, exposing the misery of her
house ? and how did she know that something might
not happen which would make her presence a protection to them ? She gazed out from the window
through the rain, and it occurred to her that she could
always run out there and hide herself among the trees.
They would not think of looking for her there. She
would be safe there, or at least—— This idea gave
her a little comfort. How could he find her in the
dark, in the heavy rain, among her own trees ?

The rain had driven her indoors, and in the parlour
where she was, she heard them overhead. They
seemed to be moving about softly, and sometimes
crossed the passage, as if going from one room to
another. They had shared the clothes with which
Robbie had liberally provided himself on his return—
and the thought that they were busied only with
so homely an occupation as packing brought back
a little comfort to her. A man does not fash about

his clothes, she thought, who has murder in his head. She shook off her terror with a heat of shame flaming over her. Shame to have done injustice to her neighbour, how much more to her son! They were thinking of no such dreadful things: it was only the panic of her own imagination which was in fault. She said to herself that if it must be so, if Robbie left her, she would get from him a sure address, and there she would send him the money he wanted, or whatever he wanted—for was it not all his? This was what she would do: she had nothing to give him now. Perhaps, perhaps he might be deterred by that and wait till she could get it for him, while his friend went on. What a thing this would be, to get him alone, to talk to him, to represent to him how much better to take a little time, to think, to give himself a chance. She thought over all this, and shook her head while she thought; for, alas! this was what Robbie would never do.

Suddenly, it seemed in a moment, the rain stopped, the distant thunder came to an end, the battle in the skies was over. And after all the tumult and commotion of the elements, the clouds, which had poured themselves out, dispersed in rags and fragments of vapour, and let the sky look through—the most serene evening sky, with the stars faintly visible through the wistful lingering daylight—the sweetest evening, with that clearness as of weeping, and radiance as of hope returned, which is in the skies after the relief of the rain, and in a human countenance sometimes when all its tears have been shed, and there are no more to come. Was it a good omen, or was it only the resignation of despair which shone upon her out of that evening sky?

CHAPTER XXII.

Mrs Ogilvy went wearily up-stairs after the suspense and alarm of this long, long day. It was all that she could do to drag one foot after another, to keep upright; her brain was in a confusion of misery, out of which she now could distinguish no distinct senti-ment—terror and grief and suspense, and the vague wild apprehension of some unintelligible catastrophe, all mingling together. When she reached the head of the stairs she met Robbie, who told her, not looking at her, that he had bidden Janet prepare the supper earlier than usual, "for we'll have to make a start to-night," he said.

She seized his hand in her frail ones, which could scarcely hold it. "Robbie, will you go?—will you go, and break my heart?"

"It's of no use speaking, mother; let me be free of you at least, for God's sake! You will drive me mad——"

"Robbie! Robbie! my only son—my only child! I'll be dead and gone before ever you could come back."

"You'll live the longest of the two of us, mother."

"God forbid!" she said; "God forbid! But why will ye go out into the jaws of death and the mouth of hell? If the pursuers of blood are after him, they are not after you. Oh, Robbie, stay with your mother. Dinna forsake me for a strange man."

"Mother," he said, with a hoarse voice, "when your friend is in deadly danger, is that the time, think you, to forsake him?"

And Mrs Ogilvy was silent. She looked at him with a gasp in her throat. All her old teachings, the tenets of her life, came back upon her and choked her. When your friend is in deadly danger! Was it not she who had taught her son that of all the moments of life that was the last to choose to abandon a friend. She could make him no answer; she only stared at him with troubled failing eyes.

"But once he is in safety," Robbie said, with a stammer of hesitation and confusion, "once I can feel sure that—— Mother, I promise you, if I can help it, I will not go—where he is going. I—promise you." He cast a look behind him. There was no one there, but Lew's door was open, and it was possible he might hear. Robbie bent forward hastily to his mother's ear. "I cannot stand against him," he said; "I cannot: I

told you—he is my master,—didn't I tell you? But 1
will come back—I will come back—as soon as I am
free."

He trembled, too, throughout his big bulk, with agitation and excitement—more than she ever did in her
weakness. If this was so, was it not now her business
to be strong to support her boy? She went on to her
room to put on her other cap, to prepare for the evening, and the last meal they were to eat together. The
habits of life are so strong; her heart was breaking,
and yet she knew that it was time to put on her evening cap. She went into her room, too, with the feeling
that there no new agitation could come near her, that
she might kneel down a moment by her bedside, and
get a little calm and strength. But not to-night. To
her astonishment and horror, the tall figure of Lew
raised itself from the old-fashioned escritoire in which
she kept her papers and did her writing. He turned
round, and faced her with a laugh. "Oh, it is you!"
he said. "I thought it was your good son Bob. You
surprised us when we were making a little examination
by ourselves. It is always better to examine for yourself, don't you know——"

"To examine—what?"

"Where the money is, mother," he said, with another
laugh.

She had herself closed the door before she had seen
him. She was at his mercy.

"You think, then," she said, " that I've told you a lie—about money ?"

"Everybody tells lies about money, mother. I never knew one yet who did not declare he had none—until it was taken out of his pockets, or out of his boxes, or out of a nice little piece of furniture like this, which an old lady can keep in her bedroom—locked."

She took her keys out of her pocket, a neat little bunch, shining like silver, and handed them to him without a word. He received them with a somewhat startled look. It was something like the sensation of having the other cheek turned to you, after having struck the first. He had been examining the lock with a view to opening by other methods. The keys put into his hand startled him; but again he carried it off with a laugh. "Plucky old girl!" he said. And then he turned round and proceeded to open the well-worn old secretary which had enclosed all Mrs Ogilvy's little valuables, and the records of her thoughts since she was a girl. It opened as easily as any door, and gave up its little treasures, her letters, her little memorials, the records of an inno-cent woman's evanescent joys and lasting sorrows. The rough adventurer, whose very presence here was a kind of sacrilege, stooped over the little writing-board, the dainty little drawers, like a bear examining a beehive. He pulled out a drawer or two, in which there were bundles of old letters, all neatly tied up, touching them as if his hands were too big for the little ivory knobs; and then he suddenly turned round upon her, shutting the drawers again hurriedly, and flung the keys into her lap.

"Hang it all! I cannot do it. I've not come to that. Rob a rogue by day or night; that's fair enough: but turn to picking and stealing. No! take back your keys—you may have millions for me. I can't look up your little drawers, d—n you!" he cried.

"No, laddie!" said Mrs Ogilvy, looking up at him with tears in her eyes, "you're fit for better things."

He looked at her strangely. She sat quite still beside him, not moving, not even taking up her keys, which lay in her lap.

"You think so, do you?" he said. "And yet I would have killed you last night."

"Thank the Lord," said the old lady, "that delivered you from that temptation."

"That saved your life, you mean. But it wasn't the Lord. It was Bob, your son, who couldn't stand and see it after all."

"Thank the Lord still more," she said, "that wakened the old heart, his own natural heart, in my boy."

"Well that is one view to take of it," said Lew. "I should have thought it more sensible, however, to thank the Lord, as you say, for your own life."

Mrs Ogilvy rose up. The keys of her treasures fell

to the ground. What were they to her at this moment? "And what is my life to me," she said, "that I should think of it instead of better things? Do you think it matters much to me, left here alone an auld wreck on the shore, without a son, without a companion, without a hope for this world, whether I live or die? Man!" she cried, laying a hand on his arm, "it's not that I would give it for my Robbie, my own son, over and over and over! but I would give it for you. Oh, dinna think that I am making a false pretence! For you, laddie, that are none of mine, that would have killed me last night, that would kill me now for ever so little that I stood in your way."

"No!" he said in a hoarse murmur, "no!"—but she saw still the gleam of the devil in his eye, that murderous sense of power—that he had but to put forth a hand.

"If it would not be for the sin on your soul—you that are taking my son from me—you might take my life too, and welcome," she said.

She could not stand. She was restless, too, and could not bear one position. She sank upon her chair again, and, lifting up the keys, laid them down upon the open escritoire, where they lay shining between the two, neither of use nor consequence to either. Lew began to pace up and down the room, half abashed at his own weakness, half furious at his failure. She might have millions—but he could not fish them out of her drawers, not he. That was no man's work. He could have killed her last night, and he could, she divined, kill her now, with a sort of satisfaction, but not rob her escritoire.

"Mr Lew, will you leave me my son?" she said.

"No: I have nothing to do with it; he comes of his own will," cried the other. "You make yourself a fine idea of your son. Do you know he has been in with me in everything? Ah! he has his own scruples; he has not mine. He interfered last night; but he'd turn out your drawers as soon as look at you. It's a pity he's not here to do it."

"Will you leave me my son?" she repeated again; "he is all I have in the world."

"I've got less," cried Lew; "I haven't even a son, and don't want one. You are a deal better without him. Whatever he might be when he was a boy, Bob's a rover now. He never would settle down. He would do you a great deal more harm than good."

"Will you leave me my son?" she said again.

"No! I can say No as well as you, mother; but I've nothing to do with it. Ask himself, not me. Do you think this is a place for a man? What can he do? Who would he see? Nobody. It is not living—it is making believe to live. No; he won't stay here if he will be guided by me."

The door opened suddenly, and Robbie looked in. "Are you going to stay all night?" he said, gruffly.

"There's supper waiting, and no time to be lost, if——"

"If—we take that long run we were thinking of to-night. Well, let's go. Mrs Ogilvy, you're going to keep us company to-night."

"It's the last time," said her son.

"Oh, Robbie, Robbie!" she cried.

"Stop that, mother. I've said all I'm going to say."

To sit down round the table with the dishes served as usual, the lamp shining, the men eating largely, even it seemed with enjoyment, a little conversation going on—was to go from one dreadful dream to another with scarcely a pause between. Was it real that they were sitting there to-day and would be far away to-morrow? That this was her son, whom she could touch, and to-morrow he would have disappeared again into the unseen? Love is the most obdurate, the most unreasoning thing in the world. Mrs Ogilvy knew now very well what her Robbie was. There were few revelations which could have been made to her on the subject. Perhaps—oh, horrible thing to think or say!—it was better for her before he came back, when she had thought that his absence was the great sorrow of her life: she had learnt many other things since then. Perhaps in his heart the father of the prodigal learned this lesson too, and knew that, even with the best robe upon him, and the ring on

Y

his finger and the shoes on his feet, he was still hankering after the husks which the swine eat, and their company. How much easier would life be, and how many problems would disappear or be solved, if we could love only those whom we approved! But how little, how very little difference does this make. Mrs Ogilvy knew everything, divined everything, and yet the thought that he was going away made heaven and earth blank to her. She could not reconcile herself to the dreadful thought. And he, for his part, said very little. He showed no regret, but neither did he show that eagerness to take the next step which began to appear in Lew. He sat very silent, chiefly in the shade, saying nothing. Perhaps after all he was sorry; but his mother, watching him in her anguish, could not make sure even of that. Janet was, next to Lew himself, the most cheerful person in the room. She pulled her mistress's sleeve, and showed her two shining pieces of gold in her hand, with a little nod of her head towards Lew. "And Andrew has one," she whispered. "I aye said he was a real gentleman! Three golden sovereigns between us —and what have we ever done? I'll just put them by for curiosities. It's no often you see the like o' them here." The mistress looked at them with a rueful smile. Gold is not very common in rural Scotland. She had taken so much trouble to get those golden sovereigns for her departing guest! but it did not dis-

please her that he had been generous to her old servants. There was good in him—oh, there was good
in him!—he had been made for better things.

Janet had been in this radiant mood when she
cleared the table; but a few minutes after she came
in again with a scared face, and beckoned to her
mistress at the door. Mrs Ogilvy hurried out, afraid
she knew not of what, fearing some catastrophe.
Andrew stood behind Janet in the hall. "What is it,
what is it?" the mistress cried.

"Have you siller in the house, mem? is it known
that you have siller in the house?"

"Me—siller? are you out of your senses? I have
no siller in the house—nothing beyond the ordinary,"
Mrs Ogilvy cried.

"It's just this," said Janet, "there's a heap of waiff
characters creeping up about the house. I canna think
it's just for the spoons and the tea-service and that, that
are aye here; but I thought if you had been sending
for money, and thae burglars had got wit of it——"

"What kind of waiff characters?" said Mrs Ogilvy,
trembling.

"They are both back and front. Andrew he was
going to supper Sandy, and a man started up at his
lug. The doors and the windows are all weel fastened,
but Andrew he said I should let you ken."

"The gentlemen," said Andrew, "will maybe know
—they will maybe know——"

"How should the gentlemen know, poor laddies, mair than any one of us?" cried Janet.

It was a great thing for Andrew all his life after that the mistress approved his suggestion. "I will go and tell them," she said; "and you two go ben to your kitchen and keep very quiet, but if ye hear anything more let me know."

She went back into the lighted room, trembling, but ready for everything. The two men were seated at the table. They were not talking as usual, but sat like men full of thought, saying nothing to each other. They looked up both—Lew with much attention, Rob with a sort of sulky indifference. "It appears," said Mrs Ogilvy, speaking in a broken voice, "that there are men—all round the house."

"Men! all round the house." There was a moment of consternation, and then Lew sprang to his feet. "It has come, Bob; the hour has come, sooner than we thought."

Rob rose too, slowly; an oath, which in this terrible moment affected his mother more than all the rest, came from his lips. "I told you—you would let them take you by surprise."

"Fool again! I don't deny it," the other said, with a sort of gaiety. "Now for your gulley and Eskside, and a run for it. We'll beat them yet."

"If they've not stopped us up like blind moles," cried Robbie. "Mother, keep them in parley as long

as you can; every moment's worth an hour. You'll
have to open the door, but not till the very last."

She answered only with a little movement of her
head, and stood looking without a word, while they
caught up without another glance at her—Robbie the
cloak which he had brought with him, and Lew a
loose coat, in which he enveloped himself. Their
movements were very quiet, very still, as of men
absorbed in what they were doing, thinking of nothing
else. They hurried out of the room, Robbie first,
leading the way, and his mother's eyes following him
as if they would have burst out of the sockets. He
was far too much preoccupied to think of her, to give
her even a look. And this was their farewell, and she
might never see him more. She stood there motionless, conscious of nothing but that acute and poignant
anguish that she had taken her last look of her son,
when suddenly the air, which was trembling and
quivering with excitement and expectation, like the
air that thrills and shimmers over a blazing furnace,
was penetrated by the sound for which the whole
world seemed to have been waiting—a heavy ominous
loud knock at the outer door. Mrs Ogilvy recovered
all her faculties in a moment. She went to the open
door of the dining-room, where Andrew and Janet,
one on the heels of the other, were arriving in commotion, Andrew about to stride with a heavy step to
the door. She silenced them, and kept them back

with a movement of her hands, stamping her impatient foot at Andrew and his unnecessary haste.
She thought it would look like expectation if she
responded too soon—and had they not told her to
parley, to gain time? She stood at the dining-room
door and waited till the summons should be repeated.
And after an interval it came again, with a sound of
several voices. She put herself in motion now, coming
out into the hall, pretending to call upon Andrew,
as she would have done in former days if so disturbed.
" Bless me!" she cried; "who will that be making
such a noise at the door?"

"Will I open it, mem?" Andrew said.

"No, no; let me speak to them first. Who is it?"
Mrs Ogilvy said, raising her calm voice; "who is
making such a disturbance at my door at this hour of
the night?"

"Open in the Queen's name," cried somebody outside.

"Ay, that would I willingly," cried Mrs Ogilvy;
"but who are ye that are taking her sacred Majesty's
name? None of her servants, I'm sure, or you would
not disturb an honest family at this hour of the
night."

"Open to the police, at your peril," said another
voice.

"The police—in this house? No, no," she cried,
standing white and trembling, but holding out like a

lion. "You will not deceive me with that—in this house."

"Open the door, or we'll break it in. Here, you speak to her!"—"Mem," said a new voice, very tremulous but familiar, "it is me, Peter Young, with the men from Edinburgh. It's maybe some awfu' mistake; but you must let us in—you maun open the door."

"You, Peter Young!" cried Mrs Ogilvy, "you are not the man to disturb my house in the middle of the night. It ill becomes you after all you've got from the Hewan. Just tell these idle folk there is nothing to be gotten here, and bid them go away."

"This is folly," said a more imperative voice. "Break in the door if she will not open it. We can't stand all the night parleying here."

Then Mrs Ogilvy heard, her ears preternaturally sharp in the crisis, a sound as of women's voices, which gave her a momentary hope. Was it a trick that was being played upon her after all? for if it was for life or death why should there be women's voices there?

And then another voice arose which was even more reassuring. It was the minister who spoke. The minister dragged hither against his will, but beginning to feel piously that it was the hand of providence, and that he had been directed not by Mrs Ainslie, but by some special messenger from heaven—

if indeed she was not one. " Mrs Ogilvy," the minister
said, " it must be, as Peter says, some dreadful mistake—but it certainly is the police from Edinburgh,
and you must let them in."

" Who is that that is speaking? is it the minister
that is speaking? are ye all in a plot to disturb the
rest of a quiet family? No," with a sudden exclamation, " ye will not break in my door. I will open it,
since ye force me to open it. I am coming, I am
coming."

Andrew rushed forward, to pull back with all ex-
pedition the bolts and bars. But his mistress stamped
her foot at him once more, and dismissed him behind
backs with a look—from which he did not recover
for many a long day—and coming forward herself,
began to draw back with difficulty and very slowly
the innocent bolts and bars. They might have been
the fastenings of a fortress from the manner in which
she laboured at them, with her unaccustomed hands.
" And me ready to do it in a moment," Andrew said,
aggrieved, while she kept asking herself, the words
buzzing in her ears, like flies coming and going,
" Have I kept them long enough? have I given my
lads their time? Oh, if they got out that quiet they
should be safe by now." There was the bolt at the
bottom and the top, and there was the chain, and then
the key to turn. The door was driven in upon her at
last by the sudden entrance of a number of impatient

men, a great gust of fresh air, a ray of moonlight straight from the skies: and Mr Logan and his companions, Susie pale and crying, and Mrs Ainslie pale too—but with eyes sparkling and all the keen enjoyment of an exciting catastrophe in her face.

"We have a warrant for the arrest of Lew or Lewis Winterman, *alias*, &c., &c., accused of murder," said the leader of the party, "who we have reason to believe has been for some weeks harboured here."

Mrs Ogilvy disengaged herself from the man whose sudden push inwards had almost carried her away. She came forward into the midst in her white cap and shawl, a wonderful centre to all these dark figures. "There is no such person in my house," she said.

And then there came a cry and tumult from behind, and through the door of the dining-room, which stood wide open, making it a part of the scene, there suddenly appeared another group of whirling struggling figures, steadily pushing back before them the two fugitives, who had crept their way out, only to be met and overpowered, and brought back to answer as they could for themselves. Then, and only then, Mrs Ogilvy's strength failed her. The light for a moment went out of her eyes. All that she had done had been in vain, in vain.

CHAPTER XXIII.

THE two men stood with the background of dark figures behind, while the inspector who was at the head of the party advanced towards them. Robbie, with his long beard and his cloak over his shoulder, was the one upon whom all eyes were fixed. One of the policemen held him firm by the arm. His countenance was dark, his air sullen, like a wild beast taken in the toils. The other by his side, almost spruce in his loose coat, his clean-shaven face seeking no shadow, facing the enemy with a half-smile upon it, easy, careless, fearing no evil—produced an effect quite contrary to that which the dark and bearded brigand made upon the officers of the law. Who could doubt that it was he who was the son of the house, "led away" by the truculent ruffian by his side? There was no mention of Robbie's name in the warrant. And the sight of Robbie's mother, and her defence of her threshold, had touched the hearts

even of the police. To take away this ruffian, to
leave her her son in peace, poor old lady, relieving
her poor little quiet house of the horror that had
stolen into it—the inspector certainly felt that he
would be doing a good service to his neighbour as
well as obeying the orders of the law.

"The one with the beard," he said, looking at a
paper which he held in his hand—"that is him.
Secure him, Green. Stand by, men; be on your
guard; he knows what he's about——ah!" The
inspector breathed more freely when the handcuffs
clicked on Robert Ogilvy's wrists, who for his part
neither resisted nor answered, but stood looking almost stupidly at the scene, and then down upon
his hands when they were secured. The other by his
side put up a hand to his face, as if overwhelmed by
the catastrophe, and fell a little backward, overcome
it seemed with distress—as Robbie ought to have done,
had this and not the ruffian in the beard been he.

Mrs Ogilvy had been leaning on Susie's shoulder,
incapable of more, her heart almost ceasing to beat,
all her strength gone; but when the words, "the one
with the beard," reached dully and slowly to her com-
prehension, she made but one bound, pushing with
both arms every one away from her, and with a shriek
appeared in the midst of the group. "It is my son,"
she cried, "my son, my son! It is Robbie Ogilvy and
no one else. It is my son, my son, my son!" She

flung herself upon him, raving as if she had suddenly
gone mad in her misery, and tried to pluck off with
her weak hands the iron bands from his wrists. Her
cries rang out, silencing every other sound. "It is my
son, my son, my son!———"

"I am very sorry, madam; it may be your son, and
still it may be the man we want," the inspector said.

And then another shrill woman's voice burst forth
from behind. "You fools, he's escaping! Don't you
see?"—the speaker clapped her hands with a sound
that rang over their heads. "Don't you see! It's
easy to take off a beard. If you waste another moment, he'll be gone!"

He had almost got beyond the last of the men,
retreating very softly backwards, while all the attention was concentrated upon Robbie and his mother.
But he allowed himself to be pushed forward again at
the sound of this voice, as if he had had no such
intention. A snarl like that of a furious dog curled
up his lip at the side for a moment; but he did not
change his aspect—the game was not yet lost.

"There are folk here," cried Mrs Ogilvy, still pluck-
ing at the handcuffs, while Robbie stood silent, saying
nothing—"there are folk here who have known him
from his cradle, that will tell you he's Robert Ogilvy:
there are my servants—there is the minister, here
present God knows why or wherefore: they know—
he's been absent from his home many a day; but he's

Robert Ogilvy: no the other. If he's Robert Ogilvy he is not the other: if he's my son he's not that man. And he is my son, my son, my son! I swear it to you—and the minister. Mr Logan, tell them——"

Mr Logan's mind was much disturbed. He felt that providence itself had sent him here; but he was slow to make up his mind what to say. He wanted time to speak and to explain. "I have every reason to think that is Robert Ogilvy," he said; "but I never saw him with a beard; and what he may have been doing all these years——"

"Mr Inspector," cried Mrs Ainslie, panting with excitement, close to the officer's side. "Listen to me: as it chances, I know the man. There is no one here but I who knows the man. It shows how little you know if you think that idiot is Lew. I'm a respectable lady of this place, but I've been in America, and I know the man. I've seen him—I've seen him tried for his life and get off; and if you drivel on like that, he'll get off again. _That_ Lew!" she cried, with a hysterical laugh,—"Lew the devil, Lew the road-agent! That man's like a sheep. Do you hear me, do you hear me? You'll let him escape again."

Now was the time for Robbie to speak, for his mother to speak, and say, "That is the man!" But Mrs Ogilvy was absorbed tearing in vain at the hand-cuffs, repeating unconsciously her exclamation, "My son, my son!" And he stood looking down upon her and her vain struggle, and upon his own imprisoned hands. I doubt whether she knew what was passing, or was conscious of anything but of one thing—which was Robbie in those disgraceful bonds. But he in his dull soul, forced into enlightenment by the catastrophe, was very conscious of everything, and especially that he was betrayed—that he himself was being left to bear the brunt, and that his friend in his character was stealing away.

Janet had been kept back, partly by fright and astonishment, partly by the police and Andrew, the last of whom had a fast hold upon her gown, and bade her under his breath to "Keep out o't — keep out o't; we can do nothing:" but this restraint she could no longer bear. Her desire to be in the midst of everything, to be by her mistress's side, to have her share of what was going on, would have been enough for her, even if she felt, as Andrew did, that she could do no good. But Janet was of no such opinion. Was she not appealed to, as one whose testimony would put all right? She pushed her way from among the men, pulling her cotton gown, which tore audibly, out of Andrew's hand. "Sir, here am I: let me speak," she said. "This is Mr Robert Ogilvy, that I've known since ever he was born. He came home the 15th of June, the same day many weary years before as he ran away. The other gentleman is Mr Lewis, his friend, that followed him

here about a month ago at the most, a real fine good-
hearted gentleman, too, if maybe he has been a little
wild. Our gentleman is just as he was when he came
out of the deserts and wildernesses. We're not a
family that cares a great deal for appearances. But
Mr Lewis, he's of another way of thinking, and we've
had a great laughing all day at his shaving off of his
beard."

"That's what I told you!" said Mrs Ainslie, in her
excitement pulling the inspector's arm. "I told you
so! What's a beard? it is as easy to take off as a
bonnet. And he would have got clean off—look at
him, look at him!—if it hadn't been for me."

"Look after that man, you fellows there," said the
inspector's deep voice. "Don't let him get away.
Secure them both."

No one had put handcuffs on Lew's wrists; no
policeman had touched him; he had been free, with
all his wits about him, noting everything, alert, all
conscious, self-possessed. Twice he had almost got
away: the first time before Mrs Ainslie had interfered; the second when Janet with her evidence had
come forward, directing all attention once more to
Robbie—during which moment he had made his way
backward again in the most cautious way, endeavouring to get behind the backs of the men and make a
dash for the door. Almost! but what a difference
was that! The policemen, roused and startled,

hustled him forward to his "mate's" side, but still
without laying a hand upon him. All their suspicions
and observation were for the handcuffed criminal
standing silent and gloomy on the other side. Lew
maintained his careless attitude well, nodding at the
inspector, with a "Well, well, officer," as if he yielded
easily but half-contemptuously to punctilio. But
when he saw another constable draw from his pocket
another pair of handcuffs, he changed colour; his eyes
lighted up with a wild fire. Mrs Ainslie, who had got
beyond her own control, followed his movements with
the closest inspection. She burst into a laugh as he
grew pale. Her nerves were excited far beyond her
control. She cried out, without knowing, without
intending, "Ah, Lew! You have had more than
you meant. You've found more than you wanted.
Caught! caught at last. And you will not get off
this time," she cried, with the wild laugh which she
was quite unable to quench, or even to restrain.

Whether he saw what no doubt was true, that
every hope was over, and that, once conveyed to
Edinburgh, no further mistake was possible, and his
fate sealed; or whether he was moved by a swift wave
of passion, as happened to him from time to time—
and the exasperation of the woman's voice, which
worked him to madness—can never be known. He
was still quite free, untouched by any one; but the
handcuffs approaching which would make an end of

every independent act. His tall figure, and clean-
shaven, unveiled face seemed suddenly to rise and
tower over every other in the heat and pale glow
of passion. "You viper, Liz!" he thundered out.
"Music-hall Liz!" with a fierce laugh, "here's for you
— the traitor's pay!" And before any one could
breathe or speak, before a hand could be lifted, there
was a sudden flash and report, and in a moment he
had flung himself forward upon the two or three
startled men in front of him, with a rush for the open
door, and the pistol still smoking in his hand. Two
steps more, and he would have been out in the open,
in the fresh air that breathed like heaven upon him,
among the dark trees that give hiding and shelter, and
make a man, with his wits about him, a match for any
dozen. Two steps more! But rapid as he was, there
were too many of them to make such an escape possible. Before he had reached that open way, half-a-
dozen men were upon him. The struggle was but for
a moment — a wild sudden tumult of stamping feet
and loud voices; then there was again a sudden flash
and report and fall. The whole band seemed to fall
together—the men who had grappled with him being
dragged with him to the ground. They gathered themselves up one by one—everybody who could move: and
left the one on the ground who would never move
again.

He had so far succeeded in his rush that his head

z

fell outside the open door of the Hewan, where his face caught the calm line of the moonlight streaming in. The strange white radiance enveloped him, separating him from everything round—from the men who, struggling up to their feet, suddenly hushed and awestricken, stood hastily aside in the shadow, looking down upon the prisoner who had thus escaped from their hands. He lay right across the threshold in all his length and strength of limb,—motionless now, no struggle in him, quenched every resistance and alarm. It was so instantaneous, that the terrible event—that sudden, incalculable change of death, which is of all things in the world the most interesting and tremendous to all lookers-on—became doubly awful, falling, with a solemn chill and horror which paralysed them, upon the astonished men around. Dead! Yet a moment since flinging off the strongest, struggling against half-a-dozen, almost escaping from their hands. He had escaped now. None of them would willingly have laid a finger on him. They stood trembling round, who had been grappling him a minute before, keen for his subjugation. The curious moon, too still and cold for any ironical meaning, streamed on him from head to foot in the opening of the doorway, displaying him as if to the regard of men and angels, with a white blaze upon his upturned face, and here and there a strong silver line where an edge of his clothing caught the whiteness in relief. Everything else was in shadow, or in the trembling uncertainty of the indoor light. The pistol, still with a little smoke from it, which curled for a moment into the shining light and disappeared, was still in his hand.

This was the end of that strange visit to the little tranquil house, where he had introduced so much disturbance, so strange an overturning of every habit. He had taken it for his rest and refuge, like a master in a place where every custom of the tranquil life, and every principle and sentiment, cried out against him. He had made the son his slave, but yet had not made the mother his enemy. And yet a more wonderful thing had happened to Lew. He, whom nobody had loved in his life, save those whose vile affections can be bought for pay, and who dishonour the name—and for whom nobody would have wept had he not strayed into this peaceful abode and all but ruined and destroyed it—had tears shed for him here. Had he never come to the Hewan—to shed misery and terror around him, to kill and ruin, to rob and slay, as for some time at least he had intended—there would have been no lament made for the adventurer. But kind nature gained him this much in his end, though he no way deserved it. And the moonlight made him look like a hero slain in its defence upon the threshold of the outraged house,—the only house in the world where prayer had ever been said for this abandoned soul.

CHAPTER XXIV.

IT was only when that extraordinary momentary tragedy was over, and the hush of silence, overawed and thunder-stricken, had taken the place of the tumult, that it became apparent to most of the spectators that all was not over, that there was yet something to be done. "Let some one go for the nearest doctor," the inspector said quickly.

"No need for any doctors here, sir," said the men in concert.

"Go at once; you, Young, that know where to find one: and some of you go with him, to lose no time. There's a woman shot beside," said the officer in his curt tones of command.

But the woman shot was not Mrs Ainslie, at whom the pistol was levelled. These three visitors, so strangely mixed up in the *mêlée* and in the confusion of events, had been hustled about among the policemen, to the consternation of the father and daughter, who could not explain to themselves at first what was going on, nor what their companion had to do with it. As the course of the affair advanced, Mr Logan began to perceive, as has been said, that it was a special providence which had brought him here; but Susie, troubled and full of anguish, her whole heart absorbed in Robbie and his mother, and the mysterious trouble which she did not understand, which was hanging over them, stood alone, pressed back against the wall, following every movement of her friends, suffering with them. A sharp cry had come out of her very heart when the handcuffs—those dreadful signs of shame—were put upon his hands. She saw nothing, thought of nothing, but these two figures—what was any other to her?—and all that she understood or divined was that some dreadful trouble had happened to Robbie, and that she could not help him. She took no notice of her future step-mother's strange proceedings, nor of the extraordinary fact that she had forced herself into the midst of it—she, a stranger—and was adding her foolish shrill opinion to the discussion. If Susie thought of Mrs Ainslie at all, it was with a passing reflection that she loved to be in the midst of everything, which was far too trifling a thought to occupy Susie in the deep distress of sympathy in which she was. Her father moved about helplessly among the men. He thought he had been brought there by a special providence, but he did not know what to do.

Mrs Ogilvy had turned upon him almost fiercely, when he had hesitated in giving his testimony for Robbie— which was not from any lack of kindness, but solely because he wanted to say a great deal on the subject. Mrs Ogilvy by this time had come a little to herself, she had given up the foolish struggle with the hand-cuffs; and when Janet's over-frankness had drawn attention again to Lew, the mistress withdrew for a moment her own anxious looks from her son, and turned to the other, of whom she had said nothing, protecting him instinctively, even in the face of Robbie's danger. But when she looked at Lew's face, she trembled. The horror of last night came over her once more. Was that murder that was in it, the fire of hell? She had learned now what it meant when he put his hand to his pocket, and hers, perhaps, was the only eye that saw that gesture. He was looking at some one: was it at her, was it at some one behind her? Mrs Ogilvy instinctively made a step back, whether to escape in her own person, or to protect that other, she knew not, her eyes fixed on him with a fascination of terror. She stretched out her arms, with her shawl covering them like wings, facing him always, stretching forth what was like a white shield between him in his fury and all the unarmed defence-less people. She seemed to feel nothing but the sharp sound of the report, which rang through and through her. She did not know why she fell. There came a

shriek from the woman behind her, at whom that
bullet was aimed; but the real victim fell softly without a cry, with a murmur of bewilderment, and the
sharp sound still ringing, ringing in her ears. The
man seemed to spring over her where she lay; but she
knew no more of what had happened, except that soft
arms came suddenly round her, and her head was
raised on some one's breast, and Susie's voice began to
sound over her, calling her name, asking where was
she hurt. She did not know she was hurt. It all
seemed to become natural again with the sound of
Susie's voice. She did not lose consciousness, though
she fell, and though it was evident now that the white
shawl was all dabbled with red. It was hard to tell
what it all meant, but yet there seemed some apology
wanted. " He did not mean it," she said; " he did not
mean it. There is—good in him." She laid her head
back on Susie's bosom with a soft look of content.
" It is maybe—not so bad as you think," she said.

The shot was in the shoulder, and the wound bled
a great deal. No ambulance classes nor amateur
doctoring had reached so far as Eskholm; but Susie
by the light of nature did all that was possible to stop
the bleeding until the doctor came. She sent Janet
off for cushions and pillows, to make so far as she
could an impromptu bed, that the sufferer might rest
more easily. Most of the police party had been
ordered outside, though two of them still stood, a

living screen, between the group round the wounded
woman and that figure lying in the doorway, which
was not to be disturbed till the doctor came, some one
having found or fancied a faint flutter in the heart.
Mrs Ainslie, to do her justice, had been totally overwhelmed for the moment. She had flung herself down
on her knees by Mrs Ogilvy's side, weeping violently,
her face hidden in her hands. She was of no help in
the dreadful strait; but at least she was in a condition
of excitement and shattered nerves from which no help
could be expected. Mr Logan had not taken any
notice of her, though he was not yet aroused to any
questions as to her behaviour and position here. He
was moving about with soft suppressed steps from one
side to another, in an agony of desire to do his duty,
and consciousness of having been brought by a special
providence. But the minister was appalled by the
dead face in the moonlight, the great figure fallen like
a tower. When it was said there was still life in him,
he knelt down heroically by Lew's side, and tried to
whisper into his ear an entreaty that still at the
eleventh hour he should prepare to meet his God.
And then he came round and looked over his daughter's head at Mrs Ogilvy. Ought he to recall to her
mind the things that concerned her peace as long as
she was able to hear? But the words died on the
minister's lips. He was a good man, though he was
not quick to understand, or able to divine. His lips

moved with the conventional phrases which belonged
to his profession, which it was his duty to say; but he
could not utter any of them. He felt with a curious
stupefied sense of reality that most likely after all
God was here, and knew more perfectly all about it
than he.

Meanwhile, the chief person in this scene lay quite
still, not suffering as appeared, very quiet and tranquil
in her mind, Susie's arm supporting her, and her head
on Susie's breast. The bleeding had almost stopped,
partly because of the complete peace, partly from
Susie's expedients. Mrs Ogilvy, no doubt, thought
she was dying; but it did not disturb her. The loss
of blood had reduced her to that state of weakness in
which there is no struggle. Impressions passed lightly
over her brain in its confusion. Sometimes she asked
a question, and then forgot what it was, and the
answer to it together. She was aware of a coming
and going in the place, a sense of movement, the
strange voices and steps of the men about; but they
were all part of the turmoil, and she paid no attention
to them. Only she roused a little when Robbie stood
near: he looked so large, when one looked up at him
lying stretched out on the floor. He was talking to
some one gravely, standing up, a free man, talking and
moving like the master of the house. She smiled and
held out a feeble hand to him, and he came immediately and knelt down by her side. "He did not

mean it," she said.   And then, "It is maybe not so
bad as you think."   These were the little phrases
which she had got by heart.

He patted her on the sound shoulder with a large
trembling hand, and bade her be quiet, very quiet, till
the doctor came.

"You have not left me, Robbie?"

"No, mother."   His voice trembled very much,
and he stooped and kissed her.   "Never, never any
more!"

She smiled at him, lying there contented, with her
head on Susie's breast—joyful, but not surprised by
this news, for nothing could surprise her now—
and then she motioned to him to come closer, and
whispered, "Has he got away?"

The appearance of the doctor, notwithstanding his
pause and exclamation of horror at the door, was an
unspeakable relief.   That cry conveyed no information to the patient within, who did not seem even to
require an answer to her question.   There was no
question any longer of any fluttering of Lew's heart.
The slight shake of the doctor's head, the look on his
face, his rapid, low-spoken directions for the removal
of the dead man, renewed the dreadful commotion of
the night for a moment.   And then he had Mrs
Ogilvy removed on the mattress which his skilled
hands helped to place her on, into her own parlour,
where he examined her wound.   She was still quite

conscious, and told him over again her old phrases.
" He did not mean it,"—and " Maybe it will not be
so ill as you think," — with a smile which wavered
between consciousness and unconsciousness. Her
troubled brain had got those words as it were by
heart. She said them many times over during the
course of the long and feverish night, during which
she saw many visions, glimpses of her son bending
over her, smoothing her pillow, touching her with
ignorant tender hands, glimpses of Susie sitting
beside her, coming and going. They were all
dreams, she knew — but sometimes dreams are
sweet. She was ill somehow — but oh, how im-
measurably content !

This catastrophe made Robert Ogilvy a man—at
least it gave him the courage and sense which since
his arrival at home he seemed to have lost. He gave
the police inspector an account of the man who was
dead, who could no longer be extradited or tried,
in Scotland or elsewhere. He did not conceal that
he himself had been more or else connected with
the troop which Lew had led. The inspector nodded.
" We know all about that," he said ; " we know you
didn't count," which pricked Robbie all the more, half
with the sense of injured pride, to prove that now
at least he did count. His story filled up all that
the authorities had wanted to know. What Lew's
antecedents were, what his history had been, mattered

nothing in this country. They mattered very little even in that from which he came; and where already his adventures had dropped into the legends of the road which we still hear from America with wonder, as if the days of Turpin were not over. No one doubted Robert Ogilvy's word. He felt for the first time, on this night, when for a brief and terrible moment he had worn handcuffs, and borne the brand of shame—and when he had felt that he was about to be left to stand in another man's name for his life —that he was now a known person, the master, at least in a secondary sense, of a house which "counted," though it was not a great house: and that he had, what he had never been conscious before of having, a local habitation and a name. Robbie was very much overpowered by this discovery, as well as by the other incidents of the night. He was not perhaps deeply moved by grief for his friend. The man had not been his friend; he had been his master, capable of fascinating and holding him, with an influence which he could not resist. But whenever he was removed from that influence, his mind and spirit had rebelled against it. Now it seemed impossible, too wonderful to believe, that he was free, that Lew's voice would never call him back, nor Lew's will rule him again. But neither was he glad. Lew had led him very far in these few days—almost to the robbing, almost to the killing, of his mother—his mother, who had fought for them both like a lion, who had done everything and dared everything for their sakes. But the slave, the bondsman, though he felt the thrill of his freedom in his veins, did not rejoice in the death of his taskmaster. It was too recent, too terrible, too tragical for that. The sight of that familiar face lying in the moonlight was always before him—he could not get it out of his eyes. He did not attempt to go to bed, but walked up and down, sometimes going into the drawing-room where his mother lay, with a wonderful tenderness towards her, altogether new to his consciousness, and understanding of the part she had played. He had never thought of this before. It had seemed to him merely the course of nature, what was to be expected, the sort of thing women did, and were glad and proud to be permitted to do. To have a son to do everything for was her delight. Why should not the son take it as such?—she was pleasing herself. That was what he had always thought,—he awakened to a different sense, another appreciation, not perhaps very vivid, but yet genuine. She had almost been killed for her love—surely there was something in it after all, more than the course of nature. He was very sorry for her, to see her lying there with little spots of blood upon her white night-dress, and the shawl all covered with blood laid aside in the corner. Poor mother! She was old and she was weak, and most likely she would die of it. And it was Lew's doing, and all for his own sake.

The house had once more become still. The crowd of people who had so suddenly taken possession of it had surged away. No one knew how it was that Mr Logan and his daughter and the lady who was going to be his wife had appeared in that strange scene, and no one noted how at least the last-named person disappeared. One moment she was kneeling on the floor, in wild fits of convulsive weeping, her hat pushed back from her head, her light hair hanging loose, wholly lost in trouble and distress: the next she was gone. She had indeed stolen away in the commotion caused by the arrival of the doctor, when Mrs Ogilvy was taken away, and that tragic obstruction removed from the doorway. It is to be supposed that she had come to herself by that time. She managed to steal out unseen, though with a shudder crossing the threshold where Lew had lain. It was she doubly, both in her betrayal of him, and in her exasperation of him, who was the cause of all; but probably she did not realise that. She found her way somehow through the moonlight and the black shadows, along the road all slippery with the recent rain, to her own house, and there spent the night as best she might, packing up many things which she prized, clothes and trinkets, and the *bibelots*, which in their fashion and hers, she loved like her betters.

And early in the morning, by the first train, she went away—to Edinburgh, in the first place, and Eskholm saw her no more.

When the doctor's ministrations were over, for which Mr Logan waited to hear the result, the minister went into all the rooms looking for her. He had thought she was helping Susie at first; then, that she had retired somewhere in the excess of her feelings, which were more exquisite and delicate than those of common folk. He had in the excitement of the time never thought of as yet, or even begun to wonder at, the position she had assumed here, and the part she had taken. He knew that if his Elizabeth had a fault, it was that she liked to be always in the front, taking a foremost place in everything. He waited as long as he could, looking about everywhere; and then, when he was quite sure she was not to be found, and saw the doctor starting on his walk home, took his hat and went also. "You think it will not be fatal, doctor?"

"It may not be—I cannot answer for anything. She's very quiet, which is much in her favour. But how, in the name of all that is wonderful, did I find a dead man, whom I never saw in life, lying across the doorsteps of the Hewan, and a quiet old lady like Mrs Ogilvy struck almost to death with a pistol-shot?"

"It is a wonder indeed," said the minister. "I, if

ye will believe me, was led there, I cannot tell ye
how, with the idea of a common call—and found the
police all about the house.   It is just the most extraordinary special providence," said Mr Logan with
solemnity, "that I ever encountered in the course of
my life."   He began by this time to feel that he had
been of great use.   But he was a little troubled, poor
man, by the thought of his Elizabeth running home
by herself, as she must have done in the night.   He
passed her house on his way to the manse, and was
relieved to find that there was a light in her bedroom
window; but though he knocked and knocked again,
and even went so far as to throw up gravel at the
window, he could obtain no response.   He went home
full of thought.   There began to rise into his mind
recollections of things which he was not conscious of
having noticed at the time—of the energy with which
she had rushed to the front (but that was her way, he
reflected, with a faint smile) and insisted with the inspector: and then some one had called her Liz—Liz!
—who was it that had called her Liz?

Mr Logan's thoughts grew, through a night that was
not very comfortable to him more than to the other
persons involved.   The absence of Susie made things
worse.   He would not have spoken to Susie on such a
delicate subject, especially as she was already hostile;
but still, if Susie had been there—in her absence there
was an usual tumult in the house, and he had no one

to save him from it. And his mind was sorely troubled. She had taken a part last night that would not have been becoming in a minister's wife. He would speak to her about it: and was it—could it be—surely it was that robber villain, the suicide, the murderer, who had called her Liz? It added to all his troubles, that when he had finally made up his mind to go to her—she not coming to him, as was her habit in the morning—he found her gone. Away to Edinburgh with the first train, leaving her boxes packed, and a message that they would be sent for, her bewildered maid said. Mr Logan returned home, a sorely disturbed man. But he never saw more the woman who had so nearly been his wife. There was truth in the story she told her daughter and son-in-law in Edinburgh, that the scene she had witnessed had completely shattered her nerves, and that she did not think she could ever face the associations of that dreadful place again. She did not cheat anybody or rob anybody, but left her little affairs at Eskholm in Tom Blair's hands, who paid everything scrupulously. I don't know that he ever was repaid; but he saw very little of his mother-in-law after this extraordinary overturn of her fate.

Mrs Ogilvy's wound took a long time to heal, but it did heal in the end. She was very weak, but had for a long time that wonderful exemption from care which is usually the privilege of the dying, though she did not die. Perhaps there was no time of her life when

2 A

she was happier than during these weeks of illness. Susie was by her bedside night and day. Robbie came in continually, a large shadow standing over her, staying but a moment at first, then longer, sitting by her, talking to her, answering her questions. I do not know that there was soon or fundamentally a great moral improvement in Robbie; but he had been startled into anxiety and kindness, and a little went a long way with those two women, who loved him. For there was little doubt in any mind, except perhaps in his own, that Susie loved him too, with something of the same tolerant, all-explaining, all-pardoning love which was in his mother's heart. She had done so all her life, waiting for him all those years, through which he never thought of her: that did not matter to Susie,—nobody had ever touched her faithful simple heart but he. She would not perhaps have been an unhappy woman had he never come back: she would have gone on looking for him with a vague and visionary hope, which would have lent a grace to her gentle being, maiden-mother as she had been born. And even this wild episode, which she never quite understood, which she never desired to understand, made no difference to Susie. She forgave it all to the man who was dead, and shed tears over the horror of his fate; but she put easily all the blame upon him. Robbie had been faithful to the death for him, would have gone away instead of him to save him.

It covered Lew with a shining mantle of charity that
he called forth so much that was noble in his friend.

The minister, who was shamed to the heart, and
wounded in his *amour propre* beyond expression by
the desertion of Mrs Ainslie, and by the conviction,
slowly forced upon him, that she had deceived him,
and was no exquisite English lady of high pretensions
but an adventuress—felt that the only amends he
could make to himself and the world was to carry out
his intention of marrying, and that as quickly as possible. Providence, as he piously said, directed his
eyes to one of those kind old maids who fill up the
crevices of the world, and who are often so humbly
ready to take that position of nurse-housekeeper-wife,
in which perhaps they can be of more use to their
generation than in their solitude, and which satisfies,
I suppose, the wish to belong to somebody, and be the
first in some life, as well as the mother-yearning in
their hearts. Such a blessed solution of the difficulty
enchanted the parish, and satisfied the boys and the
little girls, who had now unlimited petting to look
forward to—and set Susie free. She married Robert
Ogilvy soon after his mother's recovery. Fortunately
Mrs Ogilvy was never conscious of the details of the
tragedy, and did not know ever what had lain there
in the moonlight across her threshold. I doubt if she
could have come and gone cheerfully as she did over
that door-stone had she ever known. And the young

ones full of their own life forgot—and the family of three continued in the Hewan in love and content. Robbie never became a model man. He never did anything, notwithstanding the fulness of his life and strength. He had no impulse to work—rather the reverse: his impulses were all in the way of idleness; he lounged about and occupied himself with trifles, and gardened a little, and carpentered a little, and was never weary. It fretted the two women often, sometimes the length of despair, especially Susie, who would burst out into regrets of all his talents lost, and the great things he might have done. But Mrs Ogilvy did not echo those regrets: she was well enough aware what Robbie's talents were, and the great things which he would never have done. She represented to her daughter-in-law that if he had been weary of the quiet, if he had grown moody, tired of his idleness, tired of his life, as some men do, there would then have been occasion to complain. "But he is just very happy, God bless him!" his mother said. "And you and me, Susie, we are two happy women; and the Lord be thanked for all He has done for us, and no suffered me to go down famished and fasting to the grave."

PRINTED BY WILLIAM BLACKWOOD AND SONS.

Catalogue

of

Messrs Blackwood & Sons'

Publications

PHILOSOPHICAL CLASSICS FOR ENGLISH READERS.

EDITED BY WILLIAM KNIGHT, LL.D.,

Professor of Moral Philosophy in the University of St Andrews.

In crown 8vo Volumes, with Portraits, price 3s. 6d.

Contents of the Series.

DESCARTES, by Professor Mahaffy, Dublin.—BUTLER, by Rev. W. Lucas Collins, M.A.—BERKELEY, by Professor Campbell Fraser.—FICHTE, by Professor Adamson, Owens College, Manchester. — KANT, by Professor Wallace, Oxford.—HAMILTON, by Professor Veitch, Glasgow. — HEGEL, by the Master of Balliol. — LEIBNIZ, by J.

Theodore Merz.—VICO, by Professor Flint, Edinburgh.—HOBBES, by Professor Croom Robertson.—HUME, by the Editor.—SPINOZA, by the Very Rev. Principal Caird, Glasgow. — BACON: Part I. The Life, by Professor Nichol.—BACON: Part II. Philosophy, by the same Author.—LOCKE, by Professor Campbell Fraser.

FOREIGN CLASSICS FOR ENGLISH READERS.

EDITED BY MRS OLIPHANT.

In crown 8vo, 2s. 6d.

Contents of the Series.

DANTE, by the Editor. — VOLTAIRE, by General Sir E. B. Hamley, K.C.B. —PASCAL, by Principal Tulloch. — PETRARCH, by Henry Reeve, C.B.—GOETHE, by A. Hayward, Q.C.—MOLIÈRE, by the Editor and F. Tarver, M.A.—MONTAIGNE, by Rev. W. L. Collins, M.A.—RABELAIS, by Walter Besant, M.A. — CALDERON, by E. J. Hasell. — SAINT SIMON, by Clifton W. Collins, M.A. — CERVANTES, by the

Editor. — CORNEILLE AND RACINE, by Henry M. Trollope. — MADAME DE SÉVIGNÉ, by Miss Thackeray.—LA FONTAINE, AND OTHER FRENCH FABULISTS, by Rev. W. Lucas Collins, M.A.—SCHILLER, by James Sime, M.A., Author of 'Lessing, his Life and Writings.'—TASSO, by E. J. Hasell. — ROUSSEAU, by Henry Grey Graham. — ALFRED DE MUSSET, by C. F. Oliphant.

ANCIENT CLASSICS FOR ENGLISH READERS.

EDITED BY THE REV. W. LUCAS COLLINS, M.A.

Complete in 28 Vols. crown 8vo, cloth, price 2s. 6d. each. And may also be had in 14 Volumes, strongly and neatly bound, with calf or vellum back, £3, 10s.

Contents of the Series.

HOMER: THE ILIAD, by the Editor.— HOMER: THE ODYSSEY, by the Editor.— HERODOTUS, by George C. Swayne, M.A.— XENOPHON, by Sir Alexander Grant, Bart., LL.D. — EURIPIDES, by W. B. Donne.— ARISTOPHANES, by the Editor.—PLATO, by Clifton W. Collins, M.A.—LUCIAN, by the Editor. — ÆSCHYLUS, by the Right Rev. the Bishop of Colombo. — SOPHOCLES, by Clifton W. Collins, M.A — HESIOD AND THEOGNIS, by the Rev. J. Davies, M.A.— GREEK ANTHOLOGY, by Lord Neaves.— VIRGIL, by the Editor.—HORACE, by Sir Theodore Martin, K.C.B. — JUVENAL, by Edward Walford, M.A. — PLAUTUS AND

TERENCE, by the Editor—THE COMMENTARIES OF CÆSAR, by Anthony Trollope. —TACITUS, by W. B. Donne.—CICERO, by the Editor. — PLINY'S LETTERS, by the Rev. Alfred Church, M.A., and the Rev. W. J. Brodribb, M.A. — LIVY, by the Editor.—OVID, by the Rev. A. Church, M.A. — CATULLUS, TIBULLUS, AND PROPERTIUS, by the Rev. Jas. Davies, M.A. — DEMOSTHENES, by the Rev. W. J. Brodribb, M.A.—ARISTOTLE, by Sir Alexander Grant, Bart., LL.D.—THUCYDIDES, by the Editor. — LUCRETIUS, by W. H. Mallock, M.A.—PINDAR, by the Rev. F. D. Morice, M.A.

Saturday Review.—"It is difficult to estimate too highly the value of such a series as this in giving 'English readers' an insight, exact as far as it goes, into those olden times which are so remote, and yet to many of us so close."

CATALOGUE

OF

MESSRS BLACKWOOD & SONS'

PUBLICATIONS.

ALISON.
History of Europe. By Sir ARCHIBALD ALISON, Bart., D.C.L.

1. From the Commencement of the French Revolution to the Battle of Waterloo.
LIBRARY EDITION, 14 vols., with Portraits. Demy 8vo, £10, 10s.
ANOTHER EDITION, in 20 vols. crown 8vo, £6.
PEOPLE'S EDITION, 13 vols. crown 8vo, £2, 11s.

2. Continuation to the Accession of Louis Napoleon.
LIBRARY EDITION, 8 vols. 8vo, £6, 7s. 6d.
PEOPLE'S EDITION, 8 vols. crown 8vo, 34s.

Epitome of Alison's History of Europe. Thirtieth Thousand, 7s. 6d.

Atlas to Alison's History of Europe. By A. Keith Johnston.
LIBRARY EDITION, demy 4to, £3, 3s.
PEOPLE'S EDITION, 31s. 6d.

Life of John Duke of Marlborough. With some Account of his Contemporaries, and of the War of the Succession. Third Edition. 2 vols. 8vo. Portraits and Maps, 30s.

Essays: Historical, Political, and Miscellaneous. 3 vols. demy 8vo, 45s.

ACROSS FRANCE IN A CARAVAN: BEING SOME ACCOUNT OF A JOURNEY FROM BORDEAUX TO GENOA IN THE "ESCARGOT," taken in the Winter 1889-90. By the Author of 'A Day of my Life at Eton.' With fifty Illustrations by John Wallace, after Sketches by the Author, and a Map. Cheap Edition, demy 8vo, 7s. 6d.

ACTA SANCTORUM HIBERNIÆ; Ex Codice Salmanticensi. Nunc primum integre edita opera CAROLI DE SMEDT et JOSEPHI DE BACKER, e Soc. Jesu, Hagiographorum Bollandianorum; Auctore et Sumptus Largiente JOANNE PATRICIO MARCHIONE BOTHAE. In One handsome 4to Volume, bound in half roxburghe, £2, 2s.; in paper cover, 31s. 6d.

AGRICULTURAL HOLDINGS ACT, 1883. With Notes by a MEMBER OF THE HIGHLAND AND AGRICULTURAL SOCIETY. 8vo, 3s. 6d.

AIKMAN.
Manures and the Principles of Manuring. By C. M. AIKMAN, D.Sc., F.R.S.E., &c., Professor of Chemistry, Glasgow Veterinary College; Examiner in Chemistry, University of Glasgow, &c. Crown 8vo, 6s. 6d.

Farmyard Manure: Its Nature, Composition, and Treatment. Crown 8vo 1s. 6d.

AIRD. Poetical Works of Thomas Aird. Fifth Edition, with Memoir of the Author by the Rev. JARDINE WALLACE, and Portrait. Crown 8vo, 7s. 6d.

ALLARDYCE.

Balmoral: A Romance of the Queen's Country. By ALEX-ANDER ALLARDYCE. 3 vols. crown 8vo, 25s. 6d.

Earlscourt: A Novel of Provincial Life. 3 vols. crown 8vo, 25s. 6d.

The City of Sunshine. New and Revised Edition. Crown 8vo, 6s.

Memoir of the Honourable George Keith Elphinstone, K.B., Viscount Keith of Stonehaven, Marischal, Admiral of the Red. 8vo, with Portrait, Illustrations, and Maps, 21s.

ALMOND. Sermons by a Lay Head-master. By HELY HUTCH-INSON ALMOND, M.A. Oxon., Head-master of Loretto School. Crown 8vo, 5s.

ANCIENT CLASSICS FOR ENGLISH READERS. Edited by Rev. W. LUCAS COLLINS, M.A. Price 2s. 6d. each. *For List of Vols., see p. 2.*

ANNALS OF A FISHING VILLAGE. By "A SON OF THE MARSHES." *See page 28.*

AYTOUN.

Lays of the Scottish Cavaliers, and other Poems. By W. EDMONDSTOUNE AYTOUN, D.C.L., Professor of Rhetoric and Belles-Lettres in the University of Edinburgh. New Edition. Fcap. 8vo, 3s. 6d.
    ANOTHER EDITION. Fcap. 8vo, 7s. 6d.
    CHEAP EDITION. 1s. Cloth, 1s. 3d.

An Illustrated Edition of the Lays of the Scottish Cavaliers. From designs by Sir NOEL PATON. Small 4to, in gilt cloth, 21s.

Bothwell: a Poem. Third Edition. Fcap., 7s. 6d.

Poems and Ballads of Goethe. Translated by Professor AYTOUN and Sir THEODORE MARTIN, K.C.B. Third Edition. Fcap., 6s.

Bon Gaultier's Book of Ballads. By the SAME. Fifteenth Edition. With Illustrations by Doyle, Leech, and Crowquill. Fcap. 8vo, 5s.

The Ballads of Scotland. Edited by Professor AYTOUN. Fourth Edition. 2 vols. fcap. 8vo, 12s.

Memoir of William E. Aytoun, D.C.L. By Sir THEODORE MARTIN, K.C.B. With Portrait. Post 8vo, 12s.

BACH.

On Musical Education and Vocal Culture. By ALBERT B. BACH. Fourth Edition. 8vo, 7s. 6d.

The Principles of Singing. A Practical Guide for Vocalists and Teachers. With Course of Vocal Exercises. Crown 8vo, 6s.

The Art of Singing. With Musical Exercises for Young People. Crown 8vo, 3s.

The Art Ballad: Loewe and Schubert. With Musical Illustrations. With a Portrait of LOEWE. Third Edition. Small 4to, 5s.

BAIRD LECTURES.

Theism. By Rev. Professor FLINT, D.D., Edinburgh. Eighth Edition. Crown 8vo, 7s. 6d.

Anti-Theistic Theories. By the SAME. Fifth Edition. Crown 8vo, 10s. 6d.

The Inspiration of the Holy Scriptures. By Rev. ROBERT JAMIESON, D.D. Crown 8vo, 7s. 6d.

BAIRD LECTURES.

The Early Religion of Israel. As set forth by Biblical Writers and modern Critical Historians. By Rev. Professor ROBERTSON, D.D., Glasgow. Fourth Edition. Crown 8vo, 10s. 6d.

The Mysteries of Christianity. By Rev. Professor CRAWFORD, D.D. Crown 8vo, 7s. 6d.

Endowed Territorial Work : Its Supreme Importance to the Church and Country. By Rev. WILLIAM SMITH, D.D. Crown 8vo, 6s.

BALLADS AND POEMS. By MEMBERS OF THE GLASGOW BALLAD CLUB. Crown 8vo, 7s. 6d.

BANNATYNE. Handbook of Republican Institutions in the United States of America. Based upon Federal and State Laws, and other reliable sources of information. By DUGALD J. BANNATYNE, Scotch Solicitor, New York ; Member of the Faculty of Procurators, Glasgow. Crown 8vo, 7s. 6d.

BELLAIRS.

The Transvaal War, 1880-81. Edited by Lady BELLAIRS. With a Frontispiece and Map. 8vo, 15s.

Gossips with Girls and Maidens, Betrothed and Free. New Edition. Crown 8vo, 3s. 6d. Cloth, extra gilt edges, 5s.

BELLESHEIM. History of the Catholic Church of Scotland. From the Introduction of Christianity to the Present Day. By ALPHONS BELLESHEIM, D.D., Canon of Aix-la-Chapelle. Translated, with Notes and Additions, by D. OSWALD HUNTER BLAIR, O.S.B., Monk of Fort Augustus. Complete in 4 vols. demy 8vo, with Maps. Price 12s. 6d. each.

BENTINCK. Racing Life of Lord George Cavendish Bentinck, M.P., and other Reminiscences. By JOHN KENT, Private Trainer to the Goodwood Stable. Edited by the Hon. FRANCIS LAWLEY. With Twenty-three full-page Plates, and Facsimile Letter. Third Edition. Demy 8vo, 25s.

BESANT.

The Revolt of Man. By WALTER BESANT. Tenth Edition. Crown 8vo, 3s. 6d.

Readings in Rabelais. Crown 8vo, 7s. 6d.

BEVERIDGE.

Culross and Tulliallan; or Perthshire on Forth. Its History and Antiquities. With Elucidations of Scottish Life and Character from the Burgh and Kirk-Session Records of that District. By DAVID BEVERIDGE. 2 vols. 8vo, with Illustrations, 42s.

Between the Ochils and the Forth ; or, From Stirling Bridge to Aberdour. Crown 8vo, 6s.

BICKERDYKE. A Banished Beauty. By JOHN BICKERDYKE, Author of ' Days in Thule, with Rod, Gun, and Camera,' ' The Book of the All-Round Angler,' ' Curiosities of Ale and Beer,' &c. With Illustrations. Crown 8vo, 6s.

BIRCH.

Examples of Stables, Hunting-Boxes, Kennels, Racing Establishments, &c. By JOHN BIRCH, Architect, Author of ' Country Architecture,' &c. With 30 Plates. Royal 8vo, 7s.

Examples of Labourers' Cottages, &c. With Plans for Improving the Dwellings of the Poor in Large Towns. With 34 Plates. Royal 8vo, 7s.

Picturesque Lodges. A Series of Designs for Gate Lodges, Park Entrances, Keepers', Gardeners', Bailiffs', Grooms', Upper and Under Servants' Lodges, and other Rural Residences. With 16 Plates. 4to, 12s. 6d.

BLACK. Heligoland and the Islands of the North Sea. By WILLIAM GEORGE BLACK. Crown 8vo, 4s.

BLACKIE.

Lays and Legends of Ancient Greece. By JOHN STUART BLACKIE, Emeritus Professor of Greek in the University of Edinburgh. Second Edition. Fcap. 8vo, 5s.

BLACKIE.

The Wisdom of Goethe. Fcap. 8vo. Cloth, extra gilt, 6s.

Scottish Song : Its Wealth, Wisdom, and Social Significance.
Crown 8vo. With Music. 7s. 6d.

A Song of Heroes. Crown 8vo, 6s.

BLACKMORE. The Maid of Sker. By R. D. Blackmore,
Author of 'Lorna Doone,' &c. New Edition. Crown 8vo, 6s.

BLACKWOOD.

Blackwood's Magazine, from Commencement in 1817 to October 1894. Nos. 1 to 948, forming 155 Volumes.

Index to Blackwood's Magazine. Vols. 1 to 50. 8vo, 15s.

Tales from Blackwood. First Series. Price One Shilling each,
in Paper Cover. Sold separately at all Railway Bookstalls.
They may also be had bound in 12 vols., cloth, 18s. Half calf, richly gilt, 30s.
Or the 12 vols. in 6, roxburghe, 21s. Half red morocco, 28s.

Tales from Blackwood. Second Series. Complete in Twenty-
four Shilling Parts. Handsomely bound in 12 vols., cloth, 30s. In leather back,
roxburghe style, 37s. 6d. Half calf, gilt, 52s. 6d. Half morocco, 55s.

Tales from Blackwood. Third Series. Complete in Twelve
Shilling Parts. Handsomely bound in 6 vols., cloth, 15s.; and in 12 vols., cloth,
18s. The 6 vols. in roxburghe, 21s. Half calf, 25s. Half morocco, 28s.

Travel, Adventure, and Sport. From 'Blackwood's Magazine.'
Uniform with 'Tales from Blackwood.' In Twelve Parts, each price 1s. Handsomely bound in 6 vols., cloth, 15s. And in half calf, 25s.

New Educational Series. *See separate Catalogue.*

New Uniform Series of Novels (Copyright).
Crown 8vo, cloth. Price 3s. 6d. each. Now ready :—

The Story of Margrédel. By D. Storrar Meldrum.

Miss Marjoribanks. By Mrs Oliphant.

The Perpetual Curate, and The Rector. By the Same.

Salem Chapel, and The Doctor's Family. By the Same.

A Sensitive Plant. By E. D. Gerard.

Lady Lee's Widowhood. By General Sir E. B. Hamley.

Katie Stewart, and other Stories. By Mrs Oliphant.

Valentine, and his Brother. By the Same.

Sons and Daughters. By the Same.

Marmorne. By P. G. Hamerton.

Reata. By E. D. Gerard.

Beggar my Neighbour. By the Same.

The Waters of Hercules. By the Same.

Fair to See. By L. W. M. Lockhart.

Mine is Thine. By the Same.

Doubles and Quits. By the Same.

Hurrish. By the Hon. Emily Lawless.

Altiora Peto. By Laurence Oliphant.

Piccadilly. By the Same. With Illustrations.

The Revolt of Man. By Walter Besant.

Lady Baby. By D. Gerard.

The Blacksmith of Voe. By Paul Cushing.

The Dilemma. By the Author of 'The Battle of Dorking.'

My Trivial Life and Misfortune. By A Plain Woman.

Poor Nellie. By the Same.

Others in preparation.

Standard Novels. Uniform in size and binding. Each
complete in one Volume.

FLORIN SERIES, Illustrated Boards. Bound in Cloth, 2s. 6d.

Tom Cringle's Log. By Michael Scott.

The Cruise of the Midge. By the Same.

Cyril Thornton. By Captain Hamilton.

Annals of the Parish. By John Galt.

The Provost, &c. By the Same.

Sir Andrew Wylie. By the Same.

The Entail. By the Same.

Miss Molly. By Beatrice May Butt.

Reginald Dalton. By J. G. Lockhart.

Pen Owen. By Dean Hook.

Adam Blair. By J. G. Lockhart.

Lady Lee's Widowhood. By General Sir E. B. Hamley.

Salem Chapel. By Mrs Oliphant.

The Perpetual Curate. By the Same.

Miss Marjoribanks. By the Same.

John : A Love Story. By the Same.

BLACKWOOD.
Standard Novels.
SHILLING SERIES, Illustrated Cover. Bound in Cloth, 1s. 6d.

THE RECTOR, and THE DOCTOR'S FAMILY. By Mrs Oliphant.
THE LIFE OF MANSIE WAUCH. By D. M. Moir.
PENINSULAR SCENES AND SKETCHES. By F. Hardman.

SIR FRIZZLE PUMPKIN, NIGHTS AT MESS, &c.
THE SUBALTERN.
LIFE IN THE FAR WEST. By G. F. Ruxton.
VALERIUS: A Roman Story. By J. G. Lockhart.

BON GAULTIER'S BOOK OF BALLADS. Fifteenth Edition. With Illustrations by Doyle, Leech, and Crowquill. Fcap. 8vo, 5s.

BONNAR. Biographical Sketch of George Meikle Kemp, Architect of the Scott Monument, Edinburgh. By THOMAS BONNAR, F.S.A. Scot., Author of 'The Present Art Revival,' &c. With Three Portraits and numerous Illustrations. Post 8vo, 7s. 6d.

BRADDON. Thirty Years of Shikar. By Sir EDWARD BRADDON, K.C.M.G. With numerous Illustrations. In 1 vol. demy 8vo. [*In the press.*]

BROUGHAM. Memoirs of the Life and Times of Henry Lord Brougham. Written by HIMSELF. 3 vols. 8vo, £2, 8s. The Volumes are sold separately, price 16s. each.

BROWN. The Forester: A Practical Treatise on the Planting and Tending of Forest-trees and the General Management of Woodlands. By JAMES BROWN, LL.D. Sixth Edition, Enlarged. Edited by JOHN NISBET, D.Œc., Author of 'British Forest Trees,' &c. In 2 vols. royal 8vo, with 350 Illustrations, 42s. net.

BROWN. Stray Sport. By J. MORAY BROWN, Author of 'Shikar Sketches,' 'Powder, Spur, and Spear,' 'The Days when we went Hog-Hunting.' 2 vols. post 8vo, with Fifty Illustrations, 21s.

BROWN. A Manual of Botany, Anatomical and Physiological. For the Use of Students. By ROBERT BROWN, M.A., Ph.D. Crown 8vo, with numerous Illustrations, 12s. 6d.

BROWN. The Book of the Landed Estate. Containing Directions for the Management and Development of the Resources of Landed Property. By ROBERT E. BROWN, Factor and Estate Agent. Royal 8vo, with Illustrations, 21s.

BRUCE.
In Clover and Heather. Poems by WALLACE BRUCE. New and Enlarged Edition. Crown 8vo, 4s. 6d.
A limited number of Copies of the First Edition, on large hand-made paper, 12s. 6d.
Here's a Hand. Addresses and Poems. Crown 8vo, 5s.
Large Paper Edition, limited to 100 copies, price 21s.

BRYDALL. Art in Scotland; its Origin and Progress. By ROBERT BRYDALL, Master of St George's Art School of Glasgow. 8vo, 12s. 6d.

BUCHAN. Introductory Text-Book of Meteorology. By ALEXANDER BUCHAN, LL.D., F.R.S.E., Secretary of the Scottish Meteorological Society, &c. New Edition. Crown 8vo, with Coloured Charts and Engravings. [*In preparation.*]

BUCHANAN. The Shirè Highlands (East Central Africa). By JOHN BUCHANAN, Planter at Zomba. Crown 8vo, 5s.

BURBIDGE.
Domestic Floriculture, Window Gardening, and Floral Decorations. Being practical directions for the Propagation, Culture, and Arrangement of Plants and Flowers as Domestic Ornaments. By F. W. BURBIDGE. Second Edition. Crown 8vo, with numerous Illustrations, 7s. 6d.
Cultivated Plants: Their Propagation and Improvement. Including Natural and Artificial Hybridisation, Raising from Seed, Cuttings, and Layers, Grafting and Budding, as applied to the Families and Genera in Cultivation. Crown 8vo, with numerous Illustrations, 12s. 6d.

BURGESS. Ragnarök. A Tale of the White Christ. By J. J. HALDANE BURGESS, Author of 'Rasmie's Büddie,' 'Shetland Sketches,' &c. Crown 8vo, 6s.

BURROWS. Commentaries on the History of England, from the Earliest Times to 1865. By MONTAGU BURROWS, Chichele Professor of Modern History in the University of Oxford; Captain R.N.; F.S.A., &c.; "Officier de l'Instruction Publique," France. Crown 8vo, 7s. 6d.

BURTON.
The History of Scotland: From Agricola's Invasion to the Extinction of the last Jacobite Insurrection. By JOHN HILL BURTON, D.C.L., Historiographer-Royal for Scotland. New and Enlarged Edition, 8 vols., and Index. Crown 8vo, £3, 3s.

History of the British Empire during the Reign of Queen Anne. In 3 vols. 8vo. 36s.

The Scot Abroad. Third Edition. Crown 8vo, 10s. 6d.

The Book-Hunter. New Edition. With Portrait. Crown 8vo, 7s. 6d.

BUTE.
The Roman Breviary: Reformed by Order of the Holy Œcumenical Council of Trent; Published by Order of Pope St Pius V.; and Revised by Clement VIII. and Urban VIII.; together with the Offices since granted. Translated out of Latin into English by JOHN, Marquess of Bute, K.T. In 2 vols. crown 8vo, cloth boards, edges uncut. £2, 2s.

The Altus of St Columba. With a Prose Paraphrase and Notes. In paper cover, 2s. 6d.

BUTT.
Miss Molly. By BEATRICE MAY BUTT. Cheap Edition, 2s.

Eugenie. Crown 8vo, 6s. 6d.

Elizabeth, and other Sketches. Crown 8vo, 6s.

Delicia. New Edition. Crown 8vo, 2s. 6d.

CAIRD.
Sermons. By JOHN CAIRD, D.D., Principal of the University of Glasgow. Seventeenth Thousand. Fcap. 8vo, 5s.

Religion in Common Life. A Sermon preached in Crathie Church, October 14, 1855, before Her Majesty the Queen and Prince Albert. Published by Her Majesty's Command. Cheap Edition, 3d.

CALDER. Chaucer's Canterbury Pilgrimage. Epitomised by WILLIAM CALDER. With Photogravure of the Pilgrimage Company, and other Illustrations, Glossary, &c. Crown 8vo, gilt edges, 4s. Cheaper Edition without Photogravure Plate. Crown 8vo, 2s. 6d.

CAMPBELL. Critical Studies in St Luke's Gospel: Its Demon-ology and Ebionitism. By COLIN CAMPBELL, D.D., Minister of the Parish of Dundee, formerly Scholar and Fellow of Glasgow University. Author of the 'Three First Gospels in Greek, arranged in parallel columns.' Post 8vo, 7s. 6d.

CAMPBELL. Sermons Preached before the Queen at Balmoral. By the Rev. A. A. CAMPBELL, Minister of Crathie. Published by Command of Her Majesty. Crown 8vo, 4s. 6d.

CAMPBELL. Records of Argyll. Legends, Traditions, and Re-collections of Argyllshire Highlanders, collected chiefly from the Gaelic. With Notes on the Antiquity of the Dress, Clan Colours, or Tartans of the Highlanders. By Lord ARCHIBALD CAMPBELL. Illustrated with Nineteen full-page Etchings. 4to, printed on hand-made paper, £3, 3s.

CANTON. A Lost Epic, and other Poems. By WILLIAM CANTON. Crown 8vo, 5s.

CARRICK. Koumiss; or, Fermented Mare's Milk: and its uses in the Treatment and Cure of Pulmonary Consumption, and other Wasting Diseases. With an Appendix on the best Methods of Fermenting Cow's Milk. By GEORGE L. CARRICK, M.D., L.R.C.S.E. and L.R.C.P.E., Physician to the British Embassy, St Petersburg, &c. Crown 8vo, 10s. 6d.

CARSTAIRS. British Work in India. By R. CARSTAIRS. Crown 8vo, 6s.

CAUVIN. A Treasury of the English and German Languages. Compiled from the best Authors and Lexicographers in both Languages. By JOSEPH CAUVIN, LL.D. and Ph.D., of the University of Göttingen, &c. Crown 8vo, 7s. 6d.

CAVE-BROWNE. Lambeth Palace and its Associations. By J. CAVE-BROWNE, M.A., Vicar of Detling, Kent, and for many years Curate of Lambeth Parish Church. With an Introduction by the Archbishop of Canterbury. Second Edition, containing an additional Chapter on Medieval Life in the Old Palaces. 8vo, with Illustrations, 21s.

CHARTERIS. Canonicity; or, Early Testimonies to the Existence and Use of the Books of the New Testament. Based on Kirchhoffer's 'Quellensammlung.' Edited by A. H. CHARTERIS, D.D., Professor of Biblical Criticism in the University of Edinburgh. 8vo, 18s.

CHENNELLS. Recollections of an Egyptian Princess. By her English Governess (Miss E. CHENNELLS). Being a Record of Five Years' Residence at the Court of Ismael Pasha, Khédive. Second Edition. With Three Portraits. Post 8vo, 7s. 6d.

CHESNEY. The Dilemma. By General Sir GEORGE CHESNEY, K.C.B., M.P., Author of 'The Battle of Dorking,' &c. New Edition. Crown 8vo, 3s. 6d.

CHRISTISON. Life of Sir Robert Christison, Bart., M.D., D.C.L. Oxon., Professor of Medical Jurisprudence in the University of Edinburgh. Edited by his SONS. In 2 vols. 8vo. Vol. I.—Autobiography. 16s. Vol. II.—Memoirs. 16s.

CHRONICLES OF WESTERLY: A Provincial Sketch. By the Author of 'Culmshire Folk,' 'John Orlebar,' &c. 3 vols. crown 8vo, 25s. 6d.

CHURCH SERVICE SOCIETY.
A Book of Common Order: being Forms of Worship issued by the Church Service Society. Sixth Edition. Crown 8vo, 6s. Also in 2 vols. crown 8vo, 6s. 6d.
Daily Offices for Morning and Evening Prayer throughout the Week. Crown 8vo, 3s. 6d.
Order of Divine Service for Children. Issued by the Church Service Society. With Scottish Hymnal. Cloth, 3d.

CLOUSTON. Popular Tales and Fictions: their Migrations and Transformations. By W. A. CLOUSTON, Editor of 'Arabian Poetry for English Readers,' &c. 2 vols. post 8vo, roxburghe binding, 25s.

COCHRAN. A Handy Text-Book of Military Law. Compiled chiefly to assist Officers preparing for Examination; also for all Officers of the Regular and Auxiliary Forces. Comprising also a Synopsis of part of the Army Act. By Major F. COCHRAN, Hampshire Regiment Garrison Instructor, North British District. Crown 8vo, 7s. 6d.

COLQUHOUN. The Moor and the Loch. Containing Minute Instructions in all Highland Sports, with Wanderings over Crag and Corrie, Flood and Fell. By JOHN COLQUHOUN. Cheap Edition. With Illustrations. Demy 8vo, 10s. 6d.

COLVILE. Round the Black Man's Garden. By ZÉLIE COLVILE, F.R.G.S. With 2 Maps and 50 Illustrations from Drawings by the Author and from Photographs. Demy 8vo, 16s.

CONSTITUTION AND LAW OF THE CHURCH OF SCOTLAND. With an Introductory Note by the late Principal Tulloch. New Edition, Revised and Enlarged. Crown 8vo, 3s. 6d.

COTTERILL. Suggested Reforms in Public Schools. By C. C. COTTERILL, M.A. Crown 8vo, 3s. 6d.

CRANSTOUN.

The Elegies of Albius Tibullus. Translated into English Verse, with Life of the Poet, and Illustrative Notes. By JAMES CRANSTOUN, LL.D., Author of a Translation of 'Catullus.' Crown 8vo, 6s. 6d.

The Elegies of Sextus Propertius. Translated into English Verse, with Life of the Poet, and Illustrative Notes. Crown 8vo, 7s. 6d.

CRAWFORD. An Atonement of East London, and other Poems. By HOWARD CRAWFORD, M.A. Crown 8vo, 5s.

CRAWFORD. Saracinesca. By F. MARION CRAWFORD, Author of 'Mr Isaacs,' &c. &c. Eighth Edition. Crown 8vo, 6s.

CRAWFORD.

The Doctrine of Holy Scripture respecting the Atonement. By the late THOMAS J. CRAWFORD, D.D., Professor of Divinity in the University of Edinburgh. Fifth Edition. 8vo, 12s.

The Fatherhood of God, Considered in its General and Special Aspects. Third Edition, Revised and Enlarged. 8vo, 9s.

The Preaching of the Cross, and other Sermons. 8vo, 7s. 6d.

The Mysteries of Christianity. Crown 8vo, 7s. 6d.

CROSS. Impressions of Dante, and of the New World ; with a Few Words on Bimetallism. By J. W. CROSS, Editor of 'George Eliot's Life, as related in her Letters and Journals.' Post 8vo, 6s.

CUSHING.

The Blacksmith of Voe. By PAUL CUSHING, Author of 'The Bull i' th' Thorn,' 'Cut with his own Diamond.' Cheap Edition. Crown 8vo, 3s. 6d.

DAVIES.

Norfolk Broads and Rivers ; or, The Waterways, Lagoons, and Decoys of East Anglia. By G. CHRISTOPHER DAVIES. Illustrated with Seven full-page Plates. New and Cheaper Edition. Crown 8vo, 6s.

Our Home in Aveyron. Sketches of Peasant Life in Aveyron and the Lot. By G. CHRISTOPHER DAVIES and Mrs BROUGHALL. Illustrated with full-page Illustrations. 8vo, 15s. Cheap Edition, 7s. 6d.

DE LA WARR. An Eastern Cruise in the 'Edeline.' By the Countess DE LA WARR. In Illustrated Cover. 2s.

DESCARTES. The Method, Meditations, and Principles of Philosophy of Descartes. Translated from the Original French and Latin. With a New Introductory Essay, Historical and Critical, on the Cartesian Philosophy. By Professor VEITCH, LL.D., Glasgow University. Tenth Edition. 6s. 6d.

DEWAR. Voyage of the "Nyanza," R.N.Y.C. Being the Record of a Three Years' Cruise in a Schooner Yacht in the Atlantic and Pacific, and her subsequent Shipwreck. By J. CUMMING DEWAR, late Captain King's Dragoon Guards and 11th Prince Albert's Hussars. With Two Autogravures, numerous Illustrations, and a Map. Demy 8vo, 21s.

DICKSON. Gleanings from Japan. By W. G. DICKSON, Author of 'Japan: Being a Sketch of its History, Government, and Officers of the Empire.' With Illustrations. 8vo, 16s.

DOGS, OUR DOMESTICATED : Their Treatment in reference to Food, Diseases, Habits, Punishment, Accomplishments. By 'MAGENTA.' Crown 8vo, 2s. 6d.

DOUGLAS. Chinese Stories. By ROBERT K. DOUGLAS. With numerous Illustrations by Parkinson, Forestier, and others. New and Cheaper Edition. Small demy 8vo, 5s.

DU CANE. The Odyssey of Homer, Books I.-XII. Translated into English Verse. By Sir CHARLES DU CANE, K.C.M.G. 8vo, 10s. 6d.

DUDGEON. History of the Edinburgh or Queen's Regiment Light Infantry Militia, now 3rd Battalion The Royal Scots; with an Account of the Origin and Progress of the Militia, and a Brief Sketch of the Old Royal Scots. By Major R. C. DUDGEON, Adjutant 3rd Battalion the Royal Scots. Post 8vo, with Illustrations, 10s. 6d.

DUNCAN. Manual of the General Acts of Parliament relating to the Salmon Fisheries of Scotland from 1828 to 1882. By J. BARKER DUNCAN. Crown 8vo, 5s.

DUNN. Red Cap and Blue Jacket: A Novel. By GEORGE DUNN. 3 vols. crown 8vo, 25s. 6d.

DUNSMORE. Manual of the Law of Scotland as to the Relations between Agricultural Tenants and the Landlords, Servants, Merchants, and Bowers. By W. DUNSMORE. 8vo, 7s. 6d.

DUPRÈ. Thoughts on Art, and Autobiographical Memoirs of Giovanni Duprè. Translated from the Italian by E. M. PERUZZI, with the permission of the Author. New Edition. With an Introduction by W. W. STORY. Crown 8vo, 10s. 6d.

ELIOT.

George Eliot's Life, Related in Her Letters and Journals. Arranged and Edited by her husband, J. W. CROSS. With Portrait and other Illustrations. Third Edition. 3 vols. post 8vo, 42s.

George Eliot's Life. (Cabinet Edition.) With Portrait and other Illustrations. 3 vols. crown 8vo, 15s.

George Eliot's Life. With Portrait and other Illustrations. New Edition, in one volume. Crown 8vo, 7s. 6d.

Works of George Eliot (Cabinet Edition). 21 volumes, crown 8vo, price £5, 5s. Also to be had handsomely bound in half and full calf. The Volumes are sold separately, bound in cloth, price 5s. each—viz. : Romola. 2 vols.—Silas Marner, The Lifted Veil, Brother Jacob. 1 vol.— Adam Bede. 2 vols.—Scenes of Clerical Life. 2 vols.—The Mill on the Floss. 2 vols.—Felix Holt. 2 vols.—Middlemarch. 3 vols.—Daniel Deronda. 3 vols.—The Spanish Gypsy. 1 vol.—Jubal, and other Poems, Old and New. 1 vol.—Theophrastus Such. 1 vol.—Essays. 1 vol.

Novels by George Eliot. Cheap Edition. Adam Bede. Illustrated. 3s. 6d., cloth.—The Mill on the Floss. Illustrated. 3s. 6d., cloth.—Scenes of Clerical Life. Illustrated. 3s., cloth.— Silas Marner: the Weaver of Raveloe. Illustrated. 2s. 6d., cloth.—Felix Holt, the Radical. Illustrated. 3s. 6d., cloth.—Romola. With Vignette. 3s. 6d., cloth.

Middlemarch. Crown 8vo, 7s. 6d.

Daniel Deronda. Crown 8vo, 7s. 6d.

Essays. New Edition. Crown 8vo, 5s.

Impressions of Theophrastus Such. New Edition. Crown 8vo, 5s.

The Spanish Gypsy. New Edition. Crown 8vo, 5s.

The Legend of Jubal, and other Poems, Old and New. New Edition. Crown 8vo, 5s.

Wise, Witty, and Tender Sayings, in Prose and Verse. Selected from the Works of GEORGE ELIOT. New Edition. Fcap. 8vo, 3s. 6d.

ELIOT.
The George Eliot Birthday Book. Printed on fine paper, with red border, and handsomely bound in cloth, gilt. Fcap. 8vo, 3s. 6d. And in French morocco or Russia, 5s.

ESSAYS ON SOCIAL SUBJECTS. Originally published in the 'Saturday Review.' New Edition. First and Second Series. 2 vols. crown 8vo, 6s. each.

FAITHS OF THE WORLD, The. A Concise History of the Great Religious Systems of the World. By various Authors. Crown 8vo, 5s.

FARRER. A Tour in Greece in 1880. By RICHARD RIDLEY FARRER. With Twenty-seven full-page Illustrations by Lord WINDSOR. Royal 8vo, with a Map, 21s.

FERRIER.
Philosophical Works of the late James F. Ferrier, B.A. Oxon., Professor of Moral Philosophy and Political Economy, St Andrews. New Edition. Edited by Sir ALEXANDER GRANT, Bart., D.C.L., and Professor LUSHINGTON. 3 vols. crown 8vo, 34s. 6d.

Institutes of Metaphysic. Third Edition. 10s. 6d.

Lectures on the Early Greek Philosophy. 4th Edition. 10s. 6d.

Philosophical Remains, including the Lectures on Early Greek Philosophy. New Edition. 2 vols. 24s.

FITZROY. Dogma and the Church of England. By A. I. FitzRoy. Post 8vo, 7s. 6d.

FLINT.
Historical Philosophy in France and French Belgium and Switzerland. By ROBERT FLINT, Corresponding Member of the Institute of France, Hon. Member of the Royal Society of Palermo, Professor in the University of Edinburgh, &c. 8vo, 21s.

Agnosticism. Being the Croall Lecture for 1887-88.
[In the press.

Theism. Being the Baird Lecture for 1876. Eighth Edition, Revised. Crown 8vo, 7s. 6d.

Anti-Theistic Theories. Being the Baird Lecture for 1877. Fifth Edition. Crown 8vo, 10s. 6d.

FOREIGN CLASSICS FOR ENGLISH READERS. Edited by Mrs OLIPHANT. Price 2s. 6d *For List of Volumes, see page 2.*

FOSTER. The Fallen City, and other Poems.. By WILL FOSTER. Crown 8vo, 6s.

FRANCILLON. Gods and Heroes; or, The Kingdom of Jupiter. By R. E. FRANCILLON. With 8 Illustrations. Crown 8vo, 5s.

FROM SPRING TO FALL; OR, WHEN LIFE STIRS. By "A SON OF THE MARSHES.' *See page 23.*

FULLARTON.
Merlin: A Dramatic Poem. By RALPH MACLEOD FULLARTON. Crown 8vo, 5s.

Tanhäuser. Crown 8vo, 6s.

Lallan Sangs and German Lyrics. Crown 8vo, 5s.

GALT. Novels by JOHN GALT. Fcap. 8vo, boards, each 2s.; cloth, 2s. 6d.
ANNALS OF THE PARISH.—THE PROVOST.—SIR ANDREW WYLIE.—THE ENTAIL.

GENERAL ASSEMBLY OF THE CHURCH OF SCOTLAND.
Scottish Hymnal, With Appendix Incorporated. Published
for use in Churches by Authority of the General Assembly. 1. Large type,
cloth, red edges, 2s. 6d.; French morocco, 4s. 2. Bourgeois type, limp cloth, 1s.;
French morocco, 2s. 3. Nonpareil type, cloth, red edges, 6d.; French morocco,
1s. 4d. 4. Paper covers, 3d. 5. Sunday-School Edition, paper covers, 1d.,
cloth, 2d. No. 1, bound with the Psalms and Paraphrases, French morocco, 8s.
No. 2, bound with the Psalms and Paraphrases, cloth, 2s.; French morocco, 3s.

Prayers for Social and Family Worship. Prepared by a
Special Committee of the General Assembly of the Church of Scotland. Entirely
New Edition, Revised and Enlarged. Fcap. 8vo, red edges, 2s.

Prayers for Family Worship. A Selection of Four Weeks'
Prayers. New Edition. Authorised by the General Assembly of the Church of
Scotland Fcap. 8vo, red edges, 1s. 6d.

One Hundred Prayers. Prepared by a Committee of the Gen-
eral Assembly of the Church of Scotland. 16mo, cloth limp.   [*In preparation.*

GERARD.
Reata : What's in a Name. By E. D. GERARD. Cheap
Edition. Crown 8vo, 3s. 6d.

Beggar my Neighbour. Cheap Edition. Crown 8vo, 3s. 6d.

The Waters of Hercules. Cheap Edition. Crown 8vo, 3s. 6d.

A Sensitive Plant. Crown 8vo, 3s. 6d.

GERARD.
The Land beyond the Forest. Facts, Figures, and Fancies
from Transylvania. By E. GERARD. With Maps and Illustrations. 2 vols. post
8vo, 25s.

Bis : Some Tales Retold. Crown 8vo, 6s.

A Secret Mission. 2 vols. crown 8vo, 17s.

GERARD.
Lady Baby. By DOROTHEA GERARD. Cheap Edition. Crown
8vo, 3s. 6d.

Recha. Second Edition. Crown 8vo, 6s.

The Rich Miss Riddell. Crown 8vo, 6s.

GERARD. Stonyhurst Latin Grammar. By Rev. JOHN GERARD.
Second Edition. Fcap. 8vo, 3s.

GILL.
Free Trade : an Inquiry into the Nature of its Operation.
By RICHARD GILL. Crown 8vo, 7s. 6d.

Free Trade under Protection. Crown 8vo, 7s. 6d.

GOETHE. Poems and Ballads of Goethe. Translated by Professor AYTOUN and Sir THEODORE MARTIN, K.C.B. Third Edition. Fcap. 8vo, 6s.

GOETHE'S FAUST. Translated into English Verse by Sir
THEODORE MARTIN, K.C.B. Part I. Second Edition, crown 8vo, 6s. Ninth Edition, fcap., 3s. 6d. Part II. Second Edition, Revised. Fcap. 8vo, 6s.

GORDON CUMMING.
At Home in Fiji. By C. F. GORDON CUMMING. Fourth
Edition, post 8vo. With Illustrations and Map. 7s. 6d.

A Lady's Cruise in a French Man-of-War. New and Cheaper
Edition. 8vo. With Illustrations and Map. 12s. 6d.

Fire-Fountains. The Kingdom of Hawaii : Its Volcanoes,
and the History of its Missions. With Map and Illustrations. 2 vols. 8vo, 25s.

Wanderings in China. New and Cheaper Edition. 8vo, with
Illustrations, 10s.

Granite Crags : The Yō-semité Region of California. Illustrated with 8 Engravings. New and Cheaper Edition. 8vo, 8s. 6d.

GRAHAM. The Life and Work of Syed Ahmed Khan, C.S.I.
By Lieut.-Colonel G. F. I. GRAHAM, B.S.C. 8vo, 14s.

GRAHAM. Manual of the Elections (Scot.) (Corrupt and Illegal Practices) Act, 1890. With Analysis, Relative Act of Sederunt, Appendix containing the Corrupt Practices Acts of 1883 and 1885, and Copious Index. By J. EDWARD GRAHAM, Advocate. 8vo, 4s. 6d.

GRAND.
A Domestic Experiment. By SARAH GRAND, Author of 'The Heavenly Twins,' 'Ideala: A Study from Life.' Crown 8vo, 6s.
Singularly Deluded. Crown 8vo, 6s.

GRANT. Bush-Life in Queensland. By A. C. GRANT. New Edition. Crown 8vo, 6s.

GRANT. Life of Sir Hope Grant. With Selections from his Correspondence. Edited by HENRY KNOLLYS, Colonel (H.P.) Royal Artillery, his former A.D.C., Editor of 'Incidents in the Sepoy War;' Author of 'Sketches of Life in Japan,' &c. With Portraits of Sir Hope Grant and other Illustrations. Maps and Plans. 2 vols. demy 8vo, 21s.

GRIER. In Furthest Ind. The Narrative of Mr EDWARD CARLYON of Ellswether, in the County of Northampton, and late of the Honourable East India Company's Service, Gentleman. Wrote by his own hand in the year of grace 1697. Edited, with a few Explanatory Notes, by SYDNEY C. GRIER. Post 8vo, 6s.

GUTHRIE-SMITH. Crispus: A Drama. By H. GUTHRIE-SMITH. Fcap. 4to, 5s.

HALDANE. Subtropical Cultivations and Climates. A Handy Book for Planters, Colonists, and Settlers. By R. C. HALDANE. Post 8vo, 9s.

HAMERTON.
Wenderholme: A Story of Lancashire and Yorkshire Life. By P. G. HAMERTON, Author of 'A Painter's Camp.' Crown 8vo, 6s.
Marmorne. New Edition. Crown 8vo, 3s. 6d.

HAMILTON.
Lectures on Metaphysics. By Sir WILLIAM HAMILTON, Bart., Professor of Logic and Metaphysics in the University of Edinburgh. Edited by the Rev. H. L. MANSEL, B.D., LL.D., Dean of St Paul's; and JOHN VEITCH, M.A., LL.D., Professor of Logic and Rhetoric, Glasgow. Seventh Edition. 2 vols. 8vo, 24s.
Lectures on Logic. Edited by the SAME. Third Edition, Revised. 2 vols., 24s.
Discussions on Philosophy and Literature, Education and University Reform. Third Edition. 8vo, 21s.
Memoir of Sir William Hamilton, Bart., Professor of Logic and Metaphysics in the University of Edinburgh. By Professor VEITCH, of the University of Glasgow. 8vo, with Portrait, 18s.
Sir William Hamilton: The Man and his Philosophy. Two Lectures delivered before the Edinburgh Philosophical Institution, January and February 1883. By Professor VEITCH. Crown 8vo, 2s.

HAMLEY.
The Operations of War Explained and Illustrated. By General Sir EDWARD BRUCE HAMLEY, K.C.B., K.C.M.G. Fifth Edition, Revised throughout. 4to, with numerous Illustrations, 30s.
National Defence; Articles and Speeches. Post 8vo, 6s.
Shakespeare's Funeral, and other Papers. Post 8vo, 7s 6d.
Thomas Carlyle: An Essay. Second Edition. Crown 8vo, 2s. 6d.
On Outposts. Second Edition. 8vo, 2s.
Wellington's Career; A Military and Political Summary. Crown 8vo, 2s.

HAMLEY.
Lady Lee's Widowhood. New Edition. Crown 8vo, 3s. 6d.
Cheaper Edition, 2s. 6d.
Our Poor Relations. A Philozoic Essay. With Illustrations,
chiefly by Ernest Griset. Crown 8vo, cloth gilt, 3s. 6d.
HARRADEN. In Varying Moods: Short Stories. By BEATRICE
HARRADEN, Author of 'Ships that Pass in the Night.' Ninth Edition. Crown
8vo, 3s. 6d.
HARRIS. A Journey through the Yemen, and some General
Remarks upon that Country. By WALTER B. HARRIS, F.R.G.S., Author of 'The
Land of an African Sultan; Travels in Morocco,' &c. With 3 Maps and numer-
ous Illustrations by Forestier and Wallace from Sketches and Photographs
taken by the Author. Demy 8vo, 16s.
HAWKER. The Prose Works of Rev. R. S. HAWKER, Vicar of
Morwenstow. Including 'Footprints of Former Men in Far Cornwall.' Re-
edited, with Sketches never before published. With a Frontispiece. Crown
8vo, 3s. 6d.
HAY. The Works of the Right Rev. Dr George Hay, Bishop of
Edinburgh. Edited under the Supervision of the Right Rev. Bishop STRAIN.
With Memoir and Portrait of the Author. 5 vols. crown 8vo, bound in extra
cloth, £1, 1s. The following Volumes may be had separately—viz.:
The Devout Christian Instructed in the Law of Christ from the Written
Word. 2 vols., 8s.—The Pious Christian Instructed in the Nature and Practice
of the Principal Exercises of Piety. 1 vol., 3s.
HEATLEY.
The Horse-Owner's Safeguard. A Handy Medical Guide for
every Man who owns a Horse. By G. S. HEATLEY, M.R.C.V.S. Crown 8vo, 5s.
The Stock-Owner's Guide. A Handy Medical Treatise for
every Man who owns an Ox or a Cow. Crown 8vo, 4s. 6d.
HEDDERWICK.
Lays of Middle Age; and other Poems. By JAMES HEDDER-
WICK, LL.D., Author of 'Backward Glances.' Price 3s. 6d.
HEMANS.
The Poetical Works of Mrs Hemans. Copyright Editions.
Royal 8vo, 5s. The Same with Engravings, cloth, gilt edges, 7s. 6d.
Select Poems of Mrs Hemans. Fcap., cloth, gilt edges, 3s.
HERKLESS. Cardinal Beaton: Priest and Politician. By
JOHN HERKLESS, Professor of Church History, St Andrews. With a Portrait.
Post 8vo, 7s. 6d.
HEWISON. The Isle of Bute in the Olden Time. With Illus-
trations, Maps, and Plans. By JAMES KING HEWISON, M.A., F.S.A. (Scot.),
Minister of Rothesay. Vol. I., Celtic Saints and Heroes. Crown 4to, 15s. net.
[*Vol II. in preparation.*
HOME PRAYERS. By Ministers of the Church of Scotland
and Members of the Church Service Society. Second Edition. Fcap. 8vo, 3s.
HOMER.
The Odyssey. Translated into English Verse in the Spen-
serian Stanza. By PHILIP STANHOPE WORSLEY. 3d Edition. 2 vols. fcap., 12s.
The Iliad. Translated by P. S. WORSLEY and Professor CON-
INGTON. 2 vols. crown 8vo, 21s.
HUTCHINSON. Hints on the Game of Golf. By HORACE G.
HUTCHINSON. Eighth Edition, Enlarged. Fcap. 8vo, cloth, 1s.
IDDESLEIGH.
Lectures and Essays. By the late EARL of IDDESLEIGH,
G.C.B., D.C.L., &c. 8vo, 16s.
Life, Letters, and Diaries of Sir Stafford Northcote, First
Earl of Iddesleigh. By ANDREW LANG. With Three Portraits and a View of
Pynes. Third Edition. 2 vols. post 8vo, 31s. 6d.
POPULAR EDITION. With Portrait and View of Pynes. Post 8vo, 7s. 6d.

INDEX GEOGRAPHICUS: Being a List, alphabetically arranged, of the Principal Places on the Globe, with the Countries and Subdivisions of the Countries in which they are situated, and their Latitudes and Longitudes. Imperial 8vo, pp. 676, 21s.

JEAN JAMBON. Our Trip to Blunderland ; or, Grand Excursion to Blundertown and Back. By JEAN JAMBON. With Sixty Illustrations designed by CHARLES DOYLE, engraved by DALZIEL. Fourth Thousand. Cloth, gilt edges, 6s. 6d. Cheap Edition, cloth, 3s. 6d. Boards, 2s. 6d.

JEBB. A Strange Career. The Life and Adventures of JOHN GLADWYN JEBB. By his Widow. With an Introduction by H. RIDER HAGGARD, and an Electrogravure Portrait of Mr Jebb. Small demy 8vo, 10s. 6d.

JENNINGS. Mr Gladstone : A Study. By LOUIS J. JENNINGS, M.P., Author of 'Republican Government in the United States,' 'The Croker Memoirs,' &c. Popular Edition. Crown 8vo, 1s.

JERNINGHAM.
Reminiscences of an Attaché. By HUBERT E. H. JERNINGHAM. Second Edition. Crown 8vo, 5s.
Diane de Breteuille. A Love Story. Crown 8vo, 2s. 6d.

JOHNSTON.
The Chemistry of Common Life. By Professor J. F. W. JOHNSTON. New Edition, Revised. By ARTHUR HERBERT CHURCH, M.A. Oxon.; Author of 'Food: its Sources, Constituents, and Uses,' &c. With Maps and 102 Engravings. Crown 8vo, 7s. 6d.
Elements of Agricultural Chemistry. An entirely New Edition from the Edition by Sir CHARLES A. CAMERON, M.D., F.R.C.S.I., &c. Revised and brought down to date by C. M. AIKMAN, M.A., B.Sc., F.R.S.E., Professor of Chemistry, Glasgow Veterinary College. Crown 8vo, 6s. 6d.
Catechism of Agricultural Chemistry. An entirely New Edition from the Edition by Sir CHARLES A. CAMERON. Revised and Enlarged by C. M. AIKMAN, M.A., &c. 92d Thousand. With numerous Illustrations. Crown 8vo, 1s.

JOHNSTON. Agricultural Holdings (Scotland) Acts, 1883 and 1889; and the Ground Game Act, 1880. With Notes, and Summary of Procedure, &c. By CHRISTOPHER N. JOHNSTON, M.A., Advocate. Demy 8vo, 5s.

JOKAI. Timar's Two Worlds. By MAURUS JOKAI. Authorised Translation by Mrs HEGAN KENNARD. Cheap Edition. Crown 8vo, 6s.

KEBBEL. The Old and the New : English Country Life. By T. E. KEBBEL, M.A., Author of 'The Agricultural Labourers,' 'Essays in History and Politics,' 'Life of Lord Beaconsfield.' Crown 8vo, 5s.

KING. The Metamorphoses of Ovid. Translated in English Blank Verse. By HENRY KING, M.A., Fellow of Wadham College, Oxford, and of the Inner Temple, Barrister-at-Law. Crown 8vo, 10s. 6d.

KINGLAKE.
History of the Invasion of the Crimea. By A. W. KINGLAKE. Cabinet Edition, Revised. With an Index to the Complete Work. Illustrated with Maps and Plans. Complete in 9 vols., crown 8vo, at 6s. each.
History of the Invasion of the Crimea. Demy 8vo. Vol. VI. Winter Troubles. With a Map, 16s. Vols. VII. and VIII. From the Morrow of Inkerman to the Death of Lord Raglan. With an Index to the Whole Work. With Maps and Plans. 28s.
Eothen. A New Edition, uniform with the Cabinet Edition of the 'History of the Invasion of the Crimea.' 6s.

KLEIN. Among the Gods. Scenes of India, with Legends by the Way. By AUGUSTA KLEIN. With Illustrations. In 1 vol. demy 8vo.
[In the press.

KNEIPP. My Water-Cure. As Tested through more than Thirty Years, and Described for the Healing of Diseases and the Preservation of Health. By SEBASTIAN KNEIPP, Parish Priest of Wörishofen (Bavaria). With a Portrait and other Illustrations. Authorised English Translation from the Thirtieth German Edition, by A. de F. Cheap Edition. With an Appendix, containing the Latest Developments of Pfarrer Kneipp's System, and a Preface by E. Gerard. Crown 8vo, 3s. 6d.

KNOLLYS. The Elements of Field-Artillery. Designed for the Use of Infantry and Cavalry Officers. By HENRY KNOLLYS, Colonel Royal Artillery; Author of 'From Sedan to Saarbrück,' Editor of 'Incidents in the Sepoy War,' &c. With Engravings. Crown 8vo, 7s. 6d.

LAMINGTON. In the Days of the Dandies. By the late Lord LAMINGTON. Crown 8vo. Illustrated cover, 1s.; cloth, 1s. 6d.

LANG. Life, Letters, and Diaries of Sir Stafford Northcote, First Earl of Iddesleigh. By ANDREW LANG. With Three Portraits and a View of Pynes. Third Edition. 2 vols. post 8vo, 31s. 6d.
POPULAR EDITION. With Portrait and View of Pynes. Post 8vo, 7s. 6d.

LAWLESS. Hurrish: A Study. By the Hon. EMILY LAWLESS, Author of 'A Chelsea Householder,' &c. Fourth Edition. Crown 8vo, 3s. 6d.

LEES. A Handbook of the Sheriff and Justice of Peace Small Debt Courts. With Notes, References, and Forms. By J. M. LEES, Advocate, Sheriff of Stirling, Dumbarton, and Clackmannan. 8vo, 7s. 6d.

LINDSAY. The Progressiveness of Modern Christian Thought. By the Rev. JAMES LINDSAY, M.A., B.D., B.Sc., F.R.S.E., F.G.S., Minister of the Parish of St Andrew's, Kilmarnock. Crown 8vo, 6s.

LLOYD. Ireland under the Land League. A Narrative of Personal Experiences. By CLIFFORD LLOYD, Special Resident Magistrate. Post 8vo, 6s.

LOCKHART.
Doubles and Quits. By LAURENCE W. M. LOCKHART. New Edition. Crown 8vo, 3s. 6d.
Fair to See. New Edition. Crown 8vo, 3s. 6d.
Mine is Thine. New Edition. Crown 8vo, 3s. 6d.

LOCKHART.
The Church of Scotland in the Thirteenth Century. The Life and Times of David de Bernham of St Andrews (Bishop), A.D. 1239 to 1253. With List of Churches dedicated by him, and Dates. By WILLIAM LOCKHART, A.M., D.D., F.S.A. Scot., Minister of Colinton Parish. 2d Edition. 8vo, 6s.
Dies Tristes: Sermons for Seasons of Sorrow. Crown 8vo, 6s.

LORIMER.
The Institutes of Law: A Treatise of the Principles of Jurisprudence as determined by Nature. By the late JAMES LORIMER, Professor of Public Law and of the Law of Nature and Nations in the University of Edinburgh. New Edition, Revised and much Enlarged. 8vo, 18s.
The Institutes of the Law of Nations. A Treatise of the Jural Relation of Separate Political Communities. In 2 vols. 8vo. Volume I., price 16s. Volume II., price 20s.

LOVE. Scottish Church Music. Its Composers and Sources. With Musical Illustrations. By JAMES LOVE. Post 8vo, 7s. 6d.

LUGARD. The Rise of our East African Empire: Early Efforts in Uganda and Nyasaland. By F. D. LUGARD, Captain Norfolk Regiment. With 130 Illustrations from Drawings and Photographs under the personal superintendence of the Author, and 14 specially prepared Maps. In 2 vols. large demy 8vo, 42s.

M'COMBIE. Cattle and Cattle-Breeders. By WILLIAM M'COMBIE, Tillyfour. New Edition, Enlarged, with Memoir of the Author by JAMES MACDONALD, F.R.S.E., Secretary Highland and Agricultural Society of Scotland. Crown 8vo, 3s. 6d.

M'CRIE.
> Works of the Rev. Thomas M'Crie, D.D.   Uniform Edition.
> 4 vols. crown 8vo, 24s.
> Life of John Knox.   Crown 8vo, 6s.   Another Edition, 3s. 6d.
> • Life of Andrew Melville.   Crown 8vo, 6s.
> History of the Progress and Suppression of the Reformation
> in Italy in the Sixteenth Century.   Crown 8vo, 4s.
> History of the Progress and Suppression of the Reformation
> in Spain in the Sixteenth Century.   Crown 8vo, 3s. 6d.
> Lectures on the Book of Esther.   Fcap. 8vo, 5s.

M'CRIE.   The Public Worship of Presbyterian Scotland.   Histori-
cally treated.   With copious Notes, Appendices, and Index.   The Fourteenth
Series of the Cunningham Lectures.   By the Rev. CHARLES G. M'CRIE, D.D.
Demy 8vo, 10s. 6d.

MACDONALD.   A Manual of the Criminal Law (Scotland) Procedure Act, 1887.   By NORMAN DORAN MACDONALD.   Revised by the LORD
JUSTICE-CLERK.   8vo, 10s. 6d.

MACDONALD.
> Stephens' Book of the Farm.   Fourth Edition.   Revised and
> in great part Rewritten by JAMES MACDONALD, F.R.S.E., Secretary, Highland
> and Agricultural Society of Scotland.   Complete in 3 vols., bound with leather
> back, gilt top, £3, 3s.   In Six Divisional Vols., bound in cloth, each 10s. 6d.
> Pringle's Live Stock of the Farm.   Third Edition.   Revised
> and Edited by JAMES MACDONALD.   Crown 8vo, 7s. 6d.
> M'Combie's Cattle and Cattle-Breeders.   New Edition,
> Enlarged, with Memoir of the Author by JAMES MACDONALD.   Crown 8vo, 3s. 6d.
> History of Polled Aberdeen and Angus Cattle.   Giving an
> Account of the Origin, Improvement, and Characteristics of the Breed.   By JAMES
> MACDONALD and JAMES SINCLAIR.   Illustrated with numerous Animal Portraits.
> Post 8vo, 12s. 6d.

MACDOUGALL AND DODDS.   A Manual of the Local Govern-
ment (Scotland) Act, 1894.   With Introduction, Explanatory Notes, and Copious
Index.   By J. PATTEN MACDOUGALL, Legal Secretary to the Lord Advocate, and
J. M. DODDS.   Crown 8vo, 2s. 6d. net.

M'INTOSH.   The Book of the Garden.   By CHARLES M'INTOSH,
formerly Curator of the Royal Gardens of his Majesty the King of the Belgians,
and lately of those of his Grace the Duke of Buccleuch, K.G., at Dalkeith Palace.
2 vols. royal 8vo, with 1350 Engravings.   £4, 7s. 6d.   Vol. I.   On the Formation
of Gardens and Construction of Garden Edifices, £2, 10s.   Vol. II.   Practical
Gardening, £1, 17s. 6d.

MACINTYRE.   Hindu-Koh: Wanderings and Wild Sports on
and beyond the Himalayas.   By Major-General DONALD MACINTYRE, V.C., late
Prince of Wales' Own Goorkhas, F.R.G.S.   *Dedicated to H.R.H. The Prince of
Wales.*   New and Cheaper Edition, Revised, with numerous Illustrations.   Post
8vo, 3s. 6d.

MACKAY.   A Sketch of the History of Fife and Kinross.   A
Study of Scottish History and Character.   By Æ. J. G. MACKAY, Sheriff of these
Counties.   Crown 8vo, 6s.

MACKAY.
> A Manual of Modern Geography; Mathematical, Physical,
> and Political.   By the Rev. ALEXANDER MACKAY, LL.D., F.R.G.S.   11th
> Thousand, Revised to the present time.   Crown 8vo, pp. 688, 7s. 6d.
> Elements of Modern Geography.   55th Thousand, Revised to
> the present time.   Crown 8vo, pp. 300, 3s.
> The Intermediate Geography.   Intended as an Intermediate
> Book between the Author's 'Outlines of Geography' and 'Elements of Geo-
> graphy.'   Seventeenth Edition, Revised.   Crown 8vo, pp. 238, 2s.

MACKAY.
Outlines of Modern Geography. 191st Thousand, Revised to
the present time. 18mo, pp. 128, 1s.
First Steps in Geography. 105th Thousand. 18mo, pp. 56.
Sewed, 4d.; cloth, 6d.
Elements of Physiography and Physical Geography. With
Express Reference to the Instructions issued by the Science and Art Depart-
ment. 30th Thousand, Revised. Crown 8vo, 1s. 6d.
Facts and Dates; or, The Leading Events in Sacred and Pro-
fane History, and the Principal Facts in the various Physical Sciences. For
Schools and Private Reference. New Edition. Crown 8vo, 3s. 6d.

MACKENZIE. Studies in Roman Law. With Comparative
Views of the Laws of France, England, and Scotland. By Lord MACKENZIE,
one of the Judges of the Court of Session in Scotland. Sixth Edition, Edited
by JOHN KIRKPATRICK, M.A., LL.B., Advocate, Professor of History in the
University of Edinburgh. 8vo, 12s.

MACPHERSON. Glimpses of Church and Social Life in the
Highlands in Olden Times. By ALEXANDER MACPHERSON, F.S.A. Scot. With
6 Photogravure Portraits and other full-page Illustrations. Small 4to, 25s.

M'PHERSON.
Summer Sundays in a Strathmore Parish. By J. GORDON
M'PHERSON, Ph.D., F.R.S.E., Minister of Ruthven. Crown 8vo, 5s.
Golf and Golfers. Past and Present. With an Introduction
by the Right Hon. A. J. BALFOUR, and a Portrait of the Author. Fcap. 8vo,
1s. 6d.

MACRAE. A Handbook of Deer-Stalking. By ALEXANDER
MACRAE, late Forester to Lord Henry Bentinck. With Introduction by Horatio
Ross, Esq. Fcap. 8vo, with 2 Photographs from Life. 3s. 6d.

MAIN. Three Hundred English Sonnets. Chosen and Edited
by DAVID M. MAIN. Fcap. 8vo, 6s.

MAIR. A Digest of Laws and Decisions, Ecclesiastical and
Civil, relating to the Constitution, Practice, and Affairs of the Church of Scot-
land. With Notes and Forms of Procedure. By the Rev. WILLIAM MAIR, D.D.,
Minister of the Parish of Earlston. Crown 8vo. [*New Edition in preparation.*

MARCHMONT AND THE HUMES OF POLWARTH. By
One of their Descendants. With numerous Portraits and other Illustrations.
Crown 4to, 21s. net.

MARSHALL. It Happened Yesterday. A Novel. By FREDERICK
MARSHALL, Author of 'Claire Brandon,' 'French Home Life.' Crown 8vo, 6s.

MARSHMAN. History of India. From the Earliest Period to
the present time. By JOHN CLARK MARSHMAN, C.S.I. Third and Cheaper
Edition. Post 8vo, with Map, 6s.

MARTIN.
Goethe's Faust. Part I. Translated by Sir THEODORE MARTIN,
K.C.B. Second Edition, crown 8vo, 6s. Ninth Edition, fcap. 8vo, 3s. 6d.
Goethe's Faust. Part II. Translated into English Verse.
Second Edition, Revised. Fcap. 8vo, 6s.
The Works of Horace. Translated into English Verse, with
Life and Notes. 2 vols. New Edition. Crown 8vo, 21s.
Poems and Ballads of Heinrich Heine. Done into English
Verse. Third Edition. Small crown 8vo, 5s.
The Song of the Bell, and other Translations from Schiller,
Goethe, Uhland, and Others. Crown 8vo, 7s. 6d.
Madonna Pia: A Tragedy; and Three Other Dramas. Crown
8vo, 7s. 6d.

MARTIN.
    Catullus. With Life and Notes. Second Edition, Revised
and Corrected. Post 8vo, 7s. 6d.
    The 'Vita Nuova' of Dante. Translated, with an Introduction
and Notes. Third Edition. Small crown 8vo, 5s.
    Aladdin: A Dramatic Poem. By ADAM OEHLENSCHLAEGER.
Fcap. 8vo, 5s.
    Correggio: A Tragedy. By OEHLENSCHLAEGER. With Notes.
Fcap. 8vo, 3s.

MARTIN. On some of Shakespeare's Female Characters. By
HELENA FAUCIT, Lady MARTIN. Dedicated by permission to Her Most Gracious
Majesty the Queen. Fifth Edition. With a Portrait by Lehmann. Demy
8vo, 7s. 6d.

MARWICK. Observations on the Law and Practice in regard
to Municipal Elections and the Conduct of the Business of Town Councils and
Commissioners of Police in Scotland. By Sir JAMES D. MARWICK, LL.D.,
Town-Clerk of Glasgow. Royal 8vo, 30s.

MATHESON.
    Can the Old Faith Live with the New? or, The Problem of
Evolution and Revelation. By the Rev. GEORGE MATHESON, D.D. Third Edition. Crown 8vo, 7s. 6d.
    The Psalmist and the Scientist; or, Modern Value of the Reli-
gious Sentiment. New and Cheaper Edition. Crown 8vo, 5s.
    Spiritual Development of St Paul. Third Edition. Cr. 8vo, 5s.
    The Distinctive Messages of the Old Religions. Second Edi-
tion. Crown 8vo, 5s.
    Sacred Songs. New and Cheaper Edition. Crown 8vo, 2s. 6d.

MAURICE. The Balance of Military Power in Europe. An
Examination of the War Resources of Great Britain and the Continental States.
By Colonel MAURICE, R.A., Professor of Military Art and History at the Royal
Staff College. Crown 8vo, with a Map, 6s.

MAXWELL.
    Life and Times of the Rt. Hon. William Henry Smith, M.P.
By Sir HERBERT MAXWELL, Bart., M.P., F.S.A., &c., Author of 'Passages in
the Life of Sir Lucian Elphin.' With Portraits and numerous Illustrations by
Herbert Railton, G. L. Seymour, and Others. 2 vols. demy 8vo, 25s.
    POPULAR EDITION. With a Portrait and other Illustrations. Crown 8vo, 3s. 6d.
    Scottish Land Names: Their Origin and Meaning. Being
the Rhind Lectures in Archæology for 1893. Post 8vo, 6s.
    Meridiana: Noontide Essays. Post 8vo, 7s. 6d.

MELDRUM. The Story of Margrédel: Being a Fireside History of a Fifeshire Family. By D. STORRAR MELDRUM. Cheap Edition. Crown
8vo, 3s. 6d.

MICHEL. A Critical Inquiry into the Scottish Language. With
the view of Illustrating the Rise and Progress of Civilisation in Scotland. By
FRANCISQUE-MICHEL, F.S.A. Lond. and Scot., Correspondant de l'Institut de
France, &c. 4to, printed on hand-made paper, and bound in roxburghe, 66s.

MICHIE.
    **The Larch: Being a Practical Treatise on its Culture and
General Management.** By CHRISTOPHER Y. MICHIE, Forester, Cullen House.
Crown 8vo, with Illustrations. New and Cheaper Edition, Enlarged, 5s.
    The Practice of Forestry. Crown 8vo, with Illustrations. 6s.

MIDDLETON. The Story of Alastair Bhan Comyn; or, The
Tragedy of Dunphail. A Tale of Tradition and Romance. By the Lady MIDDLE-
TON. Square 8vo, 10s. Cheaper Edition, 5s.

MILLER. Landscape Geology. A Plea for the Study of Geology
by Landscape Painters. By HUGH MILLER, of H.M. Geological Survey. Crown
8vo, 3s. Cheap Edition, paper cover, 1s.

MINTO.
A Manual of English Prose Literature, Biographical and
Critical: designed mainly to show Characteristics of Style. By W. MINTO,
M.A., Hon. LL.D. of St Andrews; Professor of Logic in the University of Aber-
deen. Third Edition, Revised. Crown 8vo, 7s. 6d.
Characteristics of English Poets, from Chaucer to Shirley.
New Edition, Revised. Crown 8vo, 7s. 6d.
Plain Principles of Prose Composition. Crown 8vo, 1s. 6d.
The Literature of the Georgian Era. Edited, with a Bio-
graphical Introduction, by Professor KNIGHT, St Andrews.   [*In the press.*

MOIR. Life of Mansie Wauch, Tailor in Dalkeith. By D. M.
MOIR. With 8 Illustrations on Steel, by the late GEORGE CRUIKSHANK. Crown
8vo, 3s. 6d. Another Edition, fcap. 8vo, 1s. 6d.

MOMERIE.
Defects of Modern Christianity, and other Sermons. By
ALFRED WILLIAMS MOMERIE, M.A., D.Sc., LL.D. Fifth Edition. Crown
8vo, 5s.
The Basis of Religion. Being an Examination of Natural
Religion. Third Edition. Crown 8vo, 2s. 6d.
The Origin of Evil, and other Sermons. Seventh Edition,
Enlarged. Crown 8vo, 5s.
Personality. The Beginning and End of Metaphysics, and
a Necessary Assumption in all Positive Philosophy. Fourth Edition, Revised.
Crown 8vo, 3s.
Agnosticism. Fourth Edition, Revised. Crown 8vo, 5s.
Preaching and Hearing; and other Sermons. Third Edition,
Enlarged. Crown 8vo, 5s.
Belief in God. Third Edition. Crown 8vo, 3s.
Inspiration; and other Sermons. Second Edition, Enlarged.
Crown 8vo, 5s.
Church and Creed. Third Edition. Crown 8vo, 4s. 6d.
The Future of Religion, and other Essays. Second Edition.
Crown 8vo, 3s. 6d.

MONTAGUE. Military Topography. Illustrated by Practical
Examples of a Practical Subject. By Major-General W. E. MONTAGUE, C.B.,
P.S.C., late Garrison Instructor Intelligence Department, Author of 'Campaign-
ing in South Africa.' With Forty-one Diagrams. Crown 8vo, 5s.

MONTALEMBERT. Memoir of Count de Montalembert. A
Chapter of Recent French History. By Mrs OLIPHANT, Author of the 'Life of
Edward Irving,' &c. 2 vols. crown 8vo, £1, 4s.

MORISON.
Doorside Ditties. By JEANIE MORISON. With a Frontis-
piece. Crown 8vo, 3s. 6d.
Æolus. A Romance in Lyrics. Crown 8vo, 3s.
There as Here. Crown 8vo, 3s.
⁎ *A limited impression on hand-made paper, bound in vellum, 7s. 6d.*
Selections from Poems. Crown 8vo, 4s. 6d.
Sordello. An Outline Analysis of Mr Browning's Poem.
Crown 8vo, 3s.
Of "Fifine at the Fair," "Christmas Eve and Easter Day,"
and other of Mr Browning's Poems. Crown 8vo, 3s.
The Purpose of the Ages. Crown 8vo, 9s.
Gordon: An Our-day Idyll. Crown 8vo, 3s.
Saint Isadora, and other Poems. Crown 8vo, 1s. 6d.

MORISON.
Snatches of Song. Paper, 1s. 6d. ; Cloth, 3s.
Pontius Pilate. Paper, 1s. 6d. ; Cloth, 3s.
Mill o' Forres. Crown 8vo, 1s.
Ane Booke of Ballades. Fcap. 4to, 1s.

MOZLEY. Essays from 'Blackwood.' By the late ANNE
MOZLEY, Author of 'Essays on Social Subjects'; Editor of 'The Letters and
Correspondence of Cardinal Newman,' 'Letters of the Rev. J. B. Mozley,' &c.
With a Memoir by her Sister, FANNY MOZLEY. Post 8vo, 7s. 6d.

MUNRO. On Valuation of Property. By WILLIAM MUNRO,
M.A., Her Majesty's Assessor of Railways and Canals for Scotland. Second
Edition, Revised and Enlarged. 8vo, 3s. 6d.

MURDOCH. Manual of the Law of Insolvency and Bankruptcy:
Comprehending a Summary of the Law of Insolvency, Notour Bankruptcy,
Composition - contracts, Trust - deeds, Cessios, and Sequestrations; and the
Winding-up of Joint-Stock Companies in Scotland; with Annotations on the
various Insolvency and Bankruptcy Statutes; and with Forms of Procedure
applicable to these Subjects. By JAMES MURDOCH, Member of the Faculty of
Procurators in Glasgow. Fifth Edition, Revised and Enlarged. 8vo, 12s. net.

MY TRIVIAL LIFE AND MISFORTUNE: A Gossip with
no Plot in Particular. By A PLAIN WOMAN. Cheap Edition. Crown 8vo, 3s. 6d.

By the SAME AUTHOR.
POOR NELLIE. Cheap Edition. Crown 8vo, 3s. 6d.

NAPIER. The Construction of the Wonderful Canon of Loga-
rithms. By JOHN NAPIER of Merchiston. Translated, with Notes, and a
Catalogue of Napier's Works, by WILLIAM RAE MACDONALD. Small 4to, 15s.
A few large-paper copies on Whatman paper, 30s.

NEAVES.
Songs and Verses, Social and Scientific. By An Old Con-
tributor to 'Maga.' By the Hon. Lord NEAVES. Fifth Edition. Fcap. 8vo, 4s.
The Greek Anthology. Being Vol. XX. of 'Ancient Classics
for English Readers.' Crown 8vo, 2s. 6d.

NICHOLSON.
A Manual of Zoology, for the use of Students. With a
General Introduction on the Principles of Zoology. By HENRY ALLEYNE
NICHOLSON, M.D., D.Sc., F.L.S., F.G.S., Regius Professor of Natural History in
the University of Aberdeen. Seventh Edition, Rewritten and Enlarged. Post
8vo, pp. 956, with 555 Engravings on Wood, 18s.
Text-Book of Zoology, for Junior Students. Fifth Edition,
Rewritten and Enlarged. Crown 8vo, with 358 Engravings on Wood, 10s. 6d.
Introductory Text-Book of Zoology, for the use of Junior
Classes. Sixth Edition, Revised and Enlarged, with 166 Engravings, 3s.
Outlines of Natural History, for Beginners : being Descrip-
tions of a Progressive Series of Zoological Types. Third Edition, with
Engravings, 1s. 6d.
A Manual of Palæontology, for the use of Students. With a
General Introduction on the Principles of Palæontology. By Professor H.
ALLEYNE NICHOLSON and RICHARD LYDEKKER, B.A. Third Edition, entirely
Rewritten and greatly Enlarged. 2 vols. 8vo, £3, 3s.
The Ancient Life-History of the Earth. An Outline of the
Principles and Leading Facts of Palæontological Science. Crown 8vo, with 276
Engravings, 10s. 6d.
On the "Tabulate Corals" of the Palæozoic Period, with
Critical Descriptions of Illustrative Species. Illustrated with 15 Lithographed
Plates and numerous Engravings. Super-royal 8vo, 21s.

NICHOLSON.
Synopsis of the Classification of the Animal Kingdom. 8vo, with 106 Illustrations, 6s.
On the Structure and Affinities of the Genus Monticulipora and its Sub-Genera, with Critical Descriptions of Illustrative Species. Illustrated with numerous Engravings on Wood and Lithographed Plates. Super-royal 8vo, 18s.

NICHOLSON.
Communion with Heaven, and other Sermons. By the late MAXWELL NICHOLSON, D.D., St Stephen's, Edinburgh. Crown 8vo, 5s. 6d.
Rest in Jesus. Sixth Edition. Fcap. 8vo, 4s. 6d.

NICHOLSON.
Thoth. A Romance. By JOSEPH SHIELD NICHOLSON, M.A., D.Sc., Professor of Commercial and Political Economy and Mercantile Law in the University of Edinburgh. Third Edition. Crown 8vo, 4s. 6d.
A Dreamer of Dreams. A Modern Romance. Second Edition. Crown 8vo, 6s.

NICOLSON AND MURE. A Handbook to the Local Government (Scotland) Act, 1889. With Introduction, Explanatory Notes, and Index. By J. BADENACH NICOLSON, Advocate, Counsel to the Scotch Education Department, and W. J. MURE, Advocate, Legal Secretary to the Lord Advocate for Scotland. Ninth Reprint. 8vo, 5s.

OLIPHANT.
Masollam : A Problem of the Period. A Novel. By LAURENCE OLIPHANT. 3 vols. post 8vo, 25s. 6d.
Scientific Religion; or, Higher Possibilities of Life and Practice through the Operation of Natural Forces. Second Edition. 8vo, 16s.
Altiora Peto. Cheap Edition. Crown 8vo, boards, 2s. 6d. ; cloth, 3s. 6d. Illustrated Edition. Crown 8vo, cloth, 6s.
Piccadilly. With Illustrations by Richard Doyle. New Edition, 3s. 6d. Cheap Edition, boards, 2s. 6d.
Traits and Travesties ; Social and Political. Post 8vo, 10s. 6d.
Episodes in a Life of Adventure ; or, Moss from a Rolling Stone. Fifth Edition. Post 8vo, 6s.
Haifa : Life in Modern Palestine. Second Edition. 8vo, 7s. 6d.
The Land of Gilead. With Excursions in the Lebanon. With Illustrations and Maps. Demy 8vo, 21s.
Memoir of the Life of Laurence Oliphant, and of Alice Oliphant, his Wife. By Mrs M. O. W. OLIPHANT. Seventh Edition. 2 vols. post 8vo, with Portraits. 21s.
POPULAR EDITION. With a New Preface. Post 8vo, with Portraits. 7s. 6d.

OLIPHANT.
Who was Lost and is Found. By Mrs OLIPHANT. Cr. 8vo, 6s.
Miss Marjoribanks. New Edition. Crown 8vo, 3s. 6d.
The Perpetual Curate, and The Rector. New Edition. Crown 8vo, 3s. 6d.
Salem Chapel, and The Doctor's Family. New Edition. Crown 8vo, 3s. 6d.
Katie Stewart, and other Stories. New Edition. Crown 8vo, cloth, 3s. 6d.
Valentine and his Brother. New Edition. Crown 8vo, 3s. 6d.
Sons and Daughters. Crown 8vo, 3s. 6d.
Katie Stewart. Illustrated boards, 2s. 6d.
Two Stories of the Seen and the Unseen. The Open Door —Old Lady Mary. Paper covers, 1s.

OLIPHANT. Notes of a Pilgrimage to Jerusalem and the Holy
Land. By F. R. OLIPHANT. Crown 8vo, 3s. 6d.

ON SURREY HILLS. By "A SON OF THE MARSHES."
See page 28.

OSWALD. By Fell and Fjord ; or, Scenes and Studies in Ice-
land. By E. J. OSWALD. Post 8vo, with Illustrations. 7s. 6d.

PAGE.
Introductory Text-Book of Geology. By DAVID PAGE, LL.D.,
Professor of Geology in the Durham University of Physical Science, Newcastle,
and Professor LAPWORTH of Mason Science College, Birmingham. With Engravings and Glossarial Index. Twelfth Edition, Revised and Enlarged. 3s. 6d.

Advanced Text-Book of Geology, Descriptive and Industrial.
With Engravings, and Glossary of Scientific Terms. Sixth Edition, Revised and
Enlarged. 7s. 6d.

Introductory Text-Book of Physical Geography. With Sketch-
Maps and Illustrations. Edited by Professor LAPWORTH, LL.D., F.G.S., &c.,
Mason Science College, Birmingham. Thirteenth Edition, Revised and Enlarged,
2s. 6d.

Advanced Text-Book of Physical Geography. Third Edition.
Revised and Enlarged by Professor LAPWORTH. With Engravings. 5s.

PATON.
Spindrift. By Sir J. NOEL PATON. Fcap., cloth, 5s.
Poems by a Painter. Fcap., cloth, 5s.

PATON. Body and Soul. A Romance in Transcendental Path-
ology. By FREDERICK NOEL PATON. Third Edition. Crown 8vo, 1s.

PATRICK. The Apology of Origen in Reply to Celsus. A
Chapter in the History of Apologetics. By the Rev. J. PATRICK, B.D. Post 8vo,
7s. 6d.

PATTERSON.
Essays in History and Art. By R. HOGARTH PATTERSON.
8vo, 12s.
The New Golden Age, and Influence of the Precious Metals
upon the World. 2 vols. 8vo, 31s. 6d.

PAUL. History of the Royal Company of Archers, the Queen's
Body-Guard for Scotland. By JAMES BALFOUR PAUL, Advocate of the Scottish
Bar. Crown 4to, with Portraits and other Illustrations. £2, 2s.

PEILE. Lawn Tennis as a Game of Skill. With latest revised
Laws as played by the Best Clubs. By Captain S. C. F. PEILE, B.S.C. Cheaper
Edition. Fcap., cloth, 1s.

PETTIGREW. The Handy Book of Bees, and their Profitable
Management. By A. PETTIGREW. Fifth Edition, Enlarged, with Engravings.
Crown 8vo, 3s. 6d.

PFLEIDERER. Philosophy and Development of Religion.
Being the Edinburgh Gifford Lectures for 1894. By OTTO PFLEIDERER, D.D.,
Professor of Theology at Berlin University. In 2 vols. post 8vo, 15s. net.

PHILOSOPHICAL CLASSICS FOR ENGLISH READERS.
Edited by WILLIAM KNIGHT, LL.D., Professor of Moral Philosophy, University
of St Andrews. In crown 8vo volumes, with Portraits, price 3s. 6d.
[*For List of Volumes, see page* 2.

POLLARD. A Study in Municipal Government : The Corpora-
tion of Berlin. By JAMES POLLARD, C.A., Chairman of the Edinburgh Public
Health Committee, and Secretary of the Edinburgh Chamber of Commerce.
Second Edition, Revised. Crown 8vo, 3s. 6d.

POLLOK. The Course of Time : A Poem. By ROBERT POLLOK,
A.M. Cottage Edition, 32mo, 8d. The Same, cloth, gilt edges, 1s. 6d. Another
Edition, with Illustrations by Birket Foster and others, fcap., cloth, 3s. 6d., or
with edges gilt, 4s.

PORT ROYAL LOGIC. Translated from the French ; with
Introduction, Notes, and Appendix. By THOMAS SPENCER BAYNES, LL.D., Professor in the University of St Andrews. Tenth Edition, 12mo, 4s.

POTTS AND DARNELL.
Aditus Faciliores : An Easy Latin Construing Book, with
Complete Vocabulary. By A. W. POTTS, M.A., LL.D., and the Rev. C. DARNELL,
M.A., Head-Master of Cargilfield Preparatory School, Edinburgh. Tenth Edition,
fcap. 8vo, 3s. 6d.

Aditus Faciliores Græci. An Easy Greek Construing Book,
with Complete Vocabulary. Fifth Edition, Revised. Fcap. 8vo, 3s.

POTTS. School Sermons. By the late ALEXANDER WM. POTTS,
LL.D., First Head-Master of Fettes College. With a Memoir and Portrait.
Crown 8vo, 7s. 6d.

PRINGLE. The Live - Stock of the Farm. By ROBERT O.
PRINGLE. Third Edition. Revised and Edited by JAMES MACDONALD. Crown
8vo, 7s. 6d.

PRYDE. Pleasant Memories of a Busy Life. By DAVID PRYDE,
M.A., LL.D., Author of 'Highways of Literature,' 'Great Men in European History,' 'Biographical Outlines of English Literature,' &c. With a Mezzotint Portrait. Post 8vo, 6s.

PUBLIC GENERAL STATUTES AFFECTING SCOTLAND
from 1707 to 1847, with Chronological Table and Index. 3 vols. large 8vo, £3, 3s.

PUBLIC GENERAL STATUTES AFFECTING SCOTLAND,
COLLECTION OF. Published Annually, with General Index.

RADICAL CURE FOR IRELAND, The. A Letter to the
People of England and Scotland concerning a new Plantation. With 2 Maps.
8vo, 7s. 6d.

RAE. The Syrian Church in India. By GEORGE MILNE RAE,
M.A., D.D., Fellow of the University of Madras ; late Professor in the Madras
Christian College. With 6 full-page Illustrations. Post 8vo, 10s. 6d.

RAMSAY. Scotland and Scotsmen in the Eighteenth Century.
Edited from the MSS. of JOHN RAMSAY, Esq. of Ochtertyre, by ALEXANDER
ALLARDYCE, Author of 'Memoir of Admiral Lord Keith, K.B.,' &c. 2 vols.
8vo, 31s. 6d.

RANKIN. The Zambesi Basin and Nyassaland. By DANIEL J.
RANKIN, F.R.S.G.S., M.R.A.S. With 3 Maps and 10 full-page Illustrations.
Post 8vo, 10s. 6d.

RANKIN.
A Handbook of the Church of Scotland. By JAMES RANKIN,
D.D., Minister of Muthill ; Author of 'Character Studies in the Old Testament,'
&c. An entirely New and much Enlarged Edition. Crown 8vo, with 2 Maps,
7s. 6d.

The First Saints. Post 8vo, 7s. 6d.

The Creed in Scotland. An Exposition of the Apostles'
Creed. With Extracts from Archbishop Hamilton's Catechism of 1552, John
Calvin's Catechism of 1556, and a Catena of Ancient Latin and other Hymns.
Post 8vo, 7s. 6d.

The Worthy Communicant. A Guide to the Devout Obser-
vance of the Lord's Supper. Limp cloth, 1s. 3d.

The Young Churchman. Lessons on the Creed, the Com-
mandments, the Means of Grace, and the Church. Limp cloth, 1s. 3d.

First Communion Lessons. 24th Edition. Paper Cover, 2d.

RECORDS OF THE TERCENTENARY FESTIVAL OF THE
UNIVERSITY OF EDINBURGH. Celebrated in April 1884. Published under
the Sanction of the Senatus Academicus. Large 4to, £2, 12s. 6d.

ROBERTSON. The Early Religion of Israel. As set forth by
Biblical Writers and Modern Critical Historians. Being the Baird Lecture for
1888-89. By JAMES ROBERTSON, D.D., Professor of Oriental Languages in the
University of Glasgow. Fourth Edition. Crown 8vo, 10s. 6d.

ROBERTSON.
Orellana, and other Poems. By J. LOGIE ROBERTSON,
M.A. Fcap. 8vo. Printed on hand-made paper. 6s.
A History of English Literature. For Secondary Schools.
Crown 8vo, 3s.

ROBERTSON. Our Holiday among the Hills. By JAMES and
JANET LOGIE ROBERTSON. Fcap. 8vo, 3s. 6d.

ROBERTSON. Essays and Sermons. By the late W. ROBERT-
son, B.D., Minister of the Parish of Sprouston. With a Memoir and Portrait.
Crown 8vo, 5s. 6d.

RODGER. Aberdeen Doctors at Home and Abroad. The Story
of a Medical School. By ELLA HILL BURTON RODGER. Demy 8vo, 10s. 6d.

ROSCOE. Rambles with a Fishing-Rod. By E. S. ROSCOE.
Crown 8vo, 4s. 6d.

ROSS. Old Scottish Regimental Colours. By ANDREW ROSS,
S.S.C., Hon. Secretary Old Scottish Regimental Colours Committee. Dedicated
by Special Permission to Her Majesty the Queen. Folio. £2, 12s. 6d.

RUTLAND.
Notes of an Irish Tour in 1846. By the DUKE OF RUTLAND,
G.C.B. (Lord JOHN MANNERS). New Edition. Crown 8vo, 2s. 6d.
Correspondence between the Right Honble. William Pitt
and Charles Duke of Rutland, Lord - Lieutenant of Ireland, 1781-1787. With
Introductory Note by JOHN DUKE OF RUTLAND. 8vo, 7s. 6d.

RUTLAND.
Gems of German Poetry. Translated by the DUCHESS OF
RUTLAND (Lady JOHN MANNERS). [*New Edition in preparation.*
Impressions of Bad-Homburg. Comprising a Short Account
of the Women's Associations of Germany under the Red Cross. Crown 8vo, 1s. 6d.
Some Personal Recollections of the Later Years of the Earl
of Beaconsfield, K.G. Sixth Edition. 6d.
Employment of Women in the Public Service. 6d.
Some of the Advantages of Easily Accessible Reading and
Recreation Rooms and Free Libraries. With Remarks on Starting and Main-
taining them. Second Edition. Crown 8vo, 1s.
A Sequel to Rich Men's Dwellings, and other Occasional
Papers. Crown 8vo, 2s. 6d.
Encouraging Experiences of Reading and Recreation Rooms,
Aims of Guilds, Nottingham Social Guide, Existing Institutions, &c., &c.
Crown 8vo, 1s.

SCHEFFEL. The Trumpeter. A Romance of the Rhine. By
JOSEPH VICTOR VON SCHEFFEL. Translated from the Two Hundredth German
Edition by JESSIE BECK and LOUISA LORIMER. With an Introduction by Sir
THEODORE MARTIN, K.C.B. Long 8vo, 3s. 6d.

SCHILLER. Wallenstein. A Dramatic Poem. By FRIEDRICH
VON SCHILLER. Translated by C. G. N. LOCKHART. Fcap. 8vo, 7s. 6d.

SCOTCH LOCH FISHING. By "BLACK PALMER." Crown 8vo, interleaved with blank pages, 4s.

SCOUGAL. Prisons and their Inmates; or, Scenes from a Silent World. By FRANCIS SCOUGAL. Crown 8vo, boards, 2s.

SELLAR'S Manual of the Acts relating to Education in Scotland. By J. EDWARD GRAHAM, B.A. Oxon., Advocate. Ninth Edition. Demy 8vo, 12s. 6d.

SETH.

Scottish Philosophy. A Comparison of the Scottish and German Answers to Hume. Balfour Philosophical Lectures, University of Edinburgh. By ANDREW SETH, LL.D., Professor of Logic and Metaphysics in Edinburgh University. Second Edition. Crown 8vo, 5s.

Hegelianism and Personality. Balfour Philosophical Lectures. Second Series. Second Edition. Crown 8vo, 5s.

SETH. A Study of Ethical Principles. By JAMES SETH, M.A., Professor of Philosophy in Brown University, U.S.A. Post 8vo, 10s. 6d. net.

SHADWELL. The Life of Colin Campbell, Lord Clyde. Illustrated by Extracts from his Diary and Correspondence. By Lieutenant-General SHADWELL, C.B. With Portrait, Maps, and Plans. 2 vols. 8vo, 36s.

SHAND.

Half a Century; or, Changes in Men and Manners. By ALEX. INNES SHAND, Author of 'Kilcarra,' 'Against Time,' &c. Second Edition. 8vo, 12s. 6d.

Letters from the West of Ireland. Reprinted from the 'Times.' Crown 8vo, 5s.

SHARPE. Letters from and to Charles Kirkpatrick Sharpe. Edited by ALEXANDER ALLARDYCE, Author of 'Memoir of Admiral Lord Keith, K.B.,' &c. With a Memoir by the Rev. W. K. R. BEDFORD. In 2 vols. 8vo. Illustrated with Etchings and other Engravings. £2, 12s. 6d.

SIM. Margaret Sim's Cookery. With an Introduction by L. B. WALFORD, Author of 'Mr Smith: A Part of his Life,' &c. Crown 8vo, 5s.

SIMPSON. The Wild Rabbit in a New Aspect; or, Rabbit-Warrens that Pay. A book for Landowners, Sportsmen, Land Agents, Farmers, Gamekeepers, and Allotment Holders. A Record of Recent Experiments conducted on the Estate of the Right Hon. the Earl of Wharncliffe at Wortley Hall. By J. SIMPSON. Small crown 8vo, 5s.

SKELTON.

Maitland of Lethington; and the Scotland of Mary Stuart. A History. By JOHN SKELTON, Advocate, C.B., LL.D., Author of 'The Essays of Shirley.' Limited Edition, with Portraits. Demy 8vo, 2 vols., 28s. net.

The Handbook of Public Health. A Complete Edition of the Public Health and other Sanitary Acts relating to Scotland. Annotated, and with the Rules, Instructions, and Decisions of the Board of Supervision brought up to date with relative forms. Second Edition. With Introduction, containing the Administration of the Public Health Act in Counties. 8vo, 8s. 6d.

The Local Government (Scotland) Act in Relation to Public Health. A Handy Guide for County and District Councillors, Medical Officers, Sanitary Inspectors, and Members of Parochial Boards. Second Edition. With a new Preface on appointment of Sanitary Officers. Crown 8vo, 2s.

SKRINE. Columba: A Drama. By JOHN HUNTLEY SKRINE, Warden of Glenalmond; Author of 'A Memory of Edward Thring.' Fcap. 4to, 6s.

SMITH. For God and Humanity. A Romance of Mount Carmel. By HASKETT SMITH, Author of 'The Divine Epiphany,' &c. 3 vols. post 8vo, 25s. 6d.

SMITH.

Thorndale; or, The Conflict of Opinions. By WILLIAM SMITH, Author of 'A Discourse on Ethics,' &c. New Edition. Crown 8vo, 10s. 6d.

Gravenhurst; or, Thoughts on Good and Evil. Second Edition. With Memoir and Portrait of the Author. Crown 8vo, 8s.

The Story of William and Lucy Smith. Edited by GEORGE MERRIAM. Large post 8vo, 12s. 6d.

SMITH. Memoir of the Families of M'Combie and Thoms, originally M'Intosh and M'Thomas. Compiled from History and Tradition. By WILLIAM M'COMBIE SMITH. With Illustrations. 8vo, 7s. 6d.

SMITH. Greek Testament Lessons for Colleges, Schools, and Private Students, consisting chiefly of the Sermon on the Mount and the Parables of our Lord. With Notes and Essays. By the Rev. J. HUNTER SMITH, M.A., King Edward's School, Birmingham. Crown 8vo, 6s.

SMITH. The Secretary for Scotland. Being a Statement of the Powers and Duties of the new Scottish Office. With a Short Historical Introduction, and numerous references to important Administrative Documents. By W. C. SMITH, LL.B., Advocate. 8vo, 6s.

"SON OF THE MARSHES, A."

From Spring to Fall; or, When Life Stirs. By "A SON OF THE MARSHES. Crown 8vo, 3s. 6d.

Within an Hour of London Town: Among Wild Birds and their Haunts. Edited by J. A. OWEN. Cheap Uniform Edition. Crown 8vo, 3s. 6d.

With the Woodlanders, and By the Tide. Cheap Uniform Edition. Crown 8vo, 3s. 6d.

On Surrey Hills. Cheap Uniform Edition. Crown 8vo, 3s. 6d.

Annals of a Fishing Village. Cheap Uniform Edition. Crown 8vo, 3s. 6d.

SORLEY. The Ethics of Naturalism. Being the Shaw Fellowship Lectures, 1884. By W. R. SORLEY, M.A., Fellow of Trinity College, Cambridge, Professor of Logic and Philosophy in University College of South Wales. Crown 8vo, 6s.

SPEEDY. Sport in the Highlands and Lowlands of Scotland with Rod and Gun. By TOM SPEEDY. Second Edition, Revised and Enlarged. With Illustrations by Lieut.-General Hope Crealocke, C.B., C.M.G., and others. 8vo, 15s.

SPROTT. The Worship and Offices of the Church of Scotland. By GEORGE W. SPROTT, D.D., Minister of North Berwick. Crown 8vo, 6s.

STATISTICAL ACCOUNT OF SCOTLAND. Complete, with Index. 15 vols. 8vo, £16, 16s.

STEPHENS.

The Book of the Farm; detailing the Labours of the Farmer, Farm-Steward, Ploughman, Shepherd, Hedger, Farm-Labourer, Field-Worker, and Cattle-man. Illustrated with numerous Portraits of Animals and Engravings of Implements, and Plans of Farm Buildings. Fourth Edition. Revised, and in great part Rewritten by JAMES MACDONALD, F.R.S.E., Secretary, Highland and Agricultural Society of Scotland. Complete in Six Divisional Volumes, bound in cloth, each 10s. 6d., or handsomely bound, in 3 volumes, with leather back and gilt top, £3, 3s.

The Book of Farm Implements and Machines. By J. SLIGHT and R. SCOTT BURN, Engineers. Edited by HENRY STEPHENS. Large 8vo, £2, 2s.

Catechism of Agriculture. [*New Edition in preparation.*]

STEVENSON. British Fungi. (Hymenomycetes.) By Rev.
JOHN STEVENSON, Author of 'Mycologia Scotia,' Hon. Sec. Cryptogamic Society
of Scotland. Vols. I. and II., post 8vo, with Illustrations, price 12s. 6d. net each.

STEWART.
Advice to Purchasers of Horses. By JOHN STEWART, V.S.
New Edition. 2s. 6d.
Stable Economy. A Treatise on the Management of Horses
in relation to Stabling, Grooming, Feeding, Watering, and Working. Seventh
Edition. Fcap. 8vo, 6s. 6d.

STEWART. A Hebrew Grammar, with the Pronunciation, Syl-
labic Division and Tone of the Words, and Quantity of the Vowels. By Rev.
DUNCAN STEWART, D.D. Fourth Edition. 8vo, 3s. 6d.

STEWART. Boethius : An Essay. By HUGH FRASER STEWART,
M.A., Trinity College, Cambridge. Crown 8vo, 7s. 6d.

STODDART. Sir Philip Sidney : Servant of God. By ANNA M.
STODDART. Illustrated by MARGARET L. HUGGINS. With a New Portrait of
Sir Philip Sidney. Small 4to, with a specially designed Cover. 5s.

STODDART. Angling Songs. By THOMAS TOD STODDART.
New Edition, with a Memoir by ANNA M. STODDART. Crown 8vo, 7s. 6d.

STORMONTH.
Etymological and Pronouncing Dictionary of the English
Language. Including a very Copious Selection of Scientific Terms. For use in
Schools and Colleges, and as a Book of General Reference. By the Rev. JAMES
STORMONTH. The Pronunciation carefully revised by the Rev. P. H. PHELP, M.A.
Cantab. Eleventh Edition, with Supplement. Crown 8vo, pp. 800. 7s. 6d.
Dictionary of the English Language, Pronouncing, Etymo-
logical, and Explanatory. Revised by the Rev. P. H. PHELP. Library Edition.
New and Cheaper Edition, with Supplement. Imperial 8vo, handsomely bound
in half morocco, 21s.
The School Etymological Dictionary and Word-Book. Fourth
Edition. Fcap. 8vo, pp. 254. 2s.

STORY.
Nero ; A Historical Play. By W. W. STORY, Author of
'Roba di Roma.' Fcap. 8vo, 6s.
Vallombrosa. Post 8vo, 5s.
Poems. 2 vols., 7s. 6d.
Fiammetta. A Summer Idyl. Crown 8vo, 7s. 6d.
Conversations in a Studio. 2 vols. crown 8vo, 12s. 6d.
Excursions in Art and Letters. Crown 8vo, 7s. 6d.
A Poet's Portfolio : Later Readings. 18mo, 3s. 6d.

STURGIS.
John-a-Dreams. A Tale. By JULIAN STURGIS. New Edi-
tion. Crown 8vo, 3s. 6d.
Little Comedies, Old and New. Crown 8vo, 7s. 6d.

SUTHERLAND (DUCHESS OF). How I Spent my Twentieth
Year. Being a Record of a Tour Round the World, 1886-87. By the DUCHESS
OF SUTHERLAND (MARCHIONESS OF STAFFORD). With Illustrations. Crown 8vo,
7s. 6d.

SUTHERLAND. Handbook of Hardy Herbaceous and Alpine
Flowers, for General Garden Decoration. Containing Descriptions of upwards
of 1000 Species of Ornamental Hardy Perennial and Alpine Plants ; along with
Concise and Plain Instructions for their Propagation and Culture. By WILLIAM
SUTHERLAND, Landscape Gardener ; formerly Manager of the Herbaceous Depart-
ment at Kew. Crown 8vo, 7s. 6d.

TAYLOR. The Story of my Life. By the late Colonel MEADOWS TAYLOR, Author of 'The Confessions of a Thug,' &c., &c. Edited by his Daughter. New and Cheaper Edition, being the Fourth. Crown 8vo, 6s.

THOLUCK. Hours of Christian Devotion. Translated from the German of A. Tholuck, D.D., Professor of Theology in the University of Halle. By the Rev. ROBERT MENZIES, D.D. With a Preface written for this Translation by the Author. Second Edition. Crown 8vo, 7s. 6d.

THOMSON. South Sea Yarns. By Basil Thomson. With 10 Full-page Illustrations. Crown 8vo, 6s.

The Diversions of a Prime Minister. In 1 vol. With Illustrations. Small demy 8vo.   [*In the press.*

THOMSON.

Handy Book of the Flower-Garden: being Practical Directions for the Propagation, Culture, and Arrangement of Plants in Flower-Gardens all the year round. With Engraved Plans. By DAVID THOMSON, Gardener to his Grace the Duke of Buccleuch, K.T., at Drumlanrig. Fourth and Cheaper Edition. Crown 8vo, 5s.

The Handy Book of Fruit-Culture under Glass: being a series of Elaborate Practical Treatises on the Cultivation and Forcing of Pines, Vines, Peaches, Figs, Melons, Strawberries, and Cucumbers. With Engravings of Hothouses, &c. Second Edition, Revised and Enlarged. Crown 8vo, 7s. 6d.

THOMSON. A Practical Treatise on the Cultivation of the Grape Vine. By WILLIAM THOMSON, Tweed Vineyards. Tenth Edition. 8vo, 5s.

THOMSON. Cookery for the Sick and Convalescent. With Directions for the Preparation of Poultices, Fomentations, &c. By BARBARA THOMSON. Fcap. 8vo, 1s. 6d.

THORBURN. Asiatic Neighbours. By S. S. THORBURN, Bengal Civil Service, Author of 'Bannú; or, Our Afghan Frontier,' 'Musalmans and Money-Lenders in the Punjab.' With Four Maps. Demy 8vo, 12s. net.

THORNTON. Opposites. A Series of Essays on the Unpopular Sides of Popular Questions. By LEWIS THORNTON. 8vo, 12s. 6d.

TOM CRINGLE'S LOG. A New Edition, with Illustrations. Crown 8vo, cloth gilt, 5s. Cheap Edition, 2s.

TRANSACTIONS OF THE HIGHLAND AND AGRICULTURAL SOCIETY OF SCOTLAND. Published annually, price 5s.

TRAVEL, ADVENTURE, AND SPORT. From 'Blackwood's Magazine.' Uniform with 'Tales from Blackwood.' In 12 Parts, each price 1s. Handsomely bound in 6 vols., cloth, 15s.; half calf, 25s.

TRAVERS. Mona Maclean, Medical Student. A Novel. By GRAHAM TRAVERS. Ninth Edition. Crown 8vo, 6s.

TULLOCH.

Rational Theology and Christian Philosophy in England in the Seventeenth Century. By JOHN TULLOCH, D.D., Principal of St Mary's College in the University of St Andrews; and one of her Majesty's Chaplains in Ordinary in Scotland. Second Edition. 2 vols. 8vo, 16s.

Modern Theories in Philosophy and Religion. 8vo, 15s.

Luther, and other Leaders of the Reformation. Third Edition, Enlarged. Crown 8vo, 3s. 6d.

Memoir of Principal Tulloch, D.D., LL.D. By Mrs OLIPHANT, Author of 'Life of Edward Irving.' Third and Cheaper Edition. 8vo, with Portrait, 7s. 6d.

TWEEDIE. The Arabian Horse: His Country and People. By Major-General W. TWEEDIE, C.S.I., Bengal Staff Corps; for many years H.B.M.'s Consul-General, Baghdad, and Political Resident for the Government of India in Turkish Arabia. In one vol. royal 4to, with Seven Coloured Plates and other Illustrations, and a Map of the Country. Price £3, 3s. net.

VEITCH.
The History and Poetry of the Scottish Border : their Main
Features and Relations. By JOHN VEITCH, LL.D., Professor of Logic and
Rhetoric in the University of Glasgow. New and Enlarged Edition. 2 vols.
demy 8vo, 16s.
Institutes of Logic. Post 8vo, 12s. 6d.
The Feeling for Nature in Scottish Poetry. From the Ear-
liest Times to the Present Day. 2 vols. fcap. 8vo, in roxburghe binding, 15s.
Merlin and other Poems. Fcap. 8vo, 4s. 6d.
Knowing and Being. Essays in Philosophy. First Series.
Crown 8vo, 5s.

VIRGIL. The Æneid of Virgil. Translated in English Blank
Verse by G. K. RICKARDS, M.A., and Lord RAVENSWORTH. 2 vols. fcap. 8vo, 10s.

WACE. The Christian Faith and Recent Agnostic Attacks.
By the Rev. HENRY WACE, D.D., Principal of King's College, London ; Preacher
of Lincoln's Inn ; Chaplain to the Queen. In one vol. post 8vo. [*In preparation.*

WADDELL. An Old Kirk Chronicle : Being a History of Auld-
hame, Tyninghame, and Whitekirk, in East Lothian. From Session Records,
1615 to 1850. By Rev. P. HATELY WADDELL, B.D., Minister of the United
Parish. Small Paper Edition, 200 Copies. Price £1. Large Paper Edition, 50
Copies. Price £1, 10s.

WALFORD. Four Biographies from 'Blackwood' : Jane Taylor,
Hannah More, Elizabeth Fry, Mary Somerville. By L. B. WALFORD. Crown
8vo, 5s.

WALKER. The Teaching of Jesus in His Own Words. By the
Rev. JOHN C. WALKER. Crown 8vo, 3s. 6d.

WARREN'S (SAMUEL) WORKS :—
Diary of a Late Physician. Cloth, 2s. 6d. ; boards, 2s.
Ten Thousand A-Year. Cloth, 3s. 6d. ; boards, 2s. 6d.
Now and Then. The Lily and the Bee. Intellectual and
Moral Development of the Present Age. 4s. 6d.
Essays : Critical, Imaginative, and Juridical. 5s.

WEBSTER. The Angler and the Loop - Rod. By DAVID
WEBSTER. Crown 8vo, with Illustrations, 7s. 6d.

WENLEY.
Socrates and Christ : A Study in the Philosophy of Religion.
By R. M. WENLEY, M.A., D.Sc., Lecturer on Mental and Moral Philosophy in
Queen Margaret College, Glasgow; formerly Examiner in Philosophy in the
University of Glasgow. Crown 8vo, 6s.
Aspects of Pessimism. Crown 8vo, 6s.

WERNER. A Visit to Stanley's Rear-Guard at Major Bartte-
lot's Camp on the Aruhwimi. With an Account of River-Life on the Congo.
By J. R. WERNER, F.R.G.S., Engineer, late in the Service of the Etat Indepen-
dant du Congo. With Maps, Portraits, and other Illustrations. 8vo, 16s.

WESTMINSTER ASSEMBLY. Minutes of the Westminster
Assembly, while engaged in preparing their Directory for Church Government,
Confession of Faith, and Catechisms (November 1644 to March 1649). Edited
by the Rev. Professor ALEX. T. MITCHELL, of St Andrews, and the Rev. JOHN
STRUTHERS, LL.D. With a Historical and Critical Introduction by Professor
Mitchell. 8vo, 15s.

WHITE.
The Eighteen Christian Centuries. By the Rev. JAMES
WHITE. Seventh Edition. Post 8vo, with Index, 6s.
History of France, from the Earliest Times. Sixth Thousand.
Post 8vo, with Index, 6s.

WHITE.
Archæological Sketches in Scotland—Kintyre and Knapdale.
By Colonel T. P. WHITE, R.E., of the Ordnance Survey. With numerous Illustrations. 2 vols. folio, £4, 4s. Vol. I., Kintyre, sold separately, £2, 2s.
The Ordnance Survey of the United Kingdom. A Popular
Account. Crown 8vo, 5s.

WILLIAMSON. The Horticultural Exhibitor's Handbook. A
Treatise on Cultivating, Exhibiting, and Judging Plants, Flowers, Fruits, and
Vegetables. By W. WILLIAMSON, Gardener. Revised by MALCOLM DUNN, Gardener to his Grace the Duke of Buccleuch and Queensberry, Dalkeith Park.
Crown 8vo, 3s. 6d.

WILLIAMSON. Poems of Nature and Life. By DAVID R.
WILLIAMSON, Minister of Kirkmaiden. Fcap. 8vo, 3s.

WILLIAMSON. Light from Eastern Lands on the Lives of
Abraham, Joseph, and Moses. By the Rev. ALEX. WILLIAMSON, Author of 'The
Missionary Heroes of the Pacific,' 'Sure and Comfortable Words,' 'Ask and
Receive,' &c. Crown 8vo, 3s. 6d.

WILLS AND GREENE. Drawing-Room Dramas for Children.
By W. G. WILLS and the Hon. Mrs GREENE. Crown 8vo, 6s.

WILSON.
Works of Professor Wilson. Edited by his Son-in-Law,
Professor FERRIER. 12 vols. crown 8vo, £2, 8s.
Christopher in his Sporting-Jacket. 2 vols., 8s.
Isle of Palms, City of the Plague, and other Poems. 4s.
Lights and Shadows of Scottish Life, and other Tales. 4s.
Essays, Critical and Imaginative. 4 vols., 16s.
The Noctes Ambrosianæ. 4 vols., 16s.
Homer and his Translators, and the Greek Drama. Crown
8vo, 4s.

WITHIN AN HOUR OF LONDON TOWN. Among Wild
Birds and their Haunts. By "A SON OF THE MARSHES." *See page* 28.

WITH THE WOODLANDERS, AND BY THE TIDE. By
"A SON OF THE MARSHES." *See page* 28.

WORSLEY.
Poems and Translations. By PHILIP STANHOPE WORSLEY,
M.A. Edited by EDWARD WORSLEY. Second Edition, Enlarged. Fcap. 8vo, 6s.
Homer's Odyssey. Translated into English Verse in Spenserian Stanza. By P. S. Worsley. Third Edition. 2 vols. fcap., 12s.
Homer's Iliad. Translated by P. S. Worsley and Prof. Conington. 2 vols. crown 8vo, 21s.

YATE. England and Russia Face to Face in Asia. A Record of
Travel with the Afghan Boundary Commission. By Captain A. C. YATE, Bombay
Staff Corps. 8vo, with Maps and Illustrations, 21s.

YATE. Northern Afghanistan; or, Letters from the Afghan
Boundary Commission. By Major C. E. YATE, C.S.I., C.M.G. Bombay Staff
Corps, F.R.G.S. 8vo, with Maps, 18s.

YOUNG. A Story of Active Service in Foreign Lands. Compiled from Letters sent home from South Africa, India, and China, 1856-1882. By
Surgeon-General A. GRAHAM YOUNG, Author of 'Crimean Cracks.' Crown 8vo,
Illustrated, 7s. 6d.

YULE. Fortification: For the use of Officers in the Army, and
Readers of Military History. By Colonel YULE, Bengal Engineers. 8vo, with
Numerous Illustrations, 10s.

www.ingramcontent.com/pod-product-compliance
Lightning Source LLC
Chambersburg PA
CBHW031350290326
41932CB00044B/869